Diamonds and Holes
in My Shoes

Also by Deirdre Purcell

Fiction
A Place of Stones
That Childhood Country
Falling for a Dancer
Francey
Sky
Love Like Hate Adore
Entertaining Ambrose
Marble Gardens
Last Summer in Arcadia
Children of Eve
Tell Me Your Secret

Adult literacy novellas
Jesus and Billy are off to Barcelona
Has Anyone Here Seen Larry?

Short story contributions
Ladies' Night at Finbar's Hotel
Moments (for 2004 tsunami charities)
Irish Girls Are Back in Town
(for St Vincent de Paul and Barnardos)

Non-fiction
The Dark Hunger (with photographer, Pat Langan, for Concern)
The Time of My Life (ghostwriter for Gay Byrne)
On Lough Derg (with photographer, Liam Blake)
Be Delighted: A Tribute to Maureen Potter

DEIRDRE
PURCELL

*Diamonds and Holes
in My Shoes*

HODDER
HEADLINE
IRELAND

First published in 2006 by Hodder Headline Ireland

1

A CIP catalogue record for this title is available from the British Library.

ISBN 978 0 340 89845 1

Typeset Garamond by Anú Design, Tara
Cover and text design by Anú Design, Tara
Printed and bound in Great Britain by Clay's Ltd, St Ives plc

Hodder Headline Ireland's policy is to use papers that are natural, renewable
and recyclable products and made from wood grown in sustainable forests.
The logging and manufacturing processes are expected to conform to
the environmental regulations of the country of origin.

Hodder Headline Ireland
8 Castlecourt Centre, Castleknock, Dublin 15, Ireland

A division of Hodder Headline, 338 Euston Road, London NW1 3BH, England

Contents

For Mamma and Dadda
(Maureen i Bill, Sempre Amics de Sitges)

Introduction:
Daisy in a Storm

My burning ambition as a child was to become the first professional female jockey in Ireland. I never got to sit on a horse but, for many years, practised rising to the trot on the arm of our old settee that I'd fitted with stirrups made of rough twine.

From the time he was a leggy foal, I looked after Brown Jack. I broke him (gently) to the saddle but he was temperamental and would let no one but me up on his handsome back.

His owner and trainer had high hopes of success in the Derby – but they were reluctant to let me, a novice, ride him; nevertheless the trainer, Sam 'One Eye' McTavish, bowed to the inevitable and eventually persuaded the reluctant owner that it was me or nobody, 'Och, he'll accept nowt but the wee bairn. It's her or nothing.' (Sam had moved around a lot and his accent was hard to pin down.)

The day of the race was bright and clear but, as I was unloading Jack from his trailer, I broke my leg in a freakish accident. It seemed like my dreams, and Brown Jack's, were over. But in the bee-bawing ambulance on the way to hospital, I hatched a plan.

That afternoon, back at the racecourse, with everyone busy, I managed secretly to saddle Jack. He sensed exactly what was happening and stood as still as a plinth while I mounted him and strapped my plaster cast to my stirrup leather on one side. When the coast was clear, we walked quietly to a spot behind a high hedge, near the starting gate. We managed this feat without anyone noticing.

When the field set off, to the surprise of race officials and the distant cheers of the crowd in the stand, we burst from our hiding place and set off in pursuit.

We closed fast—

We passed stragglers, picking them off,

One—

Two—

Three—

My girth snapped!

Brown Jack understood what had happened. He slowed to a canter and, as those three horses swerved past us again, raised his head to indicate that I should grab on to his mane. I slipped forward out of the saddle and lay along his stretched neck. It wasn't easy to hang on because, as he accelerated again to a gallop, I had only one hand to maintain my grip on his mane because the other had to hold the trailing saddle to which the plaster cast was bound.

We were still behind the field coming up to the last bend and although we were gaining, the task did seem out of reach.

I closed my eyes and spoke gently into Brown Jack's ear, 'It's up to you now, Jack.'

And nobly he responded, streaking past the field on the outside so that at the very last second, the two of us, two bodies indivisible, won the Derby by a nose.

Naturally, there was a steward's inquiry but, within seconds, the stewards decided courage had to be rewarded and we rode bareback into the winners' enclosure to cheers and tears of admiration and joy.

I was an imaginative child.

Sadly, I never did become a jockey, and learned to ride only in my early twenties.

As for my present calling, people assume that writing fiction was something I had wanted to do all my life; this was most definitely not the case. I did write two 'plays' at the ages of eight and ten (for something to do in the summer holidays) but never attempted anything else before my first novel was published in 1991 when I was forty-six years old.

So authorship, while the longest served, is but the most recent in a long line of occupations and, before becoming a writer I had switched jobs so many times that I was wont to see myself as a daisy in a storm, never initiating the moves, merely reacting to others' offers and ideas.

I was shocked, therefore, when Emer O'Kelly, critic, journalist and former colleague in the RTÉ newsroom, shattered this nonchalant belief.

We were enjoying our annual Christmas Eve visit in her sitting room where the log fire crackled and the champagne bubbles fizzed – Emer is the quintessential hostess. The talk turned to the qualities of courage and determination in people we mutually admire. It became personal and I found myself wittering about what a mouse I was: how I always swung this way and that depending on which way the wind blew, how I hated saying no to anyone and how, for fear of disobliging people, I always found my tongue agreeing enthusiastically to schemes and projects while my heart and mind shouted, 'No, no, *no!*'

Well, I was not allowed to get very far with that as a piece of self-analysis. Ms O'Kelly, who is never less than forthright in her opinions, raised an eyebrow and, with a regal wave, stopped me in mid-flow and stated, in tones of great certitude, 'But you are the most single-minded person I know!'

Emer has no doubt forgotten this episode and it is probable she has no idea how much that short pronouncement affected me for, as I slunk away from her doorstep that day, I reckoned that if this was how I presented myself to her – ergo to the outside world – I was going to have to revise my opinion of myself. This would be a seriously disorienting task.

Single-minded?

Moi?

How unladylike! How treacherously disloyal to my convent education! How un-*nice*!

Being nice is a habit I find difficult to relinquish. For instance, even these days I don't find it easy to use the word 'career' in the context of my own life; to me it still sounds like a harsh, unforgiving word because during my formative years, to aspire to a 'career' eschewed femininity and modesty. 'Careers' were for men, who took care of women who 'took' jobs to tide them over until marriage. Spinsters worked in careers because they had to.

But the result of Emer's remark was that I was forced to consider my butterfly professional life in a completely different light. Now, at the age of sixty and embarking on a memoir, perhaps I'll find that there was a pattern all along.

If I can remember what's relevant! The problem with memory after a certain age is not that you can't remember, it is that, when the memory does strike, it is ephemeral and will not stick. Or, very commonly, that it is slow to react to a summons.

Like most of my friends of the same age (safety in numbers, what?), I have gone through periods of fearing that the 'senior moments', when, for instance, the name of even an everyday object temporarily eludes the tongue, might herald the onset of Alzheimer's or dementia.

Unlike some of them, however, I refuse to be medically tested, on the 'Auntie Nora principle' forged by the aunt of one of my friends. This redoubtable woman, on being diagnosed with heart trouble, came home from hospital having survived 'a turn' to announce to her family, 'The doctor says I'm to have no more bad news.' This worked a treat and for the rest of her happy, serene life, her family could not have been more solicitous in minding her and shielding her from the more unpleasant facets of the world.

What a brilliant wheeze, I thought, and so adapted it to suit myself, rationalising that, by this stage of life, memory is a flibbertigibbet merely because its storage banks are stuffed to bursting and, as a result, it now has to discriminate between warehousing what's important and what's not. It cannot be bothered with irritating detail – the whereabouts of spectacles, combs or keys, the original reason for trips to the shed...

I comfort myself with an article I read somewhere (don't remember where!) that satisfactorily explains everything. After fifty, apparently, a change occurs in the brain where the section that's in charge of focus-cum-concentration begins to weaken, allowing the 'distraction' section to become dominant. It could be baloney, but it's good enough for me. Whereas we used to be able to think about five different concepts in parallel, this has reduced to two or, at the most, three.

So when I find myself standing halfway up the stairs wondering why I'd decided to go up, I don't scold myself or strain to retrieve the reason for the expedition. Instead, I congratulate myself on being a deep thinker and indulge the Great Thought that has slipped in to replace the mission.

I have never made a secret of my age. Don't see the point, really: if someone is truly bent on finding it, my birth cert is available cheaply in the General Register Office down there in Lombard Street East. But I do truly hate reading that sixty is the new fifty. It is not. It is sixty. And for me, as for other sexagenarians, the signpost bearing that figure is pointing its stubby arm to the edge of a cliff. We have spent most of our years and are now travelling at increasing speed. Many turnoffs along the route have been blocked off and, except for how we deal with what is thrust upon us for reasons of ill health, finance or family, personal choices are diminishing with bewildering rapidity. The word on that signpost is 'realism'. We have no choice but to suck it and see.

This does not mean we cannot choose to change partner, domicile, personality, body shape or even sex; or that satisfaction, tranquillity and happiness have been left behind. It is just that, from now on, whatever decisions we make are within earshot of that inexorable countdown.

In my case, although there's a lot more to do, I do accept that

I'll never travel up the Amazon in a kayak – physically still possible, but unlikely. It is unlikely too that I'll live in Australia or, again, in America, but these are dreams I won't give up completely just yet. And I might still fulfil that cliché of crossing America on a Harley. Or maybe – sacrilege! – on an uber-comfortable Honda Gold Wing...

For sure, though, I won't play in an orchestra or own a house with a swimming pool, become a size 10 or have a Waltons-style family – all ambitions typical of those I held when I thought I had plenty of time. (Patricia Madigan, my best friend since childhood, insists that since all my novels seem to involve dysfunctional families in one guise or another, albeit families wherein redemption is always beckoning, I am in retrospect trying to create for myself my own *Little House on the Prairie* or *Darling Buds of May*; I am destined to keep at it and at it, she says, until I get it right. She must know. She's a social worker.)

However, like most people, and not alone writers, it transpires that I do want to leave something behind me so that like the biblical sparrow, my existence might have made some mark on the earth. Remember that concept? Where eternity begins only when the friction of a sparrow's wing has obliterated our entire planet – said sparrow having touched the earth's surface once every thousand years.

And yet, to embark on a memoir does feel somewhat narcissistic, because, again in the context of being ladylike, I was reared in an era when 'blowing your own trumpet' was seen as one of the deadliest of female sins by teachers and parents. I have not managed to shake this off.

So, let's get it over with. Just in case, by writing about myself at such length, I might get carried away with my own importance, maybe now is the time to reveal an image from 1998.

As an established novelist, I had been invited to give a public reading at Ballymun Library in the week following a similar performance by Roddy Doyle and, because I am a huge fan of libraries, I agreed to do it despite warning the librarian that, 'I'm no Roddy Doyle—'

'You'll be grand.' The librarian had been gently dismissive of my fears. 'This is a very enthusiastic crowd. They're dying to meet you. They love your books. We've publicised the series very well. The place'll be jammed. You'll see!'

Drip! Drip! Drip!

It is the appointed day and, somewhere, someone has not turned off a tap. I look out at ninety-five empty chairs arranged in a big, empty space.

Five chairs are occupied: one each by my mother and my father, two by neighbours of theirs whom they have brought along to show how popular and brilliant their daughter is and – sitting a little apart, no doubt thoroughly embarrassed – a single member of the public. This is obviously someone who hadn't read the date correctly and who had thought he was coming to hear Roddy.

In my ears, the sound of the drip grows until it sounds like bullets in a bucket. I am fiddling with my bottle of mineral water. I am pouring it noisily. I am smiling inanely. I am pretending I don't care. I am grinning for Ireland.

'Well, everyone?' the hapless librarian, voice dropping into the void, finally succumbs to reality as she surveys the 'jam' of people. 'I guess if we're all here, we should make a start? Yeah?' She turns to me.

'Good morning, everyone,' peeps the voice from behind the celebrity desk, 'Thank you all for coming...' I pick up my novel, festooned with little yellow stickers, and open it.

Drip! Drip! Drip!

And how about the dull drizzly morning in August 1965 on the northside of Dublin? I am twenty years old and gorgeously comfy, snuggled under the blankets in this childhood bedroom where the patterns of grey and green foliage on the wallpaper are familiar and dear. Dreamily, I remember that there is something special about this day, but my brain is too fuzzy to grasp quite what it is. Then, cold as a douche, reality whooshes to the surface. Today is the day of a first rehearsal called especially for me in my new job as a permanent member of the Abbey Theatre's acting company. I am a fully fledged professional actress. With that realisation comes serious apprehension.

This rehearsal is to 'read me in' to a show already in repertory. I am to be inserted into the experienced cast to replace an actress who has played the part for so many years she is now deemed too old to play 'juves' – juveniles, lead roles for the young. Understandably, she is not greatly amused at the handover. Her husband is in the cast. So are many of her close friends in the acting company. They're the ones I've to face.

But that is not all: they have all done this play so often that they could be resentful that instead of relaxing at home, they have been called in to run through the show solely for this upstart neophyte, parachuted straight into their midst from amateursville.

I had been so nervous about these twin perils the previous evening that, knowing I would not sleep, and never having taken one before, I had accepted the offer of a sleeping pill from my mother. I hadn't wanted to be sleepy-eyed and jaded on such a significant day and, thanks to my amazing little helper, I had enjoyed a night of solid, dreamless, worryless sleep.

The house is still quiet; my alarm hasn't yet gone off, but it does seem to be bright outside and I might as well get up to face the music. A bath, a bit of titivating – I should try to make an impression on this day of all days.

How much time do I have? Lazily, I extract my arm from under the blankets to look at my watch, and apprehension gives way to horror.

The alarm had gone off but I hadn't heard it. My rehearsal was to start punctually at 10.30 a.m. in the hired function room of a hotel in Westland Row.

My bedroom is in Ballymun.

Westland Row is on the far side of the city.

There are very few buses after the morning rush hour.

It is 10.50 a.m....

Holy God...

But let's not cry for me because here I am, fifteen months earlier and nineteen years of age.

It is 17 March 1964. The air, arctic in temperature, is saturated with cheers and the high-pitched squeal of bagpipes; as I walk down the centre of Fifth Avenue, I am aware that this will be one of the more extraordinary experiences of my life. It is the St Patrick's Day Parade and, shoe-horned into an Aer Lingus uniform, I am with dozens, maybe a hundred, of my colleagues as we march, a tightly packed phalanx of smiles and green tweed, to fly the flag for our national airline.

And – oh, fantastic! – here I am, rocketed into 1986 where I am now a journalist. It is dawn in the perpetual summer of the Sudan, and in my outdoor bed within its tall muslin-draped frame, I wake to the smell of warming dust and a kindergarten cacophony from a klatch of unfamiliar birds. I am not yet used to how quickly the sun rises here: just a few minutes of rapidly pearling grey and then – abracadabra! – full sun in glaring white light. We're still at the pearly stage at the moment. There is a small breeze as the light advances and, around me, the pale muslin netting on the bed frame drifts gently. I feel weightless.

With a shock, I realise I am not alone: outside my veils stands a giant in tribal robes, rendered even taller by his towering headdress; alarmingly, one hand rests casually on the scabbard of a huge scimitar belted to a waist as thick as a tree trunk. We gaze at each other through the gauze. He smiles.

Relieved, I smile back.

Then, using sign language, he conveys through the nets that all is well. He is my guard. Doing his rounds of the Concern compound. Checking to see if the lady journalist is awake.

A perfect morning.

Morning is my time, especially when I am writing in summer and, woken by a brightening sky, can gladly get up early.

Here I am now, standing for a few moments by the French doors in the living room of our house, high over Coulagh Bay in Kilcatherine on the Béara Peninsula, one of the most beautiful places on earth. It is 5.30 a.m., on a morning beyond perfect. Wagtails bob about on the patio outside, and beyond the tangle of brambles at our boundary, a rabbit grazes on old lazy beds covered in bright new grass; she takes a moment to scratch her ears then sits upright to check for roving collies.

East-southeast, a rim of sun appears, simmering between two peaks of the Caha Mountains. I sip my second cup of good, hot coffee as the disc reddens and grows quickly, igniting a mesh of rubies and garnets on the surface of the bay and pinkening the blossom on our single proper tree, a gnarled hawthorn.

I push open the doors and the air, chill but exhilarating, hits the back of my throat like clean white wine. Somewhere to the left, bell-like through the general avian twitter and chat, echoes the call of a cuckoo. I love that sound and knowing that, as usual, I will not manage to catch sight of the bird himself, I nevertheless step outside on the off chance that I might.

Again I don't, so I finish my coffee and set to work again. What to put in? What to leave out?

I have read many memoirs, and I believe that David Niven's graceful *The Moon's a Balloon* is a perfect example of how the reader gets to enjoy not only the writer's charming personality but also learns his view of the world and of himself without feeling like a voyeur. And in her memoir, *When I Grow Up*, the late novelist Bernice Rubens does warn memoirists not to seize an opportunity for self-justification, to exact revenge or gratuitously to invade the privacy of others.

While bearing in mind that every individual sees life through a very subjective lens, 'gratuitous' is the operative word here. We are all born into families and communities. Certainly I was.

1

Swans and
Speckled Fish

Whatever about memory in general, in my experience, sense memory is copper-fastened and unfading, so that sounds, touch, sights, taste and smells, in particular, can always prompt vivid and accurate imagery and recollection. Therefore, since my very first memories of life are sensory, I know that they, at least, are real. The earliest is from when I was less than two years old and we were living in a rented gate lodge in Castleknock, Dublin, having moved there from our first home in Blanchardstown.

This first sensation is of lying on my back and being continuously jolted to the accompaniment of a thunderous rumbling sound. I was born in 1945 and, in our neutral republic, the shortages because of the European war were still evident, principal amongst them rubber for tyres. So my father had fashioned bockety wooden wheels to replace the missing ones on the pram body my parents had bought for me from a junk shop. I can also recall the desiccated, acrid taste of the wooden soother he carved for me (gives a new definition for the word 'plug') as, having hoisted myself into a standing position on the sides of my cot, I sucked busily until I made it grand and moist and slippy.

When I asked in later years about the authenticity of these memories, my mother confirmed the soother, the wheels and the potholed surfaces of the country roads and laneways where she took me for outings in the afternoons. She also confirmed that the two heart-shaped objects fringed with a sort of stiff lace, one red, one blue, that in my memory had dangled and bounced from the hood of this pram during the outings, had indeed existed and were pictures of the Sacred Heart and the Virgin Mary.

A little later, as a toddler, I remember picking off a sliver of rust from the armrest on the iron child-seat of my father's bicycle when we went for a spin – and its sweetish tang when I placed a bit on my tongue. I remember too the taste of my treat-food: a piece of bread dipped in a saucepan of warm milk from the black-lead range, then pressed into a little sugar saved for me from the rations. I was never greedy, though, always breaking off and setting aside two tiny portions for Little Nellie and Little Sheila, my two imaginary friends. And, every time it rained, we three pals were fascinated by the rhythmic bass, tenor, alto and soprano drip-drap-drop of rain into buckets, saucepans and kettles from the many holes in the roof.

The reality of that leaking roof has been established too, but even sense memory can be unreliable when interwoven with childhood imagination.

I would still have been only three years old or so when, in the summer of 1948, Little Nellie, round-faced with a perm and tiny spectacles, and Little Sheila, with freckles and chestnut hair, were my playmates by the banks of a stream at the end of a field behind our house. It was a magical place, with hidey-holes in the streamside bushes, a pair of tame, graceful swans gliding about and little speckled fishes darting through the pebbles in the placid shallows. Memory celebrates the happy hours I spent there, chatting with my two great friends, dabbling in the water. While I wasn't, they were brave enough to let the fish come up to nibble at their fingers. They were always the ones too who made me hide from the calls of my mother for me to come in for my dinner.

Well, as it turns out, the only water in the place were those leaks coming through the roof and the corrosion holes in the rain barrel outside our back door. 'Unless you're talking about that bit of a drain in that ditch?' asked my puzzled mother, when we were in reminiscent mode decades later. She frowned, trying to dredge through her own memory, 'No, it couldn't be that. The drain was at the bottom of the garden, all right, but it was stagnant and choked up with nettles and brambles…'

We left Laurel Lodge to stay for a while in my father's old home in Long Lane off Meath Street at the heart of Dublin's Liberties. Still under four, my recollections of that tiny house are jumbled and, again, mainly sensory: of a smoky dark kitchen, illuminated mostly with light from an open front door, of the smell of dung left by cattle on their way to the market, of a cacophony of street noises (coalman's bell, clopping of the rag-and-bone man's horse, rumbling handcarts, shouted conversations from one end of the street to the other). And I definitely remember being allowed to sit on the threshold to watch other children staging hoop races in which they used sticks to bowl rims of bicycle wheels or bindings from Guinness barrels up and down the road.

The next move was to Ballymun, where we rented a house at 11

Dean Swift Road, one of the terraced streets in the Associated Properties' estate. It was there my parents and their friends, the Madigans, Malones and Hendersons, renters all, formed a Ballymun Gang of Eight, a group of friends who were to stay attached for life. Once a week, or more often if necessary, Mamma and Stella Madigan walked me and her daughter, Patricia, all the way down the hill to Glasnevin to shop for groceries in Boland's, beside where the Bons Secours Hospital is now. That shop was a small cornucopia, supplying loose tea, flour and sugar from large bins, raisins, butter, vegetables, fruit, ham, cheese, Sunlight soap, Vim and polishes (Nugget for the shoes, Mansion for the floors). As a treat for Patricia and me to fight over on the way home, our mothers usually combined funds to buy us a penny bag of 'broken biscuits', confectionery deemed too damaged to reside in the row of glass-topped tins from Jacobs fixed along the front of the wooden counter.

It was in Ballymun that I saw my first fairy.

I was playing house on the back step outside the kitchen door. I had my toy saucepan that I'd filled with water and, using a blunt knife, was busily chopping the outer leaves of a head of cabbage Mamma had given me to make my own dinner when something, perhaps a shadow crossing the sun, made me look up. There, perched on the iron railing separating our back garden from next door's, was this fairy. She was small, maybe four inches in height (I think now) with sparkly silver shoes at the end of pale, shapely legs. She was wearing a gorgeous blue silk dress and a diamond tiara that flashed as the sun came out again.

We looked at one another, this fairy and I. She smiled, just once, and then – whuff! – flew away with a flicker of transparent wings. I went back to wrestling with my blunt knife and my thick, stalky cabbage. I decided I would name the fairy Laura because it sounded as though it matched the colour blue. But she never came back, so I never got to ask her if that was OK with her.

Dean Swift Road was also where I discovered Protestants because my first pal, Jean Brooks, who lived across the road from us, was one. She had long thick hair, worn in plaits, but what defined her Protestantism for short-haired, naked-eyed me, was that she wore glasses. Even still, if I don't catch the thought in time, to me, Protestants always do!

It is also because of Jean Brooks that, to this day, I believe subconsciously that Protestants are 'gooder' than us Catholics. My mother probably cemented this conviction in place because, if I stepped out of line, it was always Jean who was used as an exemplar – as in, 'Why can't you be good like Jean Brooks? And she's a Protestant!' The only explanation for this non-sequitur has to be that we Catholics have a duty to behave better than they do, to show them the error of their ways and bring them back into line.

I was four and a half years old when the power of the subconscious became truly evident. Santa Claus had delivered a 'fairy cycle', as children's two-wheeled bikes were then called. (I didn't notice that he had given it a lumpy paint job before delivering it; all I saw was that it was pale blue, my very favourite colour.) Unfortunately, I hadn't a clue how to ride it; there were no stabilisers then and, on Christmas Day, everyone was very busy with Christmas dinner and visitors and there was no one available to take me out to teach me. So, although I could spin its wheels and pedals, and could practise pulling on the brake handles, the fairy cycle spent Christmas Day lying about our sitting room.

Stephen's morning came and I woke, buzzing with anticipation. It was still pitch dark, though, and my parents were still snoring.

I couldn't wait any longer.

I dressed stealthily and somehow managed to get the tiny bike through the front door and into the road without waking them. But, alone in the cold, starlit world, ensconced on my saddle and contemplating the empty road before me, I didn't have the courage to lift my feet, rasping on the frosty concrete, to the pedals.

As I procrastinated, I took the measure of a Dean Swift Road I hadn't seen before: under the haloed street lights, the rows of shut doors and whitened front gardens behind their railings seemed full of mystery and I fell into a daydream about riding my bike through night-time skies and snowy wastelands, eventually finding myself, silk veils fluttering in the gentle zephyrs of the Far East, dawdling through the deserts (my reading at the time was an illustrated version of *1001 Arabian Nights*).

Then, from behind me, I heard an electric milk van turn into our road from Pappins, its purr enhancing rather than cutting into the reverie as, bottles tinkling like fairy bells, it shimmied past me down the hill until it reached the end and went round the corner.

Next thing, I too found myself turning right, feet dragging on the concrete to stop my momentum. I had cycled down behind the van and had not remembered doing it.

Astonished, I tried a few turns of the pedals. No problem: the bike stayed upright. I turned and tried cycling up the hill towards my house. Still no problem. No wobbles even. So I cycled down again. And up again. Up and down, up and down – until my hands, blue and numbed with cold, could no longer grip the handles properly and I had to go inside.

When my parents got up, they found me complacently munching leftover Christmas cake in the kitchen, with the fairy cycle parked against the outside wall beside the front door, just the way I'd seen Dadda park his bike.

2
Suzette

When Mamma's sister, my Aunt Sheila, married her Jimmy, who was a civil servant like Dadda, their wedding breakfast of meat sandwiches, buns, cake, tea, small quantities of beer, stout, whiskey and brandy was held at our house. Apart from chairs being borrowed from the neighbours to accommodate everyone, the only other thing I remember of that wedding is that Rita Kenny, my new Uncle Jimmy's sister, was so strong she could lift me and Patricia Madigan together, one in each arm, to pose for a photograph. At last, we had an exotic in our extended family: Rita was not only strong, she was a Knight of Malta.

There did seem to be a great deal of socialising in that house, not only with the Madigans, Malones and Hendersons, but with the Connellans across the road, the Brookses and the Tweddles – as a pilot in the fledgling Aer Lingus, Jack Tweddle was another exotic.

I remember a gathering of my mother's former waitress colleagues where I was put up on the table to do my party piece: a lusty rendition of 'Cigareetes and Whiskey and Wild Wild Weemen' ('*They drive you crazy, they drive you insane…*')

Then there were the men's Solo schools in the sitting room.

The word 'solo', incidentally, proved to be invaluable to me in cracking the reading code. From a very early age, I could recite the alphabet and recognise all the individual letters, not only from the page but also from hearing my parents spell to one another when they didn't want me to understand something, a practice I found not only frustrating but intolerable. Then, one Wednesday morning, at some point around my fourth birthday, I heard Dadda, who was on his way out to work, remind Mamma not to forget to make the sandwiches 'for the S-O-L-O tonight'.

Now I knew the men's Solo school was held on Wednesday nights.

I knew the sounds of S and O and L.

Lights on. Sounds of pennies clanging as I rushed up to my bedroom, got my books and excitedly began making connections between the sounds of the letters in the alphabet and the words on the pages. S-O-L-O spelt a word – solo.

Elementary.

I didn't tell my parents I'd cracked it. Not for a while. For the next couple of weeks, I let them spell away to each other while I figured out what it was they didn't want me to hear. It was great.

But one day, when Dadda was reading the inside of his paper, I could no longer contain my show-off tendencies and read the front-page headline aloud.

He nearly fell out of his armchair. 'What was that, Deirdre? What did you say?'

I repeated my feat.

'Good God!' He called Mamma in from the kitchen and I had

to read the headline again. She was as excited as he had been. They tested me on other headlines, and I got them mostly, if not totally, right.

I became the sensation *du jour* of their gang. For days, I basked in the neighbourhood's astonishment and pride in my precociousness as I hoovered up words and regurgitated them for general amusement. We had lovely neighbours, the Higginses, who were elderly and whose house I haunted. Mrs Higgins told Mamma – who repeated it for years and years – that on being asked one afternoon if I'd like one or two sugars in my tea, I replied from my height of two feet nothing, 'Undoubtedly, Mrs Higgins, I'd like one spoon of sugar in my tea.'

Soon, though, everyone got fed up with me and my word prowess, especially my peers, who taunted me with cries of 'Who swalleyed the diction'ry?', so I was forced to confine my brilliance to reading my own books in the confines of my own company.

That Solo school had a psychological repercussion for me as well. One Wednesday night, when it was in session, I went in as usual to say goodnight to the men and, stalling for time, begged for a sip from Dadda's Baby Power. He poured a few drops into the little tin lid and gave it to me.

I tipped the lid to my mouth and then, to the hilarity of the group, gagged and gasped as the whiskey burned across my tongue and into my throat. When I recovered sufficiently to ask Dadda why people drank such horrible stuff, he told me gravely that the priest made him drink it as a penance for his sins.

I was horrified. The stuff was so vile, Dadda's sins had to be really bad; he was bound for hell for sure.

For a long time, I spied on those Solo games, which only compounded my horror and fear: that small penitential bottle was *always* on the card table. I never confided in anyone because I didn't

9

want the shame of admitting in public what a sinful father I had; at the same time, I was grief-stricken that he was bound for eternal damnation.

So it might be a mistake to tell convenient fibs to imaginative children. Take that other time at Mass one Sunday morning when I was being 'a nuisance', fidgeting, asking too many questions.

Mass in those days was in Latin, celebrated with the priest's back firmly set against his congregation. Every so often, however, he turned around to intone, with arms outspread, '*Dominus vobiscum.*'

'Mamma, why does the priest turn around like that? Why does he wave his arms?' I pulled at her sleeve for the umpteenth time.

'To see if the people are good!' My mother's patience had run out and, for the next five or six years – I swear this is true – every time a priest turned round to face us from the altar, I cowered.

At first, I was sent to school at the Holy Faith Convent in Glasnevin, travelling there every day on the 13 bus, the terminus of which was at the top of our road. The journey entailed only three or four stops so, after a week or so, I was trusted to make it on my own. The only mishap occurred when, having disembarked, I was knocked down while crossing the road towards the school gates. Characteristically, while other children had waited for the road to be clear, I had figured I could beat the speed of an oncoming car and dashed across in front of it. I wasn't seriously hurt, suffering just a badly gashed knee – an injury I exploited for all it was worth. Anyone who had sore knees was excused kneeling for prayers, and I milked that injury until our nun yelled at me that it had been an excuse for long enough and I was to kneel and be done with it.

At first, I had been excited at the notion of being a Big Girl Now, but soon became disillusioned with the process of formal education. The nun didn't seem to appreciate that I could already read and forced me to recite the stupid 'C-A-T CAT!' 'D-O-G DOG!' mantras along with all the others; she didn't seem at all impressed with how advanced I was and, try as I might, I couldn't get her to see it.

To me, Sister also seemed obsessed with Catechism and with the priest who was coming in to examine us.

And when he did and when some of the girls got some of the answers wrong, she remained as nice as pie, beaming at us all. As soon as she had seen him through the door, however, she unleashed terror, leather strap swishing and lashing at the unfortunate miscreants.

Luckily, I wasn't a target that day, but that wasn't what mattered, I thought scornfully from the safety of my desk. While other Low Babies wept and nursed their wounded hands, I realised that Sister was a hypocrite. I despised her with all the passion of my four-year-old heart. Yes. And more than anything else in the world, I wanted to please her.

So when the time came for the annual sale of work and she asked us all to bring in some of our unwanted toys, I brought in a few items authorised by my mother: a tambourine, I seem to remember, and a couple of books. Our nun wasn't impressed, or didn't seem to be. She took my stuff without comment or thanks while lavishing praise and gratitude on the girls who had brought in huge teddy bears and dolls, many with price labels still hanging from their necks.

Because of the sale of work, we were having a half-day. When lunch-time came, I immediately ran out of the school and, not waiting for the bus, raced all the way home, a distance of about a mile and a half, most of it uphill.

'What's wrong?' My alarmed mother emerged from the kitchen

when, suffering from a stitch and sweating profusely, I crashed through the front door, open to the midday sunshine.

'Nothing!' I ran into the sitting room and snatched up my beloved Suzette, my one and only doll, who was wearing the cardigan and matching beret Mamma had knitted for her over the blue dress my grandmother had hand-stitched and smocked.

'What are you doing?' Mamma was still in the hall when I came out again.

'I'm bringing Suzette to school for the sale of work.'

'But it's the only doll you have.' She tried physically to stop me.

'I have to!' I dodged her and got out again, running as fast as my legs and stitch would allow. 'Sister said.'

The stitch became so severe that I had to halt for a minute or two on the way back, but I flew onwards again as soon as the pain had receded to a more bearable level.

Once inside the school gates, I ran into the strangely empty entrance yard in which I could see various nuns carrying trestles and so on to set up the sale of work. Our nun wasn't one of them. But then I spotted her walking with another woman. 'Here, Sister!' Panting and in a state of almost complete physical collapse, I presented Suzette. 'This is for the sale of work.'

'Oh.' Absent-mindedly, she took my darling doll without looking at her, resumed her conversation and walked away.

When I finally trailed back home again and my mother asked me what had happened, I told her off-handedly that Sister had been absolutely thrilled.

We were a small family: I have just one brother, who is a good deal younger than me and, growing up, I was embarrassed that my family was inferior to those of most of my classmates whose houses swarmed with siblings. This was the era when women who had borne twelve children or more were heroines, and I was acutely aware that, with only one brother, I was the oddity in my group and was defensive about my mother not deserving high status.

In fact, Declan and I were both only children in a sense: I was five and a half when he was born and I went off to boarding school when I was just thirteen, graduating in 1962 to go straight into work. Even during childhood holiday periods, our family never holidayed singly but always 'took a house' in Rush, or latterly Tramore, bunking in with other families from the Gang of Eight, all of whom had girls of or around my own age and boys of Declan's. My brother and I, therefore, were hardly ever thrown on one another for company and, I have to say, have only got to know each other when we chose to do so as adults.

My overriding memory of him as a child is that he was a terrible fidget. I constantly fought with my parents who, in insisting I take him to Mass with me while they stayed at home, didn't have to go through the embarrassment of being glared at by the rest of the congregation because I wasn't able to control him in our pew. The little pest even giggled every time the altar boys rang the harmonically toned Consecration bells – presaging his fascination with and talent for music.

But Declan was an early pragmatist too.

Once, we were all having tea in Mrs Phelan's who was a friend of the family, and she cooked us a fry. 'Them sausages are horrible,' said my four-year-old brother, looking askance at his plate.

Consternation. Filthy looks. Parental apologies. Frozen silence.

Two minutes later, a small voice piped up, 'This bread and jam is *lovely*!'

Declan's overriding childhood memory of me is equally dismal and is mainly of the mental torture I inflicted on him.

He remains particularly incensed by one episode. He was four years old and rankling that he still slept in a baby's cot. One day, he was as usual being a nuisance, following me where, at almost ten, I did not want him. 'Listen,' I turned on him in fury, 'why don't you go home and play on your new bed?'

His eyes lit up with transcendental delight, 'I have a new bed?'

'Yeah. Go home and play on it.'

The poor kid raced off as fast as his little legs could take him and, of course, the despised cot was all he found in his bedroom. He still hasn't forgiven me.

Memory of those holidays in Rush is largely of rain. We customarily went for the month of July, sharing with the Madigans and the Malones, with maybe day visits from other Ballymun friends. Dadda and Tom Madigan were clerical officers in the civil service; Joe Malone worked for Sunbeam Wolsey, the hosiery and knitwear manufacturer, and enjoyed the luxury of a company car. All three of the women were what were then called housewives, dissimilar in personality but having almost everything else eerily in common, including a propensity for bitching on a competitive scale about their husbands.

For the first two weeks of the month, the men came down only at weekends, leaving us children and our mothers with the run of the house – and then, for the final two, they were on leave and we were all together.

The atmosphere changed radically when the men arrived. Instead of being relaxed and hang-about, we were excursioned, brisk-walked and proper-bedtimed so that a babysitter could come in to let the adults go to the Harbour Bar – from where they returned noisily to play cards until three in the morning, filling the house thereafter with snores.

In the first Rush years, since only the Malones had a car, the

Madigans and ourselves shared a taxi for the journey to the seaside. (The highlight of one year occurred even before we'd arrived when we lost the Madigan pram off the roof of the vehicle and were able to watch through the back window as it careened through the traffic and came to rest on its side. Luckily, the damage was minimal, but for a few minutes there, we'd walked on the wild side. It was great.)

After a respectable interval (to teach me that dolls didn't grow on trees), I had acquired a replacement for Suzette and, each year, for days before this holiday, I mended and washed her clothes, then pegged them out to dry. I knitted her a new scarf, then washed and rewashed her nylon hair so she would be in good order for her hols. (Even from a young age, I was pretty well hooked on my weekly *School Friend*, in which the girls always managed to foil the atrocities of nasty prefects before going on a celebratory trip to the tuck shop. It was they who had hols and slept in dorms and whose exclamations of 'EEK!' I appropriated for myself.) I selected and reselected books and back issues of the comics, packed and repacked, making sure the miniature playing cards were included with the Ludo and the Snakes and Ladders so we kids could play Snap and Old Maid while the grown-ups played Solo.

When the taxi arrived on the great day, we Purcells and Madigans – four adults and five children – were allowed by the forbearing taxi driver to stuff and contort ourselves inside. Then we opened the windows and sweated our way through bright sunshine until we got to the holiday house, unpacked and claimed our billets. During the first walk on the harbour beach, the clouds nearly always rolled in.

Thereafter, my sense memory of Rush is of the smell of damp clothes in the cramped quarters indoors. Or outdoors, with no choice but to respond to the demands of our parents that we should get out from under their feet and 'get a bit of fresh air', of sitting cross-legged on the wet sand of the harbour beach. I can still hear the incessant fusillade of rain bouncing off the tent I made of my plastic mac by holding it over my head and tight around my face, having to open it a little wider every so often to let out the condensation.

A small girl sitting alone on a deserted beach in the pouring rain?

It sounds miserable when written so baldly, but it was fun. I discovered I liked the solitude and sense of independence. Chilly but warm and dry in my island cocoon, with the plastic warming and moulding itself stickily to my bare arms and legs, there was even enough light, albeit opalescent, by which to read. I didn't need to, however. Although I was rarely without a book somewhere close to hand, it was sufficient on those occasions to sit in my own company, listening to the loud but soothing rain with no one to order me around or make me wash the dishes or even to engage me in conversation. It was good simply to have time to think and daydream, to peer through my eye-slit at the stippled grey sea.

A change is as good as a rest, goes the saying and, at that stage of my life, when I was about eight years old, any change from school was welcome.

3

Our Teacher

I had spent only six months or so at the Holy Faith Convent when I was taken out because my parents had discovered that the nuns operated an apartheid system. We who wore blue sashes in the private part of the school were strongly discouraged from associating with the girls who wore red sashes and attended the national school on the other side of a wall.

So, still only four years old, I began travelling to Scoil na Naoíneáin, a feeder kindergarten for Scoil Mhuire. Along with the boys' school, Scoil Cholmchille, my new school was situated within the Model Schools complex in the grounds of the Department of Education in Marlborough Street where Dadda worked. In Scoil Mhuire, all subjects, even English, were taught through the Irish language, and Scoil na Naoíneáin was to prepare us for that.

Luckily, the 13 bus went all the way in to Madame Nora's, the hosiery and handbag shop on O'Connell Street. To get to the school from there entailed only a short walk down Cathedral Street where

I customarily said hello to the black-clad lady who sold holy pictures from a little tray on a stand. However, I had to remain on the *qui vive* to dodge the more startling Dublin characters who muttered and shouted to themselves in the environs of the Pro-Cathedral. For instance, I always took a wide berth around 'Bang Bang from Inchicore', part of whose beat encompassed the area around the Pro, but whose main gig was to jump onto the open platform on a bus and, brandishing a huge key, to shout, 'BANG!' while aiming at the passengers. He was essentially a harmless eccentric but I was only five years old and wary of his sudden and highly unpredictable changes of direction; if he swung that massive key at me, I was a goner. Anyway, he smelled awful. I occasionally came across flashers behind the Pro and, on the bus one afternoon, there was a man who shoved his hand under my school uniform.

Every Wednesday, Mamma went to the southside to visit her sister Sheila in Terenure, so, after school, instead of taking the 13 or the 19A home from O'Connell Street, I boarded the 54 from D'Olier Street. I liked to sit upstairs. All the better if I could get a front seat. I didn't enjoy it, though, because on many of the Wednesdays, no matter how small I scrunched myself against the wall to give him the room he seemed to need, this man, who wore a big coat and whose lips were fat and glistening, used to come and sit beside me and squish me against the wall of the bus by nudging his thigh hard against me. I thought he was very, very selfish, especially when he could see I was trying to read a book.

It never occurred to me that I could come to any harm, or even to mention any of this to anyone; I treated these flashers and gropers as an inevitable part of life, like being forced to drink Syrup of Figs or eat porridge or have my hair fine-combed for nits. I figured that these were weird, sad people, a bit simple, and filed in the same character box as Bang Bang from Inchicore, and I learned to avoid them as best I could. After a while, I always sat either on the side bench inside the door of any bus I got on or, if I couldn't get that, beside the aisle. And when on the 54 my personal pervert showed up and tried to shove me towards the wall, I learned to jump to my feet, to get out past him and go downstairs.

Yet Dublin city remained eminently negotiable at the time, even for a five- or six-year-old. There weren't that many characters that you had to worry about and, in general, I never felt a sense of danger, even when I took shortcuts through alleyways. People in bus queues tended to look after you and make sure you were able to climb onto the platforms; and if you were inclined, as I was, to jaywalk through the buses, Guinness drays and swarms of cyclists zig-zagging past Nelson's Pillar, they yanked you to safety by the collar of your coat and ate the face off you for being a stupid little twerp.

At one point, I think I was about six, I self-importantly went into McCarthy's pawnbrokers opposite the school, reaching up to the counter proudly to present a coral necklace my Auntie Nellie had given me as a souvenir of her trip to Rome with her great friend, Father Victor. I was expecting a half a crown for it at the very least.

In that era, it would appear, independent women like Nellie did forge these special, almost adoptive friendships with priests, particularly those from the mendicant orders – and it was neither untoward nor unusual that they should travel together on holiday. A Franciscan, Father Victor Sheppard was a noted scholar and theologian, based in Merchant's Quay. Nellie and he – sometimes with others – journeyed to various European cities, Paris, Assisi, Venice and, notably, Rome, where his connections assured them of proximity to the Pope during audiences. At home, they attended movies and went to theatres. In many ways, they were best friends and, although there was never a hint of impropriety, I have wondered if he was the reason she never married.

Anyhow, the pawnbroker was patient, entertaining my insistence that this was real coral and was very valuable – because my Auntie Nellie had said it was. But he refused to let me hock it. It was the first time I heard the phrase 'hen's teeth', as in, 'I'd take it if it had a few hen's teeth in it, love.'

Life in the *naoínra* itself where, under the benevolent tutelage of Bean Uí Huggard, we learned to conduct our daily lessons through Irish, was pleasant enough and I don't remember either verbal or physical assaults there. She entrusted us with serious jobs – for instance, sending us to carry notes to other teachers in the complex or, throughout the winter months, letting us take it in turn to heft the dusty sods of turf from their box so she could feed the encaged fire at the front of the classroom. We had lots of naps too: on the command, '*Téigí a chodhladh!*' we all folded our arms in front of us on the desks and dropped our heads onto them, not to be lifted again until we heard the countermand, '*Dúisigí!*'

All changed for ever in September 1952 when I was almost seven and a half. Home was no longer the cushy palace where I had been princess. Declan was two and getting all the attention, as far as I could see.

When I was well into adulthood, my mother informed me that, while I was his adored only child up to the time Declan was born, my father did a complete about-face at that point, rejected me and became interested solely in him. I don't know if this was true, I don't know either what her motivation was in telling me, perhaps to bring me onside against my father. And perhaps it did happen. Yet, although I don't remember feeling cast out, it was not until he was old and in his very last years that I succeeded at feeling somewhat easy in Dadda's presence.

Home wasn't my real problem, though.

Scoil Mhuire, big school, where we sat in pairs at scarred desks with integral inkwells, was a grey, utilitarian building set side-on to a concrete play yard behind iron railings. It had stinking outside toilets, a wide clattering staircase made of stone and classrooms partitioned from each other with glazed, folding walls. Although it stood in the same complex as the *naoínra*, my transition to it from Bean Uí Huggard's amiable regime was a huge culture shock and not just because, from now on, I had to wear a navy uniform with a *bóna bán* – white collar.

That *bóna* became one of the banes of my existence, albeit on the more trivial side. Some of us wore detachable ones pinned onto the jumpers; some wore white blouses underneath the jumpers and pulled the collars over the neckline. The difficulty arose when our new teacher, an intimidating creature with a large, muscular frame, frizzy hair and a heavy tread, swooped randomly every so often, usually on Fridays, to check if your *bóna bán* was grubby. If you were one of the unlucky ones chosen and your *bóna* was less than pristine – by Friday mine was grey – she disparaged your mother's housekeeping skills in front of the whole class, compounding the humiliation by singling out one of the inner-city girls whose *bóna* was always snow-white. She'd make the unfortunate child stand up while she scolded the rest of us and, by implication, our lazy, slobbish mothers. 'Look at that lovely *bóna*. If the mother of that poverty-stricken, numerous family could turn out her daughter's *bóna* like that…'

That teacher, who was unlike any woman I had ever seen before, initially fascinated me. She wore men's work boots and, instead of a handbag like Mamma's or my aunts', toted a battered music case.

She also chewed tobacco, spitting the juice into the cane waste-paper basket beside her desk and, every so often, disgorged a spent plug from her mouth into a plum-coloured handkerchief. I still get queasy when I imagine the lumpy, squishy feel of that thing; thank God she never gave it to me to wipe my nose, as she sometimes did with other girls.

Fascination turned to terror, however, when the roaring started. After a honeymoon period of a few weeks, our teacher grew more and more irascible. For even minor infractions, such as getting a piece of mental arithmetic wrong, she would unleash – without a warning intake of breath – a deep, baritone roar, filling the classroom with the name of the dunce.

Since that year of 1952, I have hated the name Purcell. In fact, I became averse to any word beginning with the letter *P* because of the way the plosive erupted like a missile from that woman's mouth. It didn't help that I was seated at the front of the class: as if those *P*s weren't bad enough in themselves, they could also result in a collateral spray of spittle and tobacco juice. As I write this, I have no difficulty in summoning up the sound of rattling partitions that seemed to accompany that sudden and ear-splitting, '*PUR—SÉAL!*'

Our teacher was liberal with the use of the *bata* too. This was a rough wooden baton, used as a winding tool to hold the drawstrings of our knitting bags, but also employed in the service of discipline or punishment for not knowing something we should have known. It embedded splinters on the palm of your hand.

I came to loath knitting. Sometimes, we were given knitting homework – a sock heel to be turned – and our teacher reserved a special torture for those unfortunates who either didn't complete the task or who forgot to bring it to school on the appointed day. In these cases, the offenders had to sit in the dunce's row at the back of the class and were ordered to twiddle their thumbs. The order was literal. For the entire knitting class, the miscreants, of whom I was occasionally one, were required to interlace the fingers of both hands and keep the thumbs circling around one another without cease; it's hard to describe how difficult and physically tiring that is, but if she caught you slacking, she hit you across the knuckles with the *bata*.

There was no escaping her. The system in the school was that teachers moved classes with their pupils, so we were destined to have her for six years. I became so upset at the prospect, I confided some of what I felt to my mother.

Bad mistake.

Mamma came in to protest – to my horror, right into our classroom. The teacher received her graciously and they had what seemed to be a quiet, civilised chat, none of which I could hear. There were smiling, mutual goodbyes as though everything was now settled and hunky-dory.

But, as soon as the door closed behind her, to the tittering of my classmates, our teacher held up my mother to the class as an example of how mothers should not behave, '*Thánaig an* [emphatic sneer] *máthair isteach – agus pus uirthi*!'; 'In came the [emphatic sneer] mother – and her with a pus on her.'

The word 'pus' is virtually impossible to translate. It means a sulky, ugly expression combined with a belligerent attitude. But even though my insides were dissolving with hurt and humiliation on my own behalf, but mostly on my mother's, I recognised that some of those laughing at my family were doing so because they had to please our teacher.

The upshot was that I never again confided my unhappiness at school to anyone at home; I made up my mind that the only way to survive the next six years was to be cravenly good. And just as I had tried to please my nun, with all my might, I now set about pleasing my teacher.

Naturally, I never succeeded in this, even though I came top of the class in the end-of-term exams three times a year for the entire six years – with the exception of one Easter when I was second in one paper to my pal Síle Ní Loingsigh. My teacher even refused to be impressed by my collecting money for a class end-of-year present and personally delivering it to her home.

This pusillanimity probably succeeded only in alienating her still further and goaded her into taking every opportunity to humiliate me. I seemed to represent some weird challenge to her.

One Sunday evening, I spent an inordinate amount of time on my geography assignment. I had to draw a map of Ireland, copying it from my atlas, and I took care scrupulously to include every tiny coastal indentation. The task took hours and I begged – and received – permission to stay up way past my bedtime to complete it.

Tired as I was, when eventually I lay down, I couldn't sleep. I was too excited. She would have to praise me now for sure because it really was a very good map, faithful in every detail. Even Dadda, exasperated though he'd been with me for staying up so late and as usual leaving my eccer to the last minute on a Sunday night, had been very impressed.

For once, the bus taking me to school next morning did not move fast enough for me and I practically skipped down Cathedral Street.

One by one, our teacher went through all the maps and marked them out of ten. She stopped when she came to mine and my tummy turned with delighted anticipation when she picked it up and scrutinised it. But then she held it up for the delectation of the rest of the class and announced contemptuously that I had cheated by tracing it. She dismissed my tearful denials. It was the waste-paper basket again for me. (If I got anything at all wrong, she made me stand in front of the class with my feet in her waste basket.)

When she lost her temper, that woman threw girls bodily around the classroom, against the blackboard, even heaving one through the open window into the playground. Worst day of all for me, however, came as a consequence of that single occasion when, although I came overall first, I was second to Síle in one subject. Our teacher marched me into the younger class below us, ordered me to sit at the back of their room, and explained to everyone why this was happening. I was too distressed to take in exactly what she said, but I did gather the gist, 'Look how the mighty have fallen...'

She referred to me in terms of the ultimate put-down of that time: that I was a 'know-all'. The more I put up my hand to answer, the more she ignored me. At the same time, if I didn't put up my hand, she pounced. And if I didn't know the answer to the question for which she had pounced, I was put in the waste-paper basket again.

All of this may sound fantastical, the issuings of an over-active child's imagination. But there were witnesses. Síle remembers it all and, many years later, at a book signing in Galway, I met another of my classmates, Aedín Lúcás. She and I immediately fell to reminiscing about our teacher's fear-inducing regime.

To be fair to the woman, there was perhaps some chemical interaction between her and me that neither of us understood. Given my doomed efforts to grovel for acceptance by straining not to fail, I might, perhaps, have come across as an irritating little clever clogs who had to be taken down a peg or two. It was an era when children were expected to know their place.

She vanished from our lives for a blessedly relaxed period during Fifth Class when, hardly believing our luck, we were taught by a succession of gorgeous young substitutes who laughed readily, did a lot of colouring and pinning-up of wall charts, and devised ways to keep us interested in our lessons instead of hammering us with them. It was whispered around the place that our real teacher had had a 'nervous breakdown', the first time I had heard the phrase. Picturing her insides writhing in pain as sharp nerves pricked all over the inside of her skin, I felt the first glimmering of sympathy for her. And she did appear to be different, quieter, far more subdued, when, on her first day back, she put us under instruction not to cause her any trouble because she couldn't deal with it.

The poor woman's long dead and I hope she's at peace now.

4

What Angle?

My experience of Scoil Mhuire wasn't all bad, nothing ever is. I made terrific friends there, although some engendered deep envy at the time. For instance, I coveted the home life of my pal, Síle, with whom, when the weather was fine in summer, I cycled to school. Her family lived in a small house in Finglas and her father was a teacher. To my eyes, he seemed easy-going and approachable: my mental image is of him sitting by his fireplace with an amused expression on his face as he noted the comings and goings of his large family.

Interestingly, when the time came for another of Síle's younger sisters to attend Scoil Mhuire and it became evident that our teacher would fall to her in the rotation, he sent her to a different school. He was a wise man: when Síle brought stories home, he had never come in to complain – on the basis that his intervention would make things worse in the long run. Now, when that lucky sister asked why she was not going to Scoil Mhuire, he merely told her quietly, 'You wouldn't be able to cope.'

Síle's mother had rosy cheeks and seemed actually to *like* being a housewife and, to my eye, all nine members of that family fitted happily into their tiny house like kittens in a basket. I spent as much time as I could there. I wanted to be one of them.

The exotic amongst us was my friend Adavin Ní hEidirisceóil (O'Driscoll) a glossy-haired beauty whose mother was Jewish and whose ex-Catholic father had chosen the name Adavin, a phonetic representation of the Irish for 'little atom', because it was as far removed from a Catholic name as he could manage. Many of us saw her Jewishness as a challenge and tried hard to entice her into the Pro-Cathedral to light candles or even, like the rest of us, to take short cuts to the bus stops in O'Connell Street but she remained true to her principles and while she did take the short cuts, she refused point blank to go the whole hog and light candles. Nevertheless, obviously excused Catechism class, for one exam she took the subject anyway, typically scored full marks and was then held up to the rest of us useless bunch of dullards as an example. 'Unfair!' we squawked. For we discovered that she had been given sight of the questions in advance by a substitute teacher, clearly unaware of the fiercely contested pecking order in our class.

There was Eleanor Harty, who lived in Palmerstown and whose surname was totally appropriate because they were a jolly, laughing family who, in my eyes, were amazing people because they had horses.

Then there was the truly gorgeous and dreamy Cíara Ní Shúilleabháin who, to the fierce and proprietorial pride of those of us who had counted ourselves amongst her friends, later went on to become a Rose of Tralee. She sometimes brought me home to her house in Clonskeagh where her mother, Pearl, treated Cíara, her sister Bernadette and me too, as if we were not nuisances but real people. Pearl fed us Irish stew, Marietta sandwiches (these were great because by squeezing the biscuits together, the butter oozed between the pin-sized holes) and glasses of milk with froth on them. Pearl's thank-you Christmas presents to the teacher were always the most thoughtful and the May altar flowers she sent in via her daughter were always the most luscious — lilacs, for instance, and irises.

Every year, there was always the prospect of the summer holidays after the relatively relaxed month of June, during which we were allowed to wear *ár gúnaí féin* – our own dresses – and, when the weather was fine, to have classes outside, gathering like a flock of bright butterflies around the teacher in a corner of the playground. There was Drill, also in the playground, consisting mainly of toe-touching and synchronised arm movements, '*A h-aon a dó a trí a CEATHAIR!*' counted out by Miss Medlar; it was she who also taught us Irish dancing, in which I turned out to be an expert in the slip jig and for which I won a medal, second or third I think, at a *feis* in the Mansion House.

I also won something at the Feis Matiú for a recitation in Irish of the legend of *Cearc a' Phrumpa*, complete with expansive hand-waving, soaring emphases on inappropriate syllables and alarmed-chicken imitations. '*Thuit cnó anUAS den chrann agus BHUAIL sé sa cheann í! GÁC-AC-AC-ÁC arsa Cearc a' Phrumpa, tá an SPÉIR ag TITIM!*' Cearc a' Phrumpa was the Chicken Little of our Gaelic world: a nut falls on our hen's head from a tree and, convinced the sky is falling, she spreads the bad news... '*GÁC-AC-AC-ÁC...*'

There were the annual Drill displays in the round room of the Mansion House where I was delegated by Miss Medlar to lead the whole school proudly in the marching maze; there was First Holy Communion where I managed to avoid damnation for all eternity by succeeding in not chewing the Host, although it tasted just like a very thin, stale ice-cream wafer. I had similar luck on my snowy

Confirmation day where I escaped being asked a catechism question by Archbishop McQuaid, even though I'd been put in harm's way in an aisle seat. He skipped me.

All of these good things were nevertheless just welcome distractions from the daily torment.

I became very superstitious. I went through a long, propitiatory phase of not walking on pavement cracks: any breach meant I would have a dreadful day with our teacher. I saved pennies to bribe statues of saints in the Pro-Cathedral with candles. Any morning I didn't get to give up my seat on the bus to an adult meant a bad day ahead, and I panicked if the bus wasn't full and there was no one standing. I had to resist the temptation bodily to drag people onto my bus from the street so I could give them my seat. This pre-appeasement veered close to phobia when, on a couple of those non-giving-up-of-the-seat days, I even had to jump off the bus before I got to my stop in order to vomit into the nearest gutter.

Very late in his life, my father, who worked in Education and who would undoubtedly have intervened if he had known about all this, was devastated to hear about my experiences at Scoil Mhuire. I remember exactly how it came up. He was in his late seventies and, meeting him unexpectedly in the bank in Glasnevin, I insisted on giving him a lift home in my car. The radio was on. Pat Kenny was talking to someone about the bad old days of corporal punishment in schools. Dadda, whose firm opinion was that RTÉ presenters were always unfairly harping on against the public service, snapped that, in his day, a few belts never did him any harm, which, I'm afraid, unleashed my own demons. 'I didn't know, I didn't know,' he whispered at the end of my impassioned recital, repeatedly shaking his head in disbelief so that I was desperately sorry I had opened my mouth.

I know I was merely the loser in an unlucky accident of timing:

one year later or earlier and my class would have missed that particular teacher. Mary Lynch, one of Síle's sisters, was in that younger class into which I was paraded that time. She doesn't remember it. All she remembers is that her own teacher was grand, and that as they heard the daily roaring and commotion in our class through their partition, she and her pals thanked their lucky stars that they hadn't drawn ours.

Ironically, it was common to be congratulated on getting our teacher in the six-yearly rotation as her class had the reputation of achieving wonderful results. And, true to form, after Sixth Class, the results of the Primary Cert – the official end of primary education – were terrific for us all.

In the era before fee-free secondary education, the Primary Cert also represented the end of formal schooling for many. However, Scoil Mhuire, many of whose pupils came from disadvantaged areas in the inner city, always ran an extra Seventh Class to prepare us for the scholarship entrance exams offered by the convent boarding schools around the country. Here, too, our teacher's reputation for achieving results was high. Her pupils always won more scholarships than those of any other teacher in the school.

But, for me at least, the cost was high and there have been consequences. I am in my sixties now but I still cringe at the sound of a voice raised in anger. And, although I know quite well it is a learned reaction and completely irrational, I cannot seem to overcome a fearful internal shrinking in the face of others' hostility; I rarely fight back, almost always backing off from confrontation – unless it's on behalf of others – and have to wrestle with an automatic instinct always to placate.

More immediately, by the age of thirteen, I had developed a deep fear of failure. It became a serious problem for me and I dealt with it in general by choosing not to make the effort to fulfil expectations. (In my defence, at the time, this quirk was instinctive and it was only very late in adulthood that I understood what I'd done and why.)

For instance, I was one of only three girls selected to take Honours Maths for the Leaving Cert in secondary school at Gortnor Abbey, but deliberately put up all sorts of mental blocks in refusing to understand what Mother Gabriel was on about.

'You see this angle here?'

'What angle? I can't see any angle.'

I must have driven her mad. But the poor woman persisted beyond all reason and spent hours with me, one on one, explaining concepts I continued to insist I couldn't grasp.

Looking back, I can now visualise the blocking technique I employed: I listened only with the front of my brain, if that doesn't sound too weird. I see that frontage as a pale, impermeable surface, like polished blond wood, off which Gabriel's algebraic trigonometry diagrams and other stuff I didn't want to know about could slide instantly and neatly without leaving a trace. Although she continued to do her best to dissuade me, she eventually had to yield to my demands that I be allowed to drop back to the Pass class, thus firmly scuttling the school's hopes that I could have done well enough to be offered a university scholarship.

And when classes ended a month before the first exam, and when, as young adults, we were trusted to revise and study without supervision in the dormitories or wherever we chose, I read novels and comics for most of that crucial time. The result was that while I did well enough in the Leaving Cert, I certainly didn't perform as everyone had hoped.

I didn't really mind, however, because I alone knew that I could have done it if I'd tried!

The effect of that primary teacher on my subsequent life was undoubtedly not happy. Yet, if I were a judge and she, having been convicted of bullying by a jury of her peers, were to come before me for sentencing, I would be unable to exact revenge. I am cursed with empathy. As she, the perp, awaited her just sentence, I would project ahead to what would face her in gaol. I would feel her humiliation and despair (whether she herself was in despair or not) and would not find it in myself to inflict such psychological suffering.

I had a taste of this wishy-washiness much later in the Special Criminal Court. I was a Radio Éireann announcer at the time and was called by the defence team as a minor and incidental witness in the Garda Reynolds murder case. The defendants, Noel and Marie Murray, had claimed they had not known that Garda Reynolds, who was off-duty when he was shot on Arran Quay, was a member of the force. They argued that this was revealed to them only in a subsequent radio news bulletin. This was crucial: in general, the death penalty had been abolished in Ireland, but shooting a garda remained a capital crime. The reason I was there was to confirm that I had introduced the news bulletin and to attest to the time I had done so.

Along with the general population, I had been incensed by the killing of a brave man and was happy to do my bit to contribute to a successful prosecution of the perpetrators.

But, while waiting to be called to the witness box, I was seated very close to the Murrays. I couldn't take my eyes off them. I had somehow envisaged them as Incredible Hulks, or slimy, bulgy-eyed mafiosi, but they were just an everyday, undistinguished-looking couple who stared rigidly ahead towards the judge's bench and seemed afraid even to glance at each other. Although the courtroom was warm, they were shivering, probably from stress and, while I didn't change my mind about the heinousness of the act, I could not but feel pity for them.

So I'd make a rotten judge. And, although I do think I could still weigh in as an 'ordinary' journalist, in the current raucously competitive climate, I doubt I'd make it as a newspaper columnist, since most now seem to possess unshakeable social and political convictions and are encouraged to display them. As for talk radio, I couldn't for the life of me accommodate all those calls for retribution and torrents of righteous anger. The constant demand for vengeance truly upsets me. What about mercy?

It's not that I sit on the fence, I'm as opinionated as many and somewhat more so than most, but I have a compulsion to see both sides of a story and something happens to me, a kind of melting, when I'm faced with real people as opposed to principles.

In consequence, Governor John Lonergan of Mountjoy Gaol is one of my heroes: against desperate odds, he continues to espouse rehabilitation and education for criminals, rather than 'plain vanilla' punishment. I'm with him.

5

Silk Dresses, Blue Linen

My mother's lips tightened when she mentioned her own upbringing. Her eyes slid away too, and there was never any doubt that she was resentful, even bitter.

Conversely, she was never less than tenderly nostalgic when she spoke about the place she spent most of her short childhood. Durrow, County Laois. 'Durra' to its natives, is that very pretty village, with its clean but derelict coaching inn and tidy street through which people whizz on their way from Dublin to Cork at least until the bypass opens.

What isn't generally known is that the village can boast of a Pope. Apparently, St Benedict, an early Irish saint, was born there somewhere around AD 460, made friends with St Colmcille, alongside whom he was ordained, and the two travelled to the Aran Islands to the monastery founded by St Enda on Inis Mór. In 522, Benedict travelled with Enda to Rome and, while they were there, the then Pope, St Hormisdus, died; Benedict was elected as his successor and took the name 'Pupeus'. Then, legend has it, two days later, when Enda went to say goodbye to him before setting out for Ireland, the new Pope couldn't envisage his life without his friends and his country. He ordered a new election, which resulted in the elevation of John the First. 'Durrow Man Was Pope For Two Days' says the headline over one of the articles in Edward O'Brien's publication, *An Historical and Social Diary of Durrow County Laois, 1708–1992.*

These days, no one passing through the village can fail to notice the castellated entrance to Castledurrow; its tall gate lodge with the oriel window dominates the wide village green.

It was in the room behind that window that my mother, Maureen Butler, was born in January 1918; as chauffeur to Lord Ashbrook who owned the castle, Mamma's father, Jim, was given the use of the lodge when he married one of the castle's laundry maids, Annie Cahill. Both bride and groom were local – my grandmother's family lived right opposite the gates of Castledurrow in a terraced house on Castle Street, having moved there from the nearby townland of Knockanoran.

There were three other children conceived in that room, Jack, Jim and Sheila, but Jim died in infancy. I can find no record of his birth or death.

The Ashbrook family name was Flower. They were decent people, apparently, who were to the forefront in village affairs and did their best to support all local events and charities. Viscount Flower even attempted to set up a carpet-making factory in the demesne – and to that purpose invented a type of latch-hook still in use for handmade rugs. By 1922, tenants were increasingly able to buy out their holdings, and the Flowers' fortunes declined dramatically, making the estate no longer viable. So, perhaps spurred on by the bit of bother then pertaining in Ireland, they decided to sell up and leave Castledurrow for a rented house in Merionethshire, north Wales.

Here's where my grandparent's situation becomes rather mysterious. Because the Flowers were leaving Durrow, the family chauffeur would have had to leave both His Lordship's employ and his home at the gate lodge as a matter of course. It appears, however, that, at around the same time, there was some kerfuffle involving my grandfather, who may have been accused of doing something out of order – such as taking the car out without permission.

I have a letter from Lady Gladys Ashbrook to him dated March 1923, and obviously in response to a request for a reference. She writes from her father's house in Buckinghamshire, and, addressing him, starkly, as 'Butler', tells him she had been unaware he had been dismissed: '*I cannot tell you what a shock and sorrow your letter gave me, for I never thought Lord A. would do such a shabby trick by you who have been a good and faithful servant to him for so long.*' Frustratingly, there is no explanation to what might have happened. Lady A. writes that she is '*all in the dark*', and goes on to say that while her husband will be very annoyed with her for giving the reference, she will risk it anyway because she considers my grandfather to have been '*shamefully*' treated. She sends love to Annie and the children '*tell her how sorry I am about all this*' and adds: '*I shall never care to go in a car now, that you are gone.*'

In whatever circumstances they left Durrow, it was a great blow. With my grandmother (Nanna) just one month away from giving birth to Sheila, my mother at just over four years old and Jack at only two, they moved to Kilkenny city, possibly because my grandfather, who was originally from Jenkinstown, knew his way around there. He found work in Statham's garage and they took lodgings in

Maudlin Street. Within a couple of years, they were on the move again, this time to Tullamore. He had secured a position, again as a chauffeur, to a Captain John Williams, of the firm that produced Tullamore Dew whiskey. (The initials of this man's father, D.E. Williams, from whom he took over as director, gave rise to the brilliant marketing slogan: 'Give every man his Dew...')

At some stage during this period, my grandmother became 'delicate' – the customary euphemism for a depressive illness. There is some evidence that she may have suffered from depression all her life, or it may have been post-natal, particularly after the death of her infant son. Whatever the cause, Annie left her family in Tullamore and moved back to Durrow, into the house on Castle Street where her mother still lived with Annie's brother, Mick, and her two sisters, Bab and Julia, the latter then being sent to Tullamore to look after the three children. There was another brother, Tom, who was living in Midleton, County Cork, with his wife, Betty. I never met either of them.

Nanna's health did not improve and she was sent to Kilkenny Hospital where she was treated with Electro Convulsive Therapy to both lobes, a practice that is rarely carried out in these days of more enlightened psychiatric treatment. On discharge, she went home, not to her family in Tullamore but again to Durrow.

This unusual domestic arrangement, where Julia continued to look after her sister's husband and three children while Annie stayed at home with their mother, continued until March 1931 when my grandfather caught a very bad cold but insisted, against all advice, on fulfilling his duties. It was not until he was in a state of near-collapse that he finally gave in and took to his bed.

There was widespread incidence of influenza at the time and Julia grew fearful. She sent a message to Durrow that my grandmother should perhaps think of coming up to visit.

The jury is out on why Nanna did not immediately accede to this request, although there is some evidence that she did plan to. In any event, on the Sunday following the receipt of Julia's message, she went to Mass as usual with Bab but, before he began, the priest on the altar turned to the congregation and asked them to pray for the soul of a Jim Butler.

Nanna turned to Bab, 'That's not my Jim, is it?'

It was.

My grandfather's death certificate shows that he died of influenza and that the duration of his illness had been nine days. He is buried in an unmarked grave in Durrow churchyard.

The little household in Tullamore now broke up and the two girls came back to live in the house in Castle Street. It was felt that Jack, being a boy, needed a father figure and an education and so, still only eleven, he was sent to Dublin to live with Uncle Martin Butler, his daddy's brother, and to get an education in Synge Street CBS.

Poor Julia was sent to Dublin too, into domestic service with a doctor and his family. I remember occasions on which my mother took me to visit a substantial, red-bricked house in Glasnevin where the door was opened by a wistful little person hung about with a heavy aura of tobacco. She had a deep, almost baritone voice, a head of luxuriant hair that rendered her face very small, and wore a black maid's uniform under a heavy, dark-blue apron – thick cotton perhaps, or even canvas. In my memory we were not allowed across the threshold but had to chat with her on the patterned tiles of the open porch. Julia stayed in service in that house until she became too ill to continue. She ended her days in a home.

Back in Durrow, things had changed by the time my mother and Sheila got back there from Tullamore; the Presentation Order of nuns had bought the Castledurrow demesne and had turned it into a school. So, my mother and aunt, wearing silk dresses, were now daily sent up that long avenue.

Silk dresses?

Resentment of these dresses, which, as described, must have been exquisite, was initially one of the more puzzling sources of my mother's twisted lips when she mentioned my grandmother – until I found the patience to listen properly to the reason why the memory upset her. Although Nanna had never been easy to live with, Mamma blamed bereavement, but most especially the ECT treatment, for turning the woman into an eccentric, even paranoid, tyrant. Independent to an extreme, even harmful, degree. Save for the shelter of their roof, she refused to take any financial help from her family who had little to give but who had nevertheless offered it with a heart and a half.

It was the 1920s and early 1930s, a time when the landless or jobless in Ireland had little help from the state but eked out a frugal living where they could find it; Mick earned a little as a gardener and oddjobber for the nuns up in the castle and was allowed to shoot rabbits and the occasional game bird for the pot; Bab got a few pence from selling the eggs laid by the Rhode Island Reds that picked around the kitchen floor and in the tiny yard outside the back door. In that house, even in my time, meat was reserved for visitors and Sundays and the main meal generally consisted of mashed potatoes with a pile of cabbage or turnip on the side. Sometimes, there was a small piece of bacon.

It turns out there were four tailors on my mother's side of the family and, having herself been apprenticed in childhood to one of them, Nanna was very skilled in that area. She insisted on 'paying our own way' by setting herself up as a dressmaker.

In such a small place, however, and in such straitened times, few people were treating themselves to new clothes and she could earn only a pittance from bread-and-butter work, such as alterations, or the painstaking turning of thick serge suits and tweed overcoats, shirt collars and cuffs. She certainly did not earn enough to buy the fabric for more than one silk dress each for her two daughters.

Consequently – here's where the bitterness comes in – while their pals loitered and played in the fields and trees of the demesne after school, Mamma and her sister, Sheila, were under strict orders to return home directly so the dresses could be taken off, laundered, dried and aired over the kitchen range, then pressed 'as new' to wear again the following morning. Any transgression was met with physical consequences. In addition, they were to 'keep to themselves' and 'not be telling anyone our business'. Although my mother never talked about it in detail, I got the distinct impression that Nanna's children were ruled, literally, with rods.

Mamma, for one, didn't have to endure the silk-dress routine for long. She was thirteen when her father died and, the following year, as soon as she finished school, she was sent to Dublin in search of employment and to lodge alongside Jack with Uncle Martin (another who had served in the British army during the war) and his wife, Auntie Kitty. My grandfather's brother was now a cooper with Guinness and the couple lived in one of the small, comfortable company houses in Kimmage with their two terriers. There was another uncle in Dublin too: my grandfather's brother, Jack Butler, was for many years head gardener in St Stephen's Green and lived with his family in that gorgeous little gingerbread house within the Green on the Harcourt Street corner.

By all accounts, Auntie Kitty, in particular, took her role *in loco parentis* very seriously indeed, to the extent that my poor mother, far from being released from Nanna's clutches to enjoy the delights of the city, operated under curfews and even stricter rules than she had endured at home.

Mamma got a job in the Broadway Café (latterly Cafolla's) on O'Connell Street, where she was placed behind the cake counter. Athletic, beautiful and a wonderful dancer, part of her duty was to don white gloves to partner male customers in the ballroom upstairs when there was an excess of gentlemen over ladies, perhaps when there was a ship in town.

There was nothing untoward about this; the manager of the Broadway, Mrs Hudson, was a lady of the utmost probity (Protestant, naturally!), intolerant of bad behaviour exhibited by any of her patrons, including sailors, and protective of my mother. She was proud of her venue, her wares, the live orchestra in her ballroom and her staff. She cultivated only the most civilised of customers, particularly welcoming the management and actors from the Abbey Theatre around the corner – Lennox Robinson, for instance, or Mr Yeats himself, remembered by my mother as a quiet, very courteous person, as was his beautiful friend, Maud Gonne, who sometimes accompanied him.

In due course, at the age of thirteen, Sheila too got a job in the Broadway, initially as a dishwasher. One of my mother's most frequent reminiscences was of her poor sister's reddened, chapped hands and her outraged cry of '*more* vessels?' each time the waitresses crashed through the doors into the kitchen with their laden trays.

But with both daughters gone from Durrow and earning, Nanna decided to move to the capital too. She rented a flat above a shop in James's Street, from where she could continue her dressmaking business and take both girls back to live with her.

I remember that dark flat, the fumes from the paraffin heater and gas ring competing for supremacy with the yeastiness wafting from the nearby Guinness brewery. Poor they might have been but everything shone, including the oilcloth on the table, the china cups in which Declan and I were served mashed, soft-boiled eggs, and the equally delicate plates on which lay the buttered toast she had browned on a fork over the gas ring. She usually had a tube of fruit pastilles for us as well, and a slice of 'shop cake'. Nanna always prided herself on having 'shop cake', considering it far superior to the home-baked variety.

Naturally, she made all our clothes, including, never to be forgotten, a sleeveless sheath dress of royal blue with white polka dots for me. This monstrosity originally belonged to my father's sister, Aunt Nellie, and, over my protests, was carefully cut down to size. The hand stitching on the finished product was flawless, the thing fitted me like a second skin but I was eleven years old, and appalled at having to wear something that made me look like a miniature Joan Crawford. It was fruitless to rebel: Mamma was implacable. 'You'll wear it and like it. It's *linen*. *Everyone* wants a linen dress.' It may have been her subconscious revenge on the cosmos for the wrongs done to her in the matter of silk dresses…

So, for almost an entire mortifying summer, I hobbled on hopscotch beds and under skipping ropes because the skirt was so tight; I was the butt of derision and cackles of my friends.

It may have been character forming.

6

The House
on Castle Street

Before Declan was born, I was regularly sent on holidays to Bab and Mick in Durrow.

From the time I was about four, with my name, address and destination written on a parcel label hanging from my neck on a piece of string, I was installed in the front seat of a green single-decker at its terminus on the Dublin quays and put in the charge of the conductor. I spent a lot of those journeys worrying that something would fall off the roof rack which was laden with caged pullets, day-old chicks in perforated boxes, bicycles, wedding dresses and miscellaneous goods from Clerys, Arnotts, Pims, Elverys or Brooks Thomas.

Those green buses were central to life in Ireland then. It was the same bus, reversing its route, that brought us our Durrow Christmas turkey – head, feathers and guts intact – wrapped in brown paper and tied with string secured with red sealing wax. I hated to see the poor head, opaque eyes and drooping wattles tumbling out of the paper and, when it was unceremoniously slung by its crossed legs on a butcher's hook in the passageway outside our back door, I surreptitiously went out to make myself even more miserable by gazing at it. On Christmas Eve, while I tried to keep my eyes averted from the dirty business of beheading, plucking and disembowelling, my job was to sweep up the feathers as, like snow, they drifted on to the kitchen floor.

The arrival of the bus in front of Sheppard's Auction Rooms was always a community event in Durrow, and as the conductor relinquished me to my waiting grand-uncle Mick, the rest of the crowd fussed over me, 'Look at the size of her now.'

'How's your mother doin' up there in the big smoke?'

'Don't forget to tell your granny we were asking for her.'

'How's Sheila? Hear she got married – any stir?'

The house on Castle Street, double-fronted, opened directly onto the street. To the left of the dark, windowless little hall – hall-stand at the end supporting hats, gloves and missals at the ready – was the parlour, complete with traditional aspidistra in the deep window well. As an honoured guest, I slept in there on a brass feather bed and felt like a princess because the bed was behind a set of heavy cretonne drapes hung from rings that rattled on a brass pole. I was obviously trusted too, because it was in the parlour that Uncle Mick's rifle and green bagpipes were kept in full view on the sideboard. At night, there was great peace in hearing the sound of a set of footsteps clicking by the window, or a cheerful 'good night', neighbour to neighbour.

The flagged kitchen – chequered oilcloth on the table, rough dresser, black-leaded range – was to the right of the hall. I took my first journeys to the exotic east in that kitchen while I uncovered, mouthful by mouthful, the globules hanging from the weeping tree, then the pagoda. I created stories around the figure of the little lady with the parasol. Why did she look so demure and coy? Maybe the little character poling his boat along the stream running under the arched bridge was her boyfriend. I still believe there is no taste more sublime than that of mashed potato, with a well of yellow butter spilling over into the river that winds across a willow-patterned plate.

Daytimes were filled with trips to Scott's shop to view the curls of ham or bacon sliding off Paddy Scott's shining, screeching slicer or walking with Mick in the castle demesne to pick wildflowers for Bab. There were chores: scattering mash for the hens, flinging handfuls of damp, used tea leaves on the kitchen flags before Bab's whisking broom, cutting newspaper into squares to hang on the string in the Jeyes-reeking lavatory beside the henhouse in the yard, and – my favourite – rooting in the warm roosts of straw and hay, having been summoned by the triumphant cackling of a hen, to find a newly laid egg.

There were tricky tasks, such as trying to time the sudden gush of water from the street pump outside the front door so it wouldn't overfill the bucket and spill onto my sandals; fascinating ones, where I watched in awe as, with one fluent white whoosh, the dairy-man filled the enamel jug I held out. He could estimate the cubic capacity of that jug to the nearest inch and never wasted a single drop.

On fine days, I was allowed to paddle in the Erkina river under the hump-backed stone bridge at the entrance to the village, but was a tentative adventurer as I couldn't bear to think about the wrigglers and slimy things lurking beneath the squidgy brown mud that welled up between my toes whenever I overbalanced and slipped off the wobbling pebbles. And despite my infant imaginings about speckled fish in the non-existent stream at Laurel Lodge, when I was faced with the real sort, gills and tails moving languorously as they hung in the cool shadows of the pool under the bridge, I always kept a wary eye on them. I was seriously afraid that one might take a vagary to move towards me and – horrors! – brush against my bare legs.

This, oddly, is a fear that has never left me. I have been fortunate enough to swim in the Irish Sea, the Mediterranean, the Atlantic, the Adriatic, the Aegean, the Caribbean, Lake Michigan, Lough Conn, in the Shannon and at the Meeting of the Waters in Avoca, but I have never been able to relax fully in case some slippery, scaly thing touched me.

There were excitements in Durrow: being allowed to ride on farmers' hay wagons and to throw myself into the prickly stacks during the dog days of August or, with other children I never got to know, to make a slide down the side of one. Being given tomatoes to eat directly from the plants in Dunnes' aromatic glasshouse. Attending a talent show where, amongst the accordion players and recitations, I was enthralled by the skills of an amateur ventriloquist, my first experience of a full-sized person who had genuine magic powers.

There were trips in the cab of Joe Brophy's malodorous, belching sand-lorry to his quarry, with its encrusted and permanently rotating cement mixer; I was agog at the way he could so quickly and easily form a perfect concrete block in a wooden frame. With all that blue smoke curling upwards from the cigarette that adhered permanently to his lower lip, making him squint, how could he see what he was doing?

Joe could hold entire conversations without removing this cigarette and never bothered to brush off the little cylinders of ash that fell intermittently on to his chest. A most obliging and easy-going soul, with a smoker's cough of epic fruitiness, he was a great friend of the family. As the possessor of one of the few motors in the village, he was frequently asked to meet people coming off the train at Attannagh. This was great for me because he always took me with him if I happened to be in residence on Castle Street.

But there were sadnesses too, like the awful afternoon when Bab and I saw off Mick and Roddy, their ancient Pomeranian, then had to sit and wait for the sound of the gunshot that signified the end of the dog's last walk in the demesne. I could see that poor Bab was heartbroken but was too young to find the right words to comfort her because I was heartbroken too.

Evenings with Bab and Mick were initiated by the squeak of newspaper on glass as the globe of the oil lamp was polished before it was lit. We read then: newspapers, *Ireland's Own* or *The Messenger* for them, a book for me, the three of us companionable and easy in each other's company and in the glow of the range. No need for conversation. Then the Rosary and bed.

It turns out that I was happy in Durrow and, in retrospect, I think I have worked out why: I was an honorary adult there. These childless people, Mick, Bab and Joe, treated me as though I was an equal, chatting without condescension, patronisation or the sort of attitude I normally encountered where adult superiority had to be maintained at all costs because the slightest relaxation would have meant that I was being given 'notions' above my station. I was always delighted to be part of the welcoming party in Dublin when we provided beds to Durrow people who, carrying clean shirts and underwear in parcels under their oxters and offerings of country eggs or naggins of whiskey, came up for funerals, weddings or to go to Croke Park. The delight knew no bounds when Joe and his friends, with great ceremony, presented me with a shining silver threepenny bit. I always held it tightly in my palm to warm the little rabbit embossed on it.

Bab and Mick died in relatively quick succession, and, despite her children's misgivings, Nanna moved back from Dublin to Castle Street and lived alone there for many years. She was persuaded finally to abandon the village and come to live in a granny flat my parents made for her from their garage only after one of her neighbours, not having seen her for a couple of days, peered through the letter box and saw her pinned to the ground in the little hallway under the hundredweight bag of coal she had been attempting to carry. She had had a mild stroke and had lain there, conscious but unable to move, for at least twenty-four hours.

Nevertheless, while reluctantly agreeing that perhaps the time had come to cease living alone, she dismissed any effort to persuade her into medical hands, insisting that all that was wrong with her was a touch of Bell's palsy.

I saw evidence of my grandmother's excessive, somewhat bizarre self-reliance. When she was old and living in her granny flat, her dressmaking business diminished to the occasional alteration or repair, it took my father a long time to persuade her to accept a state pension. Then, a little later, when she had finally agreed to take this pension, he had similar trouble dissuading her from handing back the paltry increase she had received after a budget, because she already had enough and didn't need it. Later again, it also took him months to stop her from paying her electricity bill: Charlie Haughey's largesse to the elderly was unnecessary *here*, thank you very much.

As for a medical card – under no circumstances would she even consider such charity. Anyhow, until the very end of her life, she refused to have anything to do with doctors, preferring to self-medicate: hot neat gin for colds, caustic soda – yes, caustic soda – used at one stage to burn off what my parents thought (and was confirmed by the obliging but bemused doctor they sneaked in to view her from the safe distance of the doorway) to be some type of skin cancer all the way round her hairline. Probably, the doctor thought, caused by her refusal to adhere to the instructions on the packets of hair dye she continually (over)used.

Dilute? Much better and blacker results if the powder was used neat.

The more I write of her, the more I see not my nanna whose life was peripheral to mine, but a real person whose spirit I never fully appreciated while she was alive and I had the chance to get to know her. We share a birthday on 22 April and, if any credence can be given to his art, an astrologer I once attended may have been right – I may be replicating at least some of her stubborn eccentricity and 'personal independence to an extreme, almost harmful degree', a likelihood increased by the scientific fact that I carry an eighth of her genes. Oh dear.

According to my mother, Nanna refused to speak to her sons-in-law when they made her girls pregnant, although, if either addressed her, she remained freezingly polite. I remember an outburst when she announced that birth control should be compulsory after having two children. She was very anti-clerical and felt that priests should keep their noses out of women's business. She rode a bicycle until she was well into her eighties and, on being told that someone of her acquaintance had recently died, remarked scornfully, 'This dyin' is getting to be all the fashion.'

At least my father made great anecdotal use of all of this, good-humouredly entertaining his weekly card school with his resident mother-in-law's latest idiosyncrasies, for instance the formal complaint she made to him, asking him to have a word with his wife. She herself, she stated, no longer knew how to cope with either of her two daughters because 'those girls are out of control'. At the time, the girls in question were well into their fifties with their own families reared.

Until the day she finally had to go into hospital, Nanna rose daily at eight o'clock, made her bed, washed, arranged her shoulder-length hair, black as a crow's wing, under its hairnet, then donned a silk or satin blouse, tweed skirt, spotless cardigan, lisle stockings, court shoes and a string of pearls. She was always breakfasted and ready to face the day before nine.

Except for very rare excursions when she could be enticed into sitting in the back garden if the sun was really scorching, she was never seen outdoors or at Mass without a wide-brimmed felt hat, dark brown or grey. She replaced it every year with one identical to the last when she took her annual excursion into Clerys in the city centre. Then, safely home, she spent a considerable amount of time bashing the crown and softening the brim of the new acquisition until it was the exact shape of its predecessor.

When visiting her in that granny flat, I always found her sitting straight as a lodge pole pine on a hard kitchen chair (she had an armchair but didn't use it) with one bar of her electric fire glowing only inches from her shins; as a consequence, they were permanently marked with a latticework of ABCs. From this chair, she would watch her small television set with her head turned at a severe ninety-degree angle to her neck and resisted all entreaties that she should turn the chair to make herself more comfortable. If she wasn't watching TV, she was reading: newspapers, biographies, detective novels, *Reader's Digest*, *Argosy* magazine – she was very well informed on current affairs.

The cause of Nanna's death was pneumonia, acquired as a result of a broken hip. The cause of the broken hip was as singular for a woman in her ninety-sixth year as the way in which she lived her life: on recovering from a bout of pleurisy, she experienced a draught at the back of her neck and traced it to an ill-fitting high window, slightly out of reach. Rather than ask for help to close it, she climbed on her chair to do it herself with predictable consequences.

By any criterion, she was odd. But Ireland used to have room for oddness: during my childhood many houses sheltered an 'odd' relative, who was not only tolerated but accepted as part of life's panoply.

But she was fascinating too. Just before her death, for instance, I learned from my mother that, at the beginning of their marriage, my grandparents ran a touring céilí band, a detail I could never have imagined – I had not once heard Nanna mention music or seen her show the slightest interest in it. I have checked it out, however, and it was true: he played the violin and she played the melodeon. My informant thinks there were four in the band, the other two being a saxophonist and a drummer.

I could have known a lot earlier. I had seen my mother become tearful on hearing the violin piece 'Meditation' from *Thais*. She had said she was upset because it had been one of her father's party pieces. I had never asked her to expand.

7

A Scribe
Is Not Born

My parents were four years behind the Madigans, Malones and Hendersons in managing to scrape together the deposit to buy one of the semi-ds in the new estates in Ballymun, a few hundred yards up the road from the house on Dean Swift Road. While they were saving, our next move was to rent at 8 Fairfield Road in Glasnevin, a small, solid red-brick house in an established middle-class area near the Botanic Gardens where we were still within walking reach of Ballymun and the Gang of Eight. Although I made new friends, I, too, maintained contact with the pals in Ballymun, particularly Patricia Madigan.

Fairfield Road was where I developed my first crush on a boy. His name was Colm Murphy and my love involved lots of fervent prayers at the May Devotions that he would notice me. And, while we all roller-skated along the paths, it involved contriving to lose my balance as frequently as possible so I could crash into him.

Fairfield Road was also the base from which, after the day's travails in Scoil Mhuire, I trekked daily to Drumcondra Library to exchange my book for another.

Authors are frequently asked why they became writers. Although I came late to the profession, I know now that one of my greatest influences was that library, a pink-bricked building I came to regard as my second home and in which the smell of ageing paper, ink, dust and binding came to mean security, order and calm in a world that had become chaotic because of my experiences at school. Each day, I walked up those steps, through the glazed doors into the quiet, brown interior, and relaxed. Nothing sudden could happen; no one would roar. On the contrary, the women behind the desk always spoke very quietly and I knew that all the sounds would be routine and dependable: the riffle of a page turning, the slow shuffle of shoes around the stacks, a muted sneeze. To me it was like an idealised church.

Rain or shine, my daily walk to the library took me through Griffith Park, a linear green oasis on both sides of the fast-flowing and flood-prone Tolka river; of course I fell in now and then, because, nose buried in either the book I was finishing or the new one I was starting as I walked home, I hadn't been looking where I was going. Luckily, I never had one of these accidents when the river was really dangerous and the most I ever suffered, apart from a wetting and the ruination of my clothes, was the loss of a shoe; it was a popular park and there was always someone around to help me scramble out if the mud was too slippy. (And, instinctively, I nearly always managed to throw my book to safety on the bank.)

I went through that library with an efficiency I have rarely demonstrated since. The children's section was to the right, just inside the doors and, starting at the *A* stacks, I worked the low-level shelves in sequence until, within a few years, I had exhausted Drumcondra's entire stock of dictionaries, children's encyclopaedias, nature books, pony books, dance books and novels. As far as I remember, it was there that I discovered Louisa May Alcott and, having avidly gobbled up the extensive Billabong series of more than thirty books, developed a permanent and still unquenched passion for wide spaces under big skies, in this case the hot Australian outback.

In saying that I had consumed the library's entire stock of children's books, I have to admit that, arrogantly, I skipped anything I considered too young for me. I also disdained biographies of saints and martyrs: their expressions in the illustrations were impossibly miserable, really. But I did make a few exceptions. I liked St Maria Goretti; although her gory martyrdom gave me nightmares, I thought she was very brave to resist the advances of that cad. I also thought that the child saint Tarcisius, who risked his life by carrying the Body of Christ through the inimical streets of Rome, was terrific. I was also so taken with St Thérèse of Lisieux that I took her name as my own for my Confirmation; perhaps, I thought, some of her Little Flowerness would rub off on me, who was far from being Little and certainly not pretty enough to be called a Flower.

After I explained that I could find nothing new to read in the children's section, the library's staff, who must have been sick of me and my proprietorial strolling around the place, nevertheless kindly allowed me into the adults' area where, on their recommendations, I started on Annie P. Smithson, D.K. Broster, Jane Austen and the Brontës.

The upshot of my library experience in Drumcondra was that, by the age of twelve, I had developed what can only be termed an addiction to reading. It was escape and stimulation, it was armchair travel and nature study, it was the wonderful world of multiple syllables; it was *stories*.

This addiction has been lifelong and I remain fearful of diving into the first paragraph of any new novel because I know that, if the first page hooks me, it will lead to the detriment of everything else in my life – my own work, appointments, obligations of all kinds. Won't stop, can't stop, until I get to the end. On holiday, I have been known to refuse the blandishments of luxury meals and fascinating excursions in order to continue reading; once, rudely, when in the Canaries with a friend, her young son and my own two children, I had been reading all night and wouldn't get out of bed to go to the beach or even the pool until I had finished a particular novel's 900-plus pages.

Fairfield Road was also where I organised my secret society, the Purple Mask, whose membership was three, just like the Silent Three in *School Friend*. (You were either a *School Friend* or a *Girl's Crystal* girl in those days; the factions were as fiercely rivalrous as any GAA inter-county neighbours.) The gang's function and purpose were obscure, but they involved wearing flowing robes made of cheap green dress lining from Clerys and there was a lot of note-passing in a code I had developed. We muttered to each other in the sinister darkness of the Yew Walk in the Botanics and made little nests for ourselves on the carpets of dropped pine needles in the niches between the giant overground roots. But our main task consisted of flitting about at dusk, Sellotaping warnings: '*BEWARE! THE PURPLE MASK!*' to lampposts on Fairfield, Mobhi, Botanic and Daneswell roads. (These were somewhat spoiled by purple blots because we'd had to hand-mix the ink by adding water to powder and it proved to be thick and unmanageable. But who cared? We were lurking, weren't we? Everyone had been duly warned.)

It was in the back garden of the Fairfield Road house that I ran my first theatre, as playwright and impresario, with a sheet along the clothesline as a curtain and with my pals and little brother as actors. As far as I remember, the script changed daily at rehearsals as my truculent, easily distracted cast objected to what I asked them to do, each member frequently pointing out that someone else had a better part. The play involved a lot of cooking and sweeping – because a broom and saucepans were the only props I could source.

The audience consisted of parents, indulgent neighbours and a few non-cast children, who sat on a row of stools and kitchen chairs in the grass. Admission cost sixpence per adult and threepence per child, with a generous free pass for babies. I think I even provided refreshments: a glass of orange squash and a Marietta biscuit.

Afterwards, even though I was convinced I deserved the lion's share, I magnanimously split the proceeds equally between all the participants. Fairness. Equal distribution of wealth. Vincent Browne, my boss many years later, would have been proud.

On the other hand, promising this was the only way I could keep my cast in line.

It was a good thing I had learned early to cut my cloth to the demands of cast and venue. Having graduated from Rush because both families had cars now, my second play was staged during one of our first holidays in Tramore when I was nine or ten years old. This was an even more modest affair because of the lack of available props, scenery and costumes in our rented cottage and the availability of just four participants: Patricia Madigan, myself and our two small brothers, Brian and Declan.

The first problem was Patricia's announcement that she wouldn't be in the play unless she could dress up and be a princess and was allowed to sing 'The Ash Grove'. This was her party piece. Meanwhile, our two fidgety little brothers were reluctant to play any part at all in the drama and had to be cajoled, then threatened, then bribed with my own pocket money.

So, cast in place but still watchful and contrary, I set about constructing my plot around my resources. I called the work: *The Lost Princess*.

Scene One involved me (The Witch, clad in a witch's robe of chenille tablecloth) and my two assistants, Fish and Chips (Declan and Brian, who had a 'no-costume' clause in their contracts), developing a dastardly plan to disable and then kidnap the lovely Princess.

Scene Two showed the lovely Princess, wearing a lace doily on her head, gazing thoughtfully into space while singing 'The Ash Grove'.

Scene Three took place around a big saucepan handily raised on a stool, where Fish, Chips and I communally stirred up a broth of witch's glue while discussing our plan to spread said witch's glue on bread and feed it to the lovely Princess in a fiendish sandwich, thereby fastening her lips together so she couldn't scream for help. Then we would carry her off to our lair.

Ahh-hh… But…

Scene Four: Fish and Chips, bearing the sandwich, were creeping up on the warbling Princess, when they hesitated, seduced by her beauty and the poignancy of 'The Ash Grove'. They took pity on her.

Scene Five involved Fish and Chips, having fallen under the influence of the lovely Princess, betraying me. They jumped on me and, having pinned me to the floor, forced me to eat my own evil sandwich, sticking *my* lips together so that, although I tried witchfully, writhing and mumbling through my tightly glued lips, I was unable to utter my wicked spells.

The End. Safety for the lovely Princess; redemption for Fish and Chips; just deserts for me.

Despite the sincere ovation accorded by our parents and Patricia's nanna, I gave up writing and directing plays. Too hard to control your people.

The Madigans and ourselves went annually to the rented cottages in Love Lane, Tramore, for the next few years. Patricia and I hung around the forbidden Pongo parlour (forerunner of Bingo) and bopped on the pavement outside the equally forbidden amusement arcade to the echoes of Bobby Darin's 'Dream Lover' emanating from within. We fought silent but vicious battles in Cunningham's chip shop, the aim of which was to psych your opponent into eating her last chip so you'd have one left.

Tom Madigan taught us both to swim in the still waters of the harbour. We took our little brothers to the Rex to see memorable films such as *Demons of the Swamp*. (Declan, whose first excursion to the cinema this was, and who spent almost the entire film cowering under his seat, cannot to this day watch a horror movie.) At the beach, we played tennis and sang lustily along to 'Que Sera Sera' with Doris Day while matching our swing boat rope-pulling to its rhythms. I rarely went on these sixpenny rides more than once a day because I was conserving some of my pocket money for the last day. To this end, I haunted Shalloe's newsagent-cum-souvenir shop, loitering along the shelves of leprechauns and sticks of Tramore rock in an effort to choose what to bring home for Nanna and Aunt Nellie as presents. The staff of Shalloe's got used to me and left me in peace. Then, no doubt with relief, on 31 July, they took my money when I had plumped eventually for something like a tiny Irish cottage made of chalk, a half-inch china cat with a threesome of quarter-inch kittens tied to her with chains or once, memorably for Nanna, a beer-bottle opener with *Souvenir of Tramore* incised on its brown plastic handle. I was desperate: she already had all the cottages and cats she could handle.

It was in Tramore that I was allowed, at the age of fifteen, to go to my first dance in the Atlantic Ballroom, where the headline band was Emile Ford and the Checkmates ('Whaddya Wanna Make Those Eyes At Me For?'). I wore white shoes, a back-combed beehive hairdo, constructed over many hours by Patricia, and a wrapover dress in stiff, apricot-coloured *peau-de-soie* Nanna had made especially for the occasion from a Butterly pattern I had been allowed to choose for myself. My father delivered me at about quarter past nine. He would pick me up at midnight.

I went in alone. Patricia, at fourteen, was considered too young. This was a disaster because, first of all, there were about ten people in the large ballroom at quarter past nine and so, sitting on a chair against the wall near the back of the hall, I stuck out like the last, most luminous apricot on the tree. And when the place did fill, about an hour and a half later, I had no one to talk to while, increasingly humiliated and miserable, I waited for someone to ask me to dance. Mind you, I was so nervous that even the underarm pads I wore couldn't stop the spread of dark perspiration stains.

I hung on grimly, though: after all the expectation and hairspray, I wasn't going to go home early and thus admit to all and sundry that I was a wallflower.

At last, just after half past eleven, a young fella approached me and we set off through the maelstrom, quickstepping – me trying to achieve the near-impossible feat of holding my hands in the correct position while keeping my elbows glued to my sides to conceal the dark patches under my arms. I was a good dancer; he certainly wasn't. As we passed the bandstand, he stepped on my feet, hard, then leaned in to shout into my ear, 'Your dress is lovely.'

'Thanks,' I shouted back.

For a moment a look of incomprehension clouded his pimply face. Then it cleared. 'Not yours! Theirs!' With a jerk of his head he indicated Emil and his black-and-white-chequerboard-bloused mates.

When that dance set was over, I thanked my partner and strolled nonchalantly back to my place at the back of the hall. On the way, I spotted Dadda by the entrance door, scanning the crowd. He was fifteen minutes early. At least I had been up on the floor and dancing when he came in.

I strolled over to him and said I'd had a great time but I didn't mind going home now.

8

Adjacent Hollows

Two years before that dance, I spent most of the summer of 1958 in Ballymun, cycling daily from Fairfield Road to call for Patricia or for Helena Buckley, who lived next door to her, and to watch the progress of the new house being built for us at 15 Willowpark Grove. From the window of what was going to be my bedroom at the front, I would have what is now described in the property supplements as 'a magnificent view of open countryside': Drew's Field, a wild green space that was a godsend for courting couples of all ages, my own contemporaries included. Unfortunately, socially stunted as I was, I never got the chance to sample the delights of its long grasses and thick, all-concealing hedges and had to live vicariously through Patricia's description of what went on there.

By the time I might have been willing or able to participate, Drew's Field was no longer available. It, and the extensive farmlands beyond it, had yielded to demands for housing, and my vista had morphed into an extension of our estate – and behind it, the flats and seven towers of the Ballymun complex.

This latter development led the original residents of Ballymun to run a local campaign urging that their part of the place be renamed a disassociative 'Glasnevin North' but, with some others, my mother and father put up an ultimately fruitless resistance to this on the grounds that it would create a them-and-us divide. Although their 'No' side was defeated, my parents refused to the end of their lives, to use the new name. ('A bit sharp with anyone erecting barriers between new and old Ballymun,' ran part of Mamma's obituary in the parish newsletter.)

Before those towers went up, though, we youngsters had the run of not only Drew's Field but an entire *rus in urbe*. We walked to Mass in St Pappin's Church along what was a country lane. The only early-morning sound on our new concrete roads was the whine of the electric milk van, competing in early summer with the whistles and calls of blackbirds, thrushes, wood pigeons and sundry other twitterers. Cows grazed on the grasslands surrounding the Albert Agricultural Training College (now the ultra-modern campus for Dublin City University).

Drew's Field being site-specific, as it were, our main hang-out as twelve- and thirteen-year-olds was in a field behind Ballymun Avenue, an as yet undeveloped site. Its tussocky, scutchy surface was uneven and afforded lots of sandy hollows wherein, if you lay down, you could be invisible to the outside world. Two of these became by default a boys' hollow and a girls' hollow and, in the summer of 1958, with Scoil Mhuire behind me and the glory of a forthcoming scholarship to a convent boarding school at Gortnor Abbey marking me out as a little bit special, I thoroughly enjoyed lying around being a teenager, a word just coming into use.

All that summer, if the rain held off, we girls sunbathed and sucked nectar from the abundant white and purple clover and, when it was cold, we drew up our legs under our cotton dresses, buttoned our cardigans and huddled together for warmth. Lying at the regulation distance from the boys, it being sufficient simply to have them within sightline if we chose to stand up and look, we talked and speculated incessantly about them. We ran minor but passionate feuds as to who was the best, Elvis or Cliff, and ridiculed Patricia who liked neither of these Titans but who had plastered her bedroom with photographs of Adam Faith.

On Mondays, we argued about the Top Twenty as revealed the evening before – if we had got to hear it in the first place: the problem was that radios were nearly always in the kitchens of our houses and, at the sacred hour, parents frequently wanted to listen to something boring on Radio Éireann.

There was only the most patchy interaction between the boys' and girls' groups that summer, although go-betweens and emissaries did shuttle cautiously between them, setting up liaisons, where two parties of the opposite sex agreed that they liked each other and would therefore officially allow themselves to be designated a couple.

But once a relationship had been theoretically established, as a girl you had to wait for him to make the first move. Apart from peer acceptance and authorisation that you could now publicly talk to your boyfriend without it being a sensation, it was up to him to make the magical 'spin' suggestion.

No one had any money and so, being unable to go to the pictures, the spin was the ultimate goal for those going together. This meant a trip into the country on bicycles, all the way up to Knocksedan, perhaps, or, if time was short, to the fields at the back of the airport. At a given spot, he would suggest dismounting. You knew exactly why, but would agree casually – 'Yeah, good idea. Why not?' – albeit with heart pounding and blood whirring so fast through your veins you could hear the fizz.

You followed him into the field – or under the bridge in Knocksedan – where, after a preliminary period during which each of you wordlessly pretended to be enjoying nature, by closely examining a daisy, for instance, or leaning into a stream or river to pluck out a perfectly ordinary pebble as though it were a gold nugget, he would put his arms around you. Then the two of you would kiss until your lips were sore and swollen. After half an hour or so, thrilled to the soles of your sandals, you cycled home together. Although you were too shy to talk about what had just happened, or indeed about anything else, all the way home, the memory of what you had just done – or in my case *not* done, of which more anon – crackled like dry kindling between the frames of the bikes.

It never went further than kissing: if a boy attempted to touch any of the forbidden body parts, or – perish the thought – make any move towards getting a hand under an item of clothing, he was slapped away and usually apologised. I think that ethos was generally accepted amongst our group, although knowing what I know now about sexual abuse, Magdalen homes and so on, it's hard to reconcile such innocence with the undercurrent of life in Ireland for so many children at that time.

Patricia, who on windy days walked backwards up Ballymun Avenue towards the hollows to protect the kiss curls she had so laboriously clipped into her strawberry blonde hair, was far more courageous and experienced than I in matters of romance.

Since our mothers, best friends too, had wheeled us out side by side during the Pappins/Dean Swift days, we had few secrets from one another. Although she was a year younger than me, she had been kissed, French-kissed even, long before I'd taken baby steps in that direction. Patricia knew the ins and outs of the etiquette pertaining to Drew's Field: she was the one whose father had cycled right into it to haul her away and lock her in her room; she was the one who had then instantly climbed through her second-storey window, slid perilously down the porch roof, and returned to the action. She was also the one who frequently locked her baby-sitting grandfather into their dining room, threatened him with dire consequences if he squealed, but made sure she was home to release him before her parents returned to find her tucked up and peacefully 'sleeping'. In response to my avid enquiries during many sleepovers in her house, Patricia was happy to explain in graphic detail, and even with physical demonstrations, how kissing was done and what it felt like. So I knew the score. I was more than ready.

But that summer of 1958, when I was thirteen, it still hadn't happened by the time I went for my first spin with my first going-together partner, the late Paddy Campion. We cycled all the way to the bridge at Knocksedan, did the dismounting, did the daisy and pebble thing in the limpid river but, when he went to put his arms around me, I instantly looked at my watch and said, assuming shock, that I'd had no idea it was the time it was and I'd be killed if I wasn't home in half an hour.

We went back up on to the bridge, turned the bikes we had left leaning on the parapet and cycled home in silence. Although it was just as potent, the crackling between us was of a very different variety from what I knew it should be. I was furious with myself, he was furious with me – we were both furious with me. I was frantically trying to figure out how I could rescue the situation. As we came down the road past Pappins' church, I almost cracked and asked him to stop so we could go into one of the fields there. But I couldn't find the words and the opportunity passed.

We said a polite goodbye to each other where our homeward paths diverged and each went home, he to continue on to Willowpark, me to Fairfield Road. He sent word thereafter that he was breaking it off.

But I harboured a secret. All during that summer of 1958, despite my brief engagement with Paddy Campion, I'd been secretly mad about somebody else.

Given the way my passion subsequently developed, and since he doesn't know a thing about it, I don't want to embarrass him or anyone connected to him by naming the boy, so I'll call him Edward.

From afar, I'd adored Edward's floppy light brown hair, his wide-set cats' eyes and vulpine teeth; he had a trick of lowering his head a little when he was talking, giving those eyes an Oriental cast, which, to me, seemed to add to his air of intelligence and certainly increased his allure. He was agile, a good footballer, in my opinion as good-looking as any film star, and so could have had any girl he wanted. I knew for sure he wouldn't be interested in a greenhorn like me.

I kept my fantasies to myself and rarely brought up his name within my own group when we were discussing the relative merits of boys. But for me, a mere 'hello' or a 'howya' from him was the equivalent of a Papal Encyclical; for days after he had paid me even that much attention, I analysed and dissected the syllables and the tone in which they were said. Had it been personal? Had there been any hidden meaning in the way he said it?

On the last day of those summer holidays, the very day before I left for boarding school and four months' absence from Ballymun, I finally succumbed and admitted my secret to my pals in our hollow.

Helena Buckley offered to be the go-between.

'Yes–no–yes–no – well, maybe… No. All right, *yes!*'

'Are you sure?'

It was the last day. Last opportunity. He might be going with someone else by the time I came back to Ballymun from the wilds of Mayo four months hence.

A further, palpitating, 'All right so – yes…' And off she went.

A lookout was posted on the tussock above our hollow – match-making was always serious business – and the rest of us lay low; but, while the others murmured speculatively to each other, I was scrunched up like a baby, every muscle clenched, far too nervous to utter a word.

The seconds dragged into minutes.

She was having to persuade him.

Or, even worse, he had laughed outright at the notion of going with me. The other boys were all laughing too… It was all a great joke…

Oh, God…

The humiliation…

Let me *die… Please.*

After an agonising ten minutes of this, the lookout suddenly dived for cover. 'She's coming back!'

Somehow, I found the courage to look over our parapet. I still remember the way the wind riffled Helena's dark hair as, slowly, she picked her way back towards us. Her expression was serious: the answer had to be no and all my pals would now know I'd been rejected. I would never show my hand again. I would never, *ever* again tell anyone I was interested in a boy…

Helena, for whom the adjectives 'calm' and 'unruffled' could have been invented, came across our tussock. She settled herself, took my arm and held it tightly with what I took to be the communication of deep sympathy. Then she looked into my eyes and said, in tones of thrilling intensity, 'Deirdre, you're going with him!'

Those words, and the tone in which they were delivered, were to rumble like background thunder through every day of every class, Mass and camogie practice during the next four months in Gortnor Abbey.

But that day, because I had to be home for my tea and was leaving early the following morning, my first date with my new partner had to be confined to a short, stumbling chat in the small parking area to the side of the Autobahn pub. We shuffled about, not touching, while expressing mutual regrets about timings and so on, then made promises that we would see each other again at Christmas.

Walking home, my brain analysing every word of that first official conversation between him and me, the rest of me screamed with frustration. Why did I have to go away just now? Why hadn't I confessed my passion last week? Why hadn't I had the guts to reach up and at least give him a peck on the cheek?

Storming with self-loathing, hormones, lust and love, I could not eat when I got home but, for once, my parents did not badger me about what was wrong. They probably figured my belligerent demeanour to be a cover-up for the very real fears engendered by the prospect of imminent departure for school.

Their assumption was partly accurate.

9

The Glindas

The scuttlebutt amongst the hardened veterans of our teacher's class, many of whom had older sisters who had gone to one of these boarding schools, was that they were tough going. Compared to what faced us in convents, Scoil Mhuire was a doddle. Nuns did not feed you. Nuns were awful, spiteful gorgons.

And so, with my luggage crammed into the small boot of our boxy Triumph Mayflower, we left Dublin and headed northwest on 7 September 1958. Everything on the convent-supplied list had been ticked off: my monogrammed knife, fork, napkin ring, dessert and teaspoons, shoe polish and brushes; name-tagged table napkin; voluminous green knickers; everyday and Sunday uniforms; indoor and outdoor shoes; slippers; suspender belts; stretchy lisle stockings; dressing gown; soap-bag; and sewing basket. I also had my few shillings to pay for my boiled egg; while all food was supplied within the terms of my scholarship, if I wanted a boiled egg for breakfast, I had to pay for it and so, faced with my stated worries about being starved, my parents had forked out. The most prized of my new possessions, however, was my letter-writing case with its Belvedere Bond contents and supply of stamps.

The journey seemed to take for ever – and, in fact, it did take most of the day as we chugged along at between twenty-five and thirty miles an hour until we reached Ballina. We then set out on the Crossmolina Road, all four of us watching out for the large white crucifix, at which, according to the nuns' directions, we should turn left into a boreen.

All too soon, the cross loomed ahead. My heart started to thump when we steered into the laneway. It beat faster and faster as we bumped along between what seemed endless bog on one side and a series of high hedges on the other. Then, having rattled across a cattle grid, we drove into another world: a wide expanse of green grass, immense blue sky and glittering, rippled lake water with the peak of Nephin Mountain purple in the distance. Even I, shaking in my new shoes at that point, was overcome with the sight. It was one thing to read in a brochure that the convent, having been converted from a historic house, was situated on the shores of Lough Conn; it was another to experience the sight.

The nuns belonged to a French order styling themselves the Religious of Jesus and Mary. The Choir nuns, our teachers, were each to be addressed as 'Mother' because their mission was to nurture and mother us as well as teach. They did take that part of their work seriously and, whereas I had been led to expect a collection of Wicked Witches of the West, they proved on the contrary to be Glindas. Good witches from the North. All of them.

The Lay nuns, whom we were to call 'Sister', were equally kind, even though we had little to do with them or their work in the kitchen and laundry. (Tentatively, I once asked one, who, with habit hitched up under a rough apron, was kneeling to scrub a stone floor, how she felt about being confined to such menial tasks but she assured me that, just as the Choir nuns had their vocations, she had hers.)

Initially, I had difficulty adjusting to my new life. I was homesick, unsettled by the intense darkness and silence outside the dormitory windows at night and kept awake by the snuffling, snoring and shifting of the more than sixty companions packed all around me into rows of beds in the Big Dormitory.

I was lonely too. Because of our Scoil Mhuire Seventh Class, I had skipped First Year and had come directly into Second Year, wherein all the friendships had already been made during the previous twelve months and, although no one was overtly snooty or hostile, I felt like the outsider I was.

My behaviour in class did not help. Accustomed to the psychological warfare of Scoil Mhuire, I was hesitant about the protocols and made mistakes – for instance, when the nun asked a question, I put my hand up if I knew the answer. After I'd done this a couple of times, I discovered through the sniffy reactions of the other girls that this was *not* the done thing. This was showing off. In Gortnor Abbey, you stared fixedly at the surface of your desk thereby avoiding the nun's gaze.

As for the general school rules – about silence, about having your beret with you at all times, about being obliged at breakfast to eat the lukewarm, grey, lumpy porridge even if it turned your stomach – it took me a couple of weeks to recognise that there were ways around most things. I quickly found out, for instance, that, in the case of the porridge, it was the principle that counted. Given a signal (we were always in silence at breakfast) that you wanted a *very* small portion, the senior girl in charge of doling it out would merely bang the back of the ladle on the bottom of your bowl to leave a greyish brown smear. Then, rules satisfied, you smirked your way back to your table where you poured in milk and sugar and spooned that up.

And I discovered a silver lining to the beret rule. Although it was strictly forbidden to eat anywhere except in the refectory, like many others, I got into the habit of smuggling out slices of white bread – in my case spread with Bovril – by packing them into the green headgear I carried folded over my belt. Then, locked into one of the toilets, I would bolt them as fast as I could, thereafter burping my way through Study. It was pure adolescent greed, but also something more: it was getting something over on Authority. Or so I thought at the time; curiously, Authority never seemed to notice the telltale crumbs in my hair.

Bit by bit, as I negotiated the rules, official and unofficial, I started to relax into the routines and surroundings and began to trust the unfamiliar concept that a teacher was neither an enemy nor a deity to be placated, but could be a real person and could be approached.

I found myself virtually adopted by Mother Joan, the elocution teacher, who was a gorgeous person, originally English, with a plummy accent (think Queen Victoria) and who was very excited to have a pupil who seemed willing to throw herself full blast into any proposal that involved speech and/or drama. In time, she prepared me for the Ballina Feis and, to the delight of everyone, I duly brought home a trophy for my impassioned delivery of *Red Hanrahan's Song about Ireland*, given with somewhat less gestural finesse than I had displayed with *Cearc a'Phrumpa* years before. I got my photo into the *Western People*.

In the dormitories, the cubicles were so small that the curtains lay against the iron beds on one side and the lockers on the other, and it was a shock to discover the arrangements for personal hygiene. Morning ablutions, for instance, were perfunctory: having filled your water jug the night before, you just splashed about a bit in the basin on top of your locker – in winter sometimes having to break ice to get at it. Bathing was authorised once a week (by rota, four pupils per hour, which meant absolutely no lolling!), initially in one of only two bathrooms that served all ninety of us. I coped with that. But, since I am afflicted with fine, greasy hair that has to be washed every day, I never resigned myself to the rule that hair washing was allowed only every third Saturday afternoon.

After the midday dinner and sports on hair-washing day, we lined up along the wooden forms placed end to end along the middle of the mud room where we kept our outdoor shoes and gabardines. We knelt on the floor at these forms and did our best with basins and jugs of water splashed out by patrolling prefects. Photographs of myself from that period mostly show me with lank, stringy hanks hanging from my head; and, although I can't say for definite that the infrequency of the hair washing was the cause of the virulent skin rashes I developed, my hunch is that constant scratching of an uncomfortable, itchy scalp was certainly a contributory factor.

Actually, I never came to terms with the general laundry arrangements and, for charity's sake, will draw a veil over them; suffice it to say that the communal air in the classrooms and assembly hall was ripe.

It also took a good while to get used to flattening myself against the wall of the narrow stairwell if a nun was passing up or down the stairs. We were not allowed to touch any part of a nun or her clothing, not even accidentally by brushing against her: nuns and their habits were consecrated and to touch them was to violate them.

I chafed against the fining system, whereby if you turned up without your beret when it was required, you paid a penny. I also thought the censorship was ridiculous. Although there was no limit to the numbers of letters you could receive, you were allowed to write only two per week, one of which had to be to your parents. These two letters were to be composed *only* during official letter-writing-shoe-polishing-sewing-and-mending time on a Saturday afternoon.

There were two rubs here: the first was that my two letters had to be to my parents and to my Aunt Nellie, leaving me no way to correspond with Patricia and my other friends in Ballymun. (I never availed of the sporadic and totally illegal unofficial system whereby correspondence was smuggled out for posting in Crossmolina by an obliging daygirl. I was afraid that if I was caught doing something so heinous, my scholarship might be revoked.)

The second rub was that, incoming or outgoing, all letters were read by the nuns. I discovered this when, shortly after arriving, I was summoned from the study hall to the headmistress' office one Sunday evening and presented with my letter home. In it, I had said, truthfully enough but with my penchant for dramatising, that I was suffering from 'a racking cough'.

'Rewrite that,' ordered Mother Claudine, a tall, imposing presence – benign despite her attempts to appear otherwise. 'You can't be worrying your poor parents like that.'

I thought it was up to me to decide whether or not to worry my parents and, in rewriting the letter, I mystified those at home by restating my health problem as 'a teeny little tiny bit of a cough', hoping they'd twig it was a complicated antonym.

Most of all, though, I hated, detested, loathed and abhorred the Sunday walks, for which, wearing our outdoor shoes, gabardines and the wretched green berets, escorted by whatever nuns or novices had drawn the short straws that afternoon, we traipsed in gappy crocodile formation across what I saw only as a damp, featureless bog. Or (even worse) we were led out past the white cross to tramp along the damp, featureless Ballina Road where the only distraction was to count the dripping telegraph poles.

This was supposedly 'free' time. I could have been reading.

Not really. Because there was one crippling lack in that school: the time or opportunity to read. Gortnor Abbey did have a library – a series of glass-fronted bookcases running along the corridor outside the classrooms – but perusal of the volumes inside was limited to official library time on Saturday afternoons, during which they had to compete for attention with all that other stuff, most of it compulsory. I felt the absence of books as badly as if a dear companion had died and found the shortness of time allocated to them so frustrating that I gave them up altogether. I couldn't cope with closing a book when I was only halfway through a chapter.

So life at G.A. wasn't perfect, but I began to feel safe, even to flourish in the regime of teachers who, silly rules apart, believed in encouraging and inspiring rather than threatening. The JM nuns coached us in tennis, netball and camogie. There was always a nun available to play scratchy 78s on the ancient turntable in the recreation hall while we danced with each other during our forty-five minutes of free time in the evenings ('Hold Your Hoult Sweet Marie' sung by Michael O'Duffy was a particular favourite, as was anything bouncy and jolly played by Andy Stewart). They encouraged music participation, so I joined the choir, took piano lessons then added the cello, eventually becoming one of the three cellists in the school orchestra. After the endurance test that was Scoil Mhuire, coming as a pupil to Gortnor was like entering a calm harbour after a storm-ridden voyage in a leaky boat. By the end of my first term, I felt

Wildlife encounter: Laurel Lodge, Castleknock.

Left: Up in the world: The new tenants of 11 Dean Swift Road. Right: 'So who're you, might I ask?'

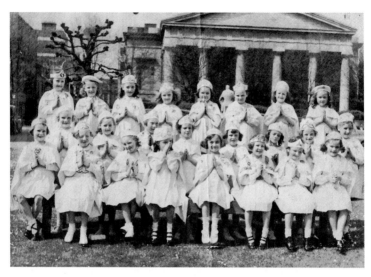

First Communion in our obligatory *gúnaí Gaelacha*. Yours truly is front row, first on the left and our future Rose of Tralee is fifth from the left on the same row.

My grandfather in his master's carriage.

The Cahills: Back: Julia, Tom and Bab – Nanna's two sisters and brother. Middle: Jack, Nanna, my great-grandmother, Mamma. Front: Tiddle Walsh (Sheila's pal) and Sheila. Note the silk dresses.

My great-grandmother outside the house on Castle Street.

A client of Drumcondra library.

Brian, Declan, Sheila Madigan, Patricia and me in Tramore, 1959.

Left: Bringing back the cup. Right: Aunt Eller and Curly on a beautiful morning at the Father Mathew Hall, 1964.

Curtain call for *Drama at Inish*: (left to right): Clive Geraghty, Eddie Golden, Aideen O'Kelly, Angela Newman, myself, Donal McCann, Geraldine Plunkett, Philip O'Flynn, Margaret O'Callaghan, Des Cave.

The salon at Molloy's pub: P.J. (front left) with Vincent Dowling, myself, Philip O'Flynn and Pat Laffan.

Cathleen: *Long Day's Journey*, 1967.

Nellie and I,
Laurel Lodge, 1948.

Clockwise from top left: Ballerina and friend: With Declan, Fairfield Road, 1955; Nellie and Simon, Glasnevin, 1976; A 6.00 a.m. wedding. Mamma and Dadda, 24 May 1942; Honeymoon in Glengarriff, West Cork.

secure enough to slacken the exhausting effort to please by always being best. Habit dies hard, however, and this was one I could not wholly relinquish. Particularly in holy matters.

Being a convent, the school was naturally a religious hothouse; we boarders competed to see who would be first down to Mass each morning and, after I settled down to the bell-driven routine and got the hang of how to wash, dress and strip my bed in three minutes, I had a long winning streak there, my crêpe soles scrunching satisfactorily on the wooden floor as I paraded to a pew, knowing that the nuns, meditating in their *prie-dieux* along the walls, had to hear me and realise that I was the first down. Again.

It wasn't all competitive though: we did pray fervently and sincerely, always aiming at our goal of at last being judged virtuous enough to enter the Sodality of Our Lady and thence to become a Child of Mary. I fell in with this communal ambition as enthusiastically as anyone. Having been a witness to one of the reception ceremonies, I too wanted to be conferred with the right to wear a huge oval medal on a blue ribbon. I too longed to wear a billowing, baby-blue cloak as I walked up the centre aisle of the candlelit chapel in the presence of all the nuns and the whole school in order to be admitted to the inner sanctum of Our Lady's special friends and devotees.

I did make it eventually. I made Prefect too, which really amazed me since I was widely regarded as a 'character'. For instance, when we were seniors, the tradition was that the younger girls put on a sketch show lampooning us. I was 'where's-me-glasses', a disorganised whirlwind who was always losing her belongings.

On the more earthy side, Gortnor Abbey reeked with adolescent hormones and, in the absence of boys, even those, like me, who were officially in love developed crushes on older girls, particular nuns, and even on our hapless chaplain, Father Lavin, who was the only male in evidence and who lived nearby with his two snuffling boxer dogs. As well as celebrating Mass and hearing our confessions, the poor man was frequently pressed into service to play table tennis with us during Recreation. Maybe he enjoyed it, although I couldn't be sure of that. He was good at the game and my memory of him is of how frequently he let rip his startling, inward-snorting laugh (think John Bruton) as, soutane cape and skirts swishing, he trounced whoever was on the other side of the table. It's a peculiar composite image: at the stage end of the hall you'd have a bunch of girls doing a four-hand reel to the music of the Kilfenora Céilí Band under the supervising eyes of the nun at the gramophone; at the other end, you'd have this snorting, black-clad dervish, whacking table-tennis balls out of reach while other girls scurried to retrieve them.

At one point, the nuns secured for us a visit from an Anne French beautician. I don't know how the woman carried it off in our class, as, with pustuled skin and hair like dirty twine, we listened solemnly while she spoke to us about the natural beauty of Irish complexions. I seem to remember that she concentrated mainly on the use of a product called Pore Grains.

We also had a visit from the great Anew McMaster, although none of us had the faintest idea who he was. Nevertheless, the whole school, plus congregation – with Mother Provincial installed on her throne in the front row – assembled to listen to the Shakespearean speeches for which he was apparently famous.

Given my interest – and later life – in drama, I should have been mightily impressed but, to tell you the truth, all I can really remember of the occasion is that my dear Mother Joan arranged for her favourite elocution pupil to visit the great thespian when he was having his tea in the parlour. But the person sitting behind the beautifully appointed table turned out to be quite an ordinary man with a red nose, who was polite but completely uninterested in anything but his meat tea, dainty sandwiches, lighter-than-air cream-filled sponge cake and glass of whiskey on the side.

With a reputation such as his, in the sunset of his career, how it must have felt to be reduced to entertaining uncomprehending adolescents in the remote boarding schools of Ireland...

Yet for me, in my bucolic eyrie while my parents and Declan were settling into Ballymun, those months from September to Christmas 1958 were a long time to be away from home for the first time with just weekly letters for sustenance. And as the date to go home for the Christmas holiday approached, butterflies in my stomach added exponentially to my habitual insomnia. I couldn't articulate my excitement so I kept it to myself, but, like a self-inflating balloon, it pushed harder and harder at the inside of my stomach and my chest.

The last day of term finished at lunch-time when the driveway in front of the school filled with cars, excited families come to collect their offspring, girls hugging, nuns waving. Five of us, whose trains for Dublin, Cork and Galway were not leaving until the following morning, were left with the run of the suddenly echoing building; food was picnic-style and even the hated berets were no longer de rigueur.

I think the best way to describe what it felt like to go home that first time is to repeat here a piece I did for RTÉ Radio One's *Sunday Miscellany* programme a couple of years ago, which was subsequently published by the broadcaster and TownHouse in a collection of pieces. It was written for voice and I have shortened and edited it a little, but I hope the gist remains clear.

Going home for Christmas—
Coming home for Christmas—

Two of the most evocative phrases in the English language. They encompass a pocket dictionary of others: joy, excitement, hope, filial duty, guilt, paying dues…

But I was only thirteen when I first came home for Christmas.

A scholarship girl from Dublin, I had spent my first term, a long fifteen weeks, in a boarding school by the shores of Lough Conn.

No visits, no outings—

Envy of other girls' ease with one another and the scrumptious Sunday sponge cakes brought in weekly by their mothers.

It's a dismal, boggy, weekday morning in late December and we serious travellers – four girls from Dublin and one from Cork – chug away from Ballina railway station.

We change trains at Manulla where the platform is even greyer. Wetter. Colder. Although we have to wait and wait, we care little. We're going home for Christmas.

The big Dublin train pulls in and we find a compartment to ourselves. We chat quietly as the drowned fields and small towns glide past our window. It is 1958, when people are still conscious of electricity bills, so the outward manifestations of the Christmas spirit are confined to glimpses of paper chains, an occasional Christmas tree or crib, a modest star on a church spire.

We take out the sandwiches the nuns have given us. I can't eat mine. I'm going home for Christmas.

Athlone. People getting on, people getting off. The chat dies away. Just seventy miles to Dublin.

Outside the train window, streaked with grime.

Darkness falls. Nothing to see now. We chunter through a blind landscape as, like keys on a piano, the swishing telegraph poles count out the miles...

Mullingar. Bustle. Lights. People embracing on the platform. Only fifty miles to Dublin.

At Maynooth, we tidy away our debris like the well-trained convent girls we are. We button coats, check shoelaces, put on our berets.

Butterflies. We're nearly home for Christmas.

The train squeals slowly into Westland Row. The others pull bags from the overhead nets, stand impatiently into the aisle. I cannot follow.

Because, as we slid alongside the platform, I had caught sight of my family – Mamma, Dadda, my seven-year-old brother in beret and good coat, his hands up holding theirs. All three were scanning the windows of the train. I am felled by tears of purest joy. They were looking for me.

I bid the others a muffled 'Happy Christmas' from under my seat as I pretend to be searching for something I have dropped; I scuffle and scrabble around the floor until I gain control.

Somehow it had not occurred to me before that my family loves me.

I had not known that I love them.

I am the last to leave that carriage, probably the train – although I don't remember that. I do remember that, as I walk towards my small family, they are as controlled as I am. Delighted to see me but mostly – and jovially –

relieved. 'We thought you weren't on it! We were nearly sending out a search party!'

There was a Christmas tree in Westland Row that year, or maybe memory has added it to my picture. There was certainly cloudy breath on cold air, and gloves and scarves and great clatter and chatter.

Our own chat on the way out of the station is about tiredness and train journeys, the Dinky crane my brother wants from Santa and the new house the three of them had moved into while I was away—

But joy, like a brilliant fish in deep water, glistens underneath.

10

Nelson's Bad Eye

Flooded. I was flooded on that homecoming day with every emotion known to me: every sense and organ overcome. And as we left the station, a new set of feelings took hold – eagerness and nervousness at the prospect of meeting my official boyfriend again.

I hoped.

The Gang of Eight always got together on special occasions – Christmas parties, birthdays, dinner-dances and suchlike – but it was rare if a week went by without social intercourse, separately or together.

My family's move to our new house meant that they were again living within a couple of hundred yards of each other and were to remain so for the rest of their lives.

Initiative and cohesion were afforded by the women, who popped in and out of each other's kitchens for gossipy or confiding visits, drinking tea (or sipping the Amicardo sherry Mamma stored with the bleach under the sink). The men played cards and, now and then, helped each other with DIY chores.

It is moot whether, left to their own devices, these men would have chosen to be friends. While they brought their Baby Powers or Jameson or bottles of beer to the Wednesday night Solo schools, it was always the wives who made the rotating diary and hospitality arrangements. There was no culinary rivalry because the fare was standard: tea, ham and salad sandwiches, Polo, Nice or custard-cream biscuits and 'ordinary' or chocolate Swiss roll. The men babysat on Thursday nights while the wives trotted out to socialise together in the Sunnybank, Addison Lodge or the Autobahn.

There were others who drifted in and out of this gang – the women were particularly assiduous in inviting the recently widowed to join them for summer holidays and parties – but the core of eight laughed and sorrowed together for decades until, one by one, they died. When the millennium turned, there were only two left alive, Rúairí Henderson and my mother. Even then, Mamma continued with the girls' weekly outing tradition, mutated now from Thursday nights to Tuesday lunch-times in Addison Lodge. No longer fit to drive, she was reliant on the goodness of a group of women who over the years had formed an outer ring of friendship with the original inner circle. They were never found wanting and remained loyal to her to the end. She lived for those Tuesdays, spending all morning dressing up and, with increasing difficulty as her sight failed, putting on her brightest makeup, reddest nail polish and tying her gayest scarf around her neck.

There was a lot of Gang socialising that first Christmas in our new house. Rúairí, Commandant Henderson, was the famous one. The others boasted that they knew him, not because he had served in the Lebanon, although they were proud of that, but because he was aide-de-camp to Dev. After Telefís Éireann was established, conversation was hushed and volume was turned up in all four households when the news came on. If Dev was somewhere about, Rúairí could not be far behind.

My mental picture of Pauline Henderson is of her sitting, arms folded across her stomach, a fond smile on her face as she listened to the chatter and laughter of the others. Bríd and Joe Malone were also relatively quiet – envied because of Joe's company car and Bríd's fine Sunbeam Wolsey knitwear – while Dadda and Tom Madigan were the practical ones. Tom's photo albums from the period are so methodically catalogued they are worthy of the Smithsonian.

Stella Madigan was the fun one: at parties and sing-songs, everyone watched her until she took off her earrings. When that happened, the party was considered a success and could really take off.

Dadda seemed to be the one they all turned to when they had a problem with officialdom. He was dogged and persistent, a natural public servant to whom sequence and order were paramount. On his own behalf – and on Mamma's because she would benefit should he pre-decease her – he fought the entire Irish administrative system for more than fifteen years to prove his eligibility for a contributory old-age pension along with his civil-service one. Something to do with a few stamps prior to 1953. He won. I suspect that, in the process, he wore down several government departments. 'If you want something fixed up, go to Bill Purcell,' was the mantra and, indeed, he proved invaluable for 'fixing up' fuel allowances, death benefits and every last penny to which not only the Gang but a wider circle of neighbours, their friends and families and *their* friends' friends and families, were entitled.

My mother was the one, I think, about whom the other seven loved to gossip and speculate. She was a doer, a joiner, an organiser but also a dreamer, restless and with a longing expression in her hazel eyes. 'Oh, you know Maureen!' the others said to each other, in and out of her hearing, 'You'd never know what Maureen'd do next!' with an indulgent smile or a glance at the heavens.

I wasn't interested in any of them that Christmas in 1958, or in their kind enquiries as to how I was getting on in County Mayo. Because, after the sheen of the first night home had worn off, the only person that concerned me was my Edward. I made excuses constantly to run errands from our new house to the shops, but I could find no sign of him around Ballymun. I still dared to hope, though, rationalising that it was too cold to hang about on the streets or in any of our fields. Anyhow, it had always been a long shot that he might be there; Patricia had been vigilant and as a result I knew that he and his family had moved to another suburb a mile and a half away.

She had his address and I could get his phone number from Directory Enquiries but, even though we now had a telephone, there was no way I could telephone a *boy* or – ohmigod – actually knock on his door.

I was in agony. Four months, spent in feverish daydreams and night-time fantasies, had been too long.

News about him during that period had been so sketchy it had served merely as a goad. It cost a lot to make an operator-assisted person-to-person call to County Mayo from the phone box outside the Autobahn; however, every few weeks, Patricia, Helena and other friends had loyally combined their pennies and queued to reassure me that our mutual girlfriend, 'Daisy', was being good (i.e. wasn't going with any other trollop) before being cut off by the merciless beeps. They also sent me letters in which Daisy featured heavily – 'met Daisy on Saturday in the chipper, she was asking for you' – as did others of the Honourable Order of the Nom-de-Plumed. 'Violet', for instance, was now the moniker of another local boy. All of this must have been highly entertaining for whatever Gortnor Abbey nun was on censorship duty when the letters came in.

Assurances notwithstanding, I knew that, in the four months that had passed, my beau had had ample opportunity to meet someone else, someone much prettier than me. Everyone was much prettier and slimmer than me: the boarding-school diet, filled out with large quantities of potatoes and all that white bread, had not been kind. What boy would want anything to do with me?

So, despite the twin exhilarations of the homecoming and exploration of our new house (sliding doors between the sitting room and the dining room! Talk about posh!), the days of Christmas dragged miserably.

The cavalry arrived in the shape of Patricia, who managed to fix it that both my love and I would be invited to a 'mixed' party – boys and girls together in the house of a girl we didn't know all that well. With my luck, it was typical that the party was not to take place until the very last night of the Christmas holidays, but it represented my best chance and I was grateful to her.

The next hurdle was my parents' permission to go. But having received an absolute guarantee that the hostess' parents would be in attendance as chaperones, they consented. I would be picked up at midnight. Sharp.

Patricia's inventiveness had not extended to finding out how my boyfriend felt about me after all this time, or even to telling him I would be going to the party. Was I still going with him? How would he behave towards me? Would he ignore me in front of everyone?

Even worse, would he pay attention to some other girl?

The omens were not good during the preliminaries when, in a jiggy atmosphere of subdued excitement and nervousness, cloaked in a pretence of casual indifference, we drank our fizzy drinks and ate our sandwiches and then, screaming and teasing each other, played games such as Nelson's Bad Eye. This involved being blindfolded and having an index finger guided into a hole gouged in a raw potato.

For that first hour or so, while I could not say for definite that Edward was deliberately ignoring me, we made no eye contact. I was dying. Someone called for yet *another* round of Nelson's Bad Eye and I could have spat at her.

Then, as if it was the most natural development at any party, our hostess announced a game of Spin the Bottle and the shrieking, giddy atmosphere imploded to become a silence so thick and sweaty it could have been fried.

We formed ourselves into a circle around the bottle on the carpet. For the first few spins, it stopped at everyone except me. I smiled gamely when it chose Edward and another girl to go outside the door. They were back in a flash and, although I took comfort from the shortness of their absence, I couldn't look at them: I was too busy nurturing the grin that showed the world I was having the time of my life.

Edward got to spin the thing next and my stomach spun with it. I thought I had seen him carefully set it to turn only halfway round and thereby stop at me.

It did.

And the flipping in my stomach became a full-blown circus act when, as I set the bottle in motion, I saw that, by pushing everyone away from each side of him and leaving himself with at least a quarter of the whole circle, my lover was manoeuvring himself to be in the receiving position. The ploy worked.

Red as a poppy, I followed him from the living room into the hallway and then, astonishingly, he opened the door of the broom cupboard under the stairs and indicated we should go inside. I reckoned that, on hearing our hostess' parents chatting quietly through the closed door of the kitchen, he didn't want them to come out and find us in our clinch.

In the claustrophic darkness of that understairs closet, the deed itself was quick and hard and sweet – and surprising. Having conjectured and consulted widely, having armed myself with Patricia's precise information, I had not anticipated that sensation could reach the soles of your feet – or that lips were warm.

I broke that first kiss because I was afraid of scandalising everyone with being missing for too long. But it was so gut-wrenchingly profound that, although I was only thirteen years old, I fell deeply in love and stayed in love for the next six years. Until Christmas 1964.

11

Facts of Life

Now and then, as a treat on Sunday nights at Gortnor Abbey, we were shown 'suitable' films, though in fits and starts because the reels had to be changed manually on the school projector. And if there was any kissing, the nun in charge put her hand over the lens, opening a small gap between two of her fingers every couple of seconds to see if it was safe enough yet to remove them. One of my more trenchant memories is of being absolutely absorbed in *A Town Like Alice*, carried away, weeping at the emotional intensity of it all – then being brutally hauled out of my reverie when the two main characters were about to embrace. The reason I remember it so vividly is that this particular kiss seemed to go on for a very long time: the nun kept opening and closing her fingers. It was like watching a movie through a nervous Venetian blind.

Food was a constant obsession. We were allowed to receive food parcels for Hallowe'en and they arrived by the lorry-load, so many that, each year, an unused classroom was pressed into service as a temporary warehouse and the corridors smelled of chocolate and oranges. (This was the same classroom in which, having caught chickenpox, I was isolated for three weeks, to be nursed by Mother Gonzaga while sulphur candles were burned outside the locked door to prevent the spread of my plague.) I always got two parcels, one from my parents and one from my Aunt Nellie.

We had three-day retreats, during which we were not allowed to speak at all but when the restrictions on buying and eating sweets were relaxed. It was on those retreats that I probably set the seeds for later problems with my teeth; I fell in love with sweets; hard, teeth-shattering and butterscotchy. Each year before the retreat, I loaded up with cartloads of them and, by the end of Day Three, I had always chomped my way through the entire supply.

It was on one of those retreats that someone broke the silence to report that she'd heard one of the missioners complain that hearing confessions from nuns was like being pecked to death by ducks. It isn't original, but it was the first time we'd heard it and, compulsory silence notwithstanding, it spread through the retreatants like a forest fire so that in every corner of the school and grounds, girls could be seen giggling uncontrollably over their copies of the *Imitation of Christ*.

Whereas in our Ballymun hollows, my friends and I had spent most of the time speculating about boys, we boarders spent hours speculating about nuns. We made illicit trips to their orchard to view the displays on their clothes-line and were thrilled beyond reason one summer when we saw not only a lineful of knickers, which was awesome enough, but *two ordinary bathing suits*. The dormitory rocked with that one for weeks.

One of the communal ambitions was to get a glimpse into their private parlour, an ambition I fulfilled once – and saw them all sitting around, just like normal people, chatting, reading, sewing. What a deflation. I had expected something far more interesting, maybe some kind of secret Masonic stuff. And while some were privileged to get a look at novices playing netball, I don't remember any of us achieving the Holy Grail: a sighting of a nun without her veil and wimple. We speculated incessantly about what colour hair each nun had, if they washed it, how short it was, did it have any shape or was it just hacked off, if they wore nightcaps in bed; even girls with older sisters in the order couldn't enlighten us on any of that.

It was probably because of Mother Joan and her advocacy that I was cast in lead roles of the school's potted versions of *Hamlet*, *Macbeth* and a play about St Patrick. I was Malvolio, too, and seem to recall giving a performance as St Genesius, patron saint of actors. It was also Mother Joan's ardent encouragement that allowed me to join the school debating team and suggest to Gael Linn that, in the course of competition, they should bring out *pop-céirníní* instead of the rusty old fiddle and *sean-nós* vinyl they seemed obsessed with. This was a commercial initiative that had no doubt been in train in any event, but they gave me a prize as an individual speaker and Mother Joan, who didn't understand a word of Irish, was delighted with me all over again and, whether deservedly or not, credited me with the idea when the first *pop-céirníní* was subsequently issued.

Mother Joseph – now plain Jo Langan, a counsellor in Liverpool – who was our English teacher, took a special interest too. I wasn't long there when she took me aside and suggested that I cease and desist from trying to be P.G. Wodehouse in my essays, a suggestion I followed by switching immediately to pastiche Jane Austen. But she kept faith in me and we're still in correspondence.

During my four years at Gortnor Abbey, there was one serious episode, considered by the nuns to be such a grave transgression that I was almost stripped of my membership in Our Lady's Sodality.

During one insomniac phase, lying awake in the dormitory with more than sixty others snoring around me, I became more and more frustrated. At home during these periods, I would have been able to switch on my light and read, but that was strictly forbidden, even if my cubicle had had anything as useful as an individual light. Or even a bloody book.

Then I heard the unmistakable sound of someone else tossing and turning. I wasn't alone in my wakefulness.

With one eye on the corner cubicle that housed the dormitory nun, I crept along the aisle between the curtains, stopping every so often to listen, until I identified which cubicle contained the non-sleeper. It turned out to be someone in my own class.

Careful not to startle her, with a finger on my lips, I stole inside. It was a very cold night and, seeking warmth, I got in beside her. We whispered and stifled our giggles for a while and then I went back to my own bed.

Over the next month or so, we repeated the adventure two or three times more, always when I discerned that she, like me, couldn't sleep.

Then one awful, terrible, dreadful night, we were caught.

What happened next was so confusing and puzzling that neither of us had even the vaguest idea what was going on. We were forbidden to sit anywhere near each other, even in the chapel, and we were not to speak a word to each other ever again. And at the next meeting of the ordinary sodality (not the elite Sodality of Our Lady), she and I were ostentatiously placed at opposite ends of the room while the nun running the session spoke about special friendships in such oblique terms that no one in the room understood what she was on about. We were left in no doubt, however, that we were in serious disgrace.

It did blow over, after a sort of quarantine period; I wasn't stripped of my Child of Mary medal so I suppose that, eventually, our genuine bafflement at the extraordinary response to what we had felt was just an infringement of an ordinary dormitory rule forced the nuns to cotton on that they had made one thousand and forty-nine out of adding two and two.

Believe it or not, I was in my late twenties, married, pregnant and living in America when I suddenly remembered that episode and realised what they had thought was going on. God love the nuns. They certainly believed I was far more knowing and sophisticated than I was, and perhaps this is because of the face I customarily presented to the world.

In Sixth Year, as a prefect, I was trusted enough to be put in charge of the sweet shop by Mother Sylvester, the nun who ran it, and we got to know each other quite well.

For some reason, Sylvester was also the nun whose duty it was to take each Sixth Year girl aside in the run-up to the Leaving Cert and to explain the facts of life – or, as I subsequently discovered, to ensure that most of us had it right and saw these facts from a Christian perspective. I watched, intrigued, as each girl emerged cherry-faced from these interviews. I couldn't wait for mine.

She came to me on a Saturday afternoon when, shop business completed, I was just about to close up.

'Now I know I don't need to have my little chat with you, Deirdre,' she began, and then, behaving like someone preaching to the converted, went on to talk about Christian values during procreation, referring in passing to which organ goes where 'and so on during the act'.

I cannot overstate my reaction. I was dumbfounded. *What* organ went *where*? I couldn't work it out. I hadn't had the *faintest clue*...

When I was eleven and in puberty, my mother had given me a leaflet from the Catholic Truth Society. It informed me that when a man and a woman love each other very much, they lie down together and 'embrace fondly', and then, if God was willing, the woman had a baby.

At that time, I was sleeping in an old-fashioned double bed, mattress sagging on its metal springs and, every Saturday morning when we didn't have to go to school, Declan, who was about six at the time, would come into my room and we would use it as a trampoline. From the time I had received this new information, I refused to allow him anywhere near the bed, for fear that, should our bouncing accidentally coincide, we could find ourselves lying down simultaneously and I might have a baby...

My information had progressed hardly at all in the interim but, assuming I was a woman of the world, Sylvester continued to be entirely matter-of-fact as, woman-to-woman, she spilled every bean in the can. She wasn't watching me closely so, as her chatty recital continued, I patted and tidied the Crunchies, Curly Wurlies, bars of chocolate and slabs of Cleeve's toffee into neat little columns. I nodded sagely while double-checking the contents of the cashbox and then, as I snapped it shut, smiled reminiscently as if I'd heard this old-hat stuff so often I was only barely listening. 'Right,' she said, when she figured she'd done her duty, and helped me latch the door of the shop.

I fled to the dormitory, pulled the curtains around my bed and lay on it to consider what I had just learned. I was reeling. The images presented by Mother had been absolutely unbelievable. I was almost seventeen years old and about to go out into the world. *And I hadn't known...*

Naturally, I didn't breathe a word to a soul. And when the other girls whispered to each other about their chats, I adopted a mysterious-but-wise Mona Lisa smile.

I may have been fooling myself about my own acting prowess. Sylvester may have been one of the wiliest women in the world, tailoring her chat to her audience: different strokes for different folks. She may have known full well that I was an innocent abroad.

I went to visit Gortnor Abbey a couple of times when I was in middle age and got a great welcome. It's a huge, bustling co-ed comprehensive now, with football fields and boys all over the place, really strange to see. But the lake is still as it always was, Nephin still broods over the landscape: my memories, encased in a rainbow-shot bubble, are secure. Sadly, though, the nuns have left, and have turned over the running of G.A. to lay people.

Gortnor was good to me in every way, not least in inviting me to live for four years in such spectacular surroundings, where in summer I could wash my hair in Lough Conn and where, I am sure, the foundations were laid for any skills I might possess in observing the beauty of the natural world. I remain very grateful, not only for the scholarship those nuns gave me but for their loving attitude to their charges.

I apologise for scuppering their high academic expectations of me and thank them for their charity in never mentioning the word 'university': no one from that school or that order has ever even hinted that my performance since leaving them has had anything but their full blessing.

I thank them mostly for restoring some of the confidence that they couldn't have known was so badly dented when I arrived there from Scoil Mhuire. Naturally, I hadn't let them, or anyone, see. The show always has to go on.

12

This Is
Gonna Be Great…

Six of the girls in my small class entered the convent at Gortnor Abbey. I would have been the seventh. Even though I was still passionately in love with Edward, I had decided that giving up this person – or the idea of this person whom I hadn't seen or heard from for more than two years – was a sacrifice I had to make to honour the crucified Christ and Our Lady.

I had gone as far as applying and had been accepted on a preliminary basis. I was in possession of a list detailing the 'trousseau' I would need to bring with me, including helpful indications as to where I could buy my undergarments and (frightening) sanitary supplies. Dowries were welcome but not necessary.

My parents put the kibosh on the enterprise. I was too young. I did not know my own mind.

I insisted I did. I argued – and wrung a concession from them that if I still felt the same way when I turned eighteen the following April, they would not stand in my way. In the meantime, I prayed that they would relent and let me go at the end of the summer. I went to Mass daily in Ballymun for the first two weeks of the holidays after completing the Leaving Cert; I lit candles to all my favourite saints and Our Lady. I sulked in my bedroom. I wore faraway holy expressions at the tea table.

Then a letter came for me. I was called to report for work at the Civil Service Commission on O'Connell Street as a clerk-typist – the lowest white-collar grade on offer.

The system at that stage for girls about to leave secondary school was that, if you weren't going for a vocation to the religious life or to nursing – or, in exceptional cases, to university – you applied in your final year at school for a clerical job in a bank, an insurance company or the civil service. There, you passed your time until you got married and had to leave your job, your departure sweetened by what was graciously called a 'marriage gratuity' – in essence your own money being given back to you.

The clerk-typist job – which luckily involved no typing at all – was the first that came up for me and, on a Monday morning in early July 1962, still planning to put in my time before I was allowed to follow my religious vocation, at £4.16s.0d. per week, I reported for work.

In my memory, everything was brown in that O'Connell Street building. Brown entrance area; brown porter's desk; brown lino on the floors; brown desks; men wearing brown jackets.

I was assigned to the Oral Irish Section.

This was contained in a small brown room, with a small high window that admitted shafts of dusty brown light. There were five brown chairs at four brown desks. Two of these desks were placed back to back for myself and the other clerk-typist, Pat Kett, so we faced one another. The third was for our clerical officer, and, nooked off a little by a half-screen, the fourth was for our staff officer.

Around the room, on narrow, head-high shelves, stood bound files containing yellow forms. On entrance to the public service – any and all branches, in fact almost everyone paid from the public purse – each person originated a yellow form clamped into one of those files. It contained his/her name, address and date of entry.

Two weeks before the fifth anniversary of that date of entry, he/she received a letter from us who beavered at the coalface of the Oral Irish Section of the Civil Service Commission. He/She was asked to report to us for a test in competency in oral Irish in order to become 'established', i.e. permanent and immovable.

The sum total of my work in that place was to write names and addresses on the envelopes containing those letters.

But I wasn't trusted to write them correctly. In bunches of twenty, I transcribed them from the forms, then took the relevant file and my bundle on the four-foot journey to a chair beside the desk of my clerical officer. From the file, one by one, I read aloud the names and addresses of the candidates while she, using a red pencil, line by line ticked those names and addresses on the envelopes. Then I took the envelopes back to my desk and, while Pat Kett read out her latest entries on the summoning letters to our clerical officer, I then inserted her previously approved bundle into my approved envelopes.

Other than that, I had very little to do, except fetch Zubes if our staff officer had a tickle in her throat or trot to Findlater's on the other side of O'Connell Street to buy a bun for her elevenses.

Findlater's was a grocery emporium, intricately tiled and smelling of different teas, salty bacon and fresh baking. Many years later, when I was interviewing Brush Sheils for the *Sunday Tribune*, he reminded me that we occasionally met at the same counter in that shop. He would have been running a similar errand to mine: as the then official messenger boy at the Commission, he was buying a bun for the supreme being in our office, Mr Duggan.

I handed up £2 at home for room and board and was allowed to keep the rest for myself. I saved for sixteen weeks to buy my first pair of stiletto-heeled shoes. They were gunmetal grey. They cost 37/6d. and I wore them until the toes curled upwards and the soles were holed and splitting from the uppers.

Pat Kett was a knitter and I too began to knit – an Aran sweater of an exceptionally complex pattern and luminously orange in colour. In slack times, therefore, all that could be heard in our room was the sound of our clacking needles.

But I realised very quickly that, just as it had in Scoil Mhuire, far from being a relaxing or rewarding activity, knitting drove me mad. Goal-oriented as I was, I found myself surreptitiously knitting when our superiors' backs were turned, even if I still had a quota of envelopes to write; at home, I stayed up late at night until my eyes could no longer focus. *I had to get the damned thing finished!*

In the December of that year, I cracked. Having worked in that room for five months, I blew an entire £2 of one week's personal fortune of £2.16s. by rushing down to Moore Street one lunch-time and buying up as many treble-layered paper chains as I could afford in the most garishly multicoloured combinations. I added balloons and pleated globes and dangling tinsel bells in silver and gold and shiny crimson. I sucked up anything that looked sparkly. I bought a monster roll of sticky tape. And when the other three came back from their lunch that day, they found me up on my desk fixing things to the walls and ceiling.

I suppose it's a fine measure of both my clerical and staff officers that, although bewildered, they let me proceed and even allowed Pat Kett to help me, so that by the time the two of us were finished in the bulb-lit late afternoon, that cubby-hole of a room looked like a corner of a Moroccan souk. I seem to remember that people came from other rooms to look at our handiwork; I think that even the great Pooh-Bah, Mr Duggan himself, dropped by on some pretext or other.

In January 1964, I was called to Aer Lingus, one of the jobs I had applied for in the rush before leaving school – but there was a complication. On the same day as I received the Aer Lingus call, I also received a call to the 'Junior Ex' – Junior Executive Officer – the first step on the executive ladder within the public service. It paid far more than the airline and offered far better 'prospects'; it could even be regarded as a profession.

But I was still only seventeen, jaundiced by my experience so far in 'the service' and when I set the excitement of working in the glamorous world of airlines against money and safety, there was no contest.

Dadda tried to persuade me otherwise. He pointed out that since I had been highly placed on the numerical list of the first Junior Exs being called that year, I would be a good candidate for quick promotion.

I challenged him by saying that I wouldn't be promoted. I'd be getting married and would have to leave...

He pointed out I'd have to do that in Aer Lingus anyhow...

As he continued to try to persuade me, I listened politely but with ears turned inward. I rejected the Junior Ex and, as requested, reported for work in Aer Lingus, next door to the Commission in O'Connell Street.

Just as it had been when I emerged from the stress of Scoil Mhuire into the calm of Gortnor Abbey, making the switch was like escaping from darkness into light. I found my colleagues, including the later Booker prize-winner John Banville, to be young like me; even the supervisors were in their twenties. The airline was at the start of its expansionary phase, still flying mainly DC3s and Viscounts, but preparing to buy BAC 1-11 jets.

I was a Grade Four, a (very) lowly cross-company grade covering general clerkship in all the administrative departments; in those pre-computer days I was assigned to Central Reservations. Specifically, The Belt.

At the front of the O'Connell Street premises sat the smart booking office with its smart staff in smart uniforms (including three, Carol Cronin, Glynis Casson and Terry Martin, who became life-long friends). This was where passengers made reservations face to face and collected tickets.

But behind this shop front lay a very long room containing The Belt: a conveyor belt, permanently rumbling under sets of parallel wooden dividers three inches high and punctuated at intervals by little stoppers, each of which bore the name of a route: Birmingham, Liverpool, Bristol/Cardiff, Glasgow, Paris, Rome, et cetera. This was now my domain.

We female Beltworkers wore uniforms too, but not the sharp suits worn out front: we wore long-sleeved shirt-dresses, overalls really, in two shades of plaid, brownish and greenish, synthetic sacks that quickly frayed, tore and lost their shape along with their buttons and hemstitching while staunchly retaining the stains (and smells) of stale sweat.

But we had power. We controlled who got the seats on every Aer Lingus flight.

In the front office, and at the top half of The Belt in front of the telephone reservations clerks, little consoles showed either a red light (flight full) or a green light (flight open) for each departure when the flight number was put in; red and green lights glowing simultaneously meant five or fewer seats available and the booking had to be 'on request' – to us. We Beltworkers had illuminated the indicator lights with red and green plugs on a giant board in a claustrophobic area called Close-Out (think of the old-fashioned telephone exchanges you've seen in movies from the 1930s and 1940s).

If your booking was successful, it was confirmed to you, and your booking card, with your name and contact details, travelled down The Belt to come to rest at the correct stopper.

Down our end, we shuttled between pegging and repegging Close-Out, scooping the booking cards from stoppers to enter passenger names manually onto cardboard flight sheets – one sheet per flight, one line per passenger and contact number – and ripping booking requests from the provincial and overseas offices out of the clattering telex machine. We also controlled the wait-lists and manually erased the cancellations.

It all sounds fearfully dull and repetitive when outlined like this – and I did hear John Banville, in the course of a radio interview some years ago, intimate as much – but for me it was Valhalla. Remember the brown job I had come from? And that I was still only eight months out of the convent? Remember that we were all young together, and that Aer Lingus was still small enough so that everyone – flight crews, baggage handlers, caterers, cleaners, clerks and management – felt he or she had a stake in its success.

And since many of the staff at our end of The Belt were *boys*, the banter quotient was high and the constant undercurrent of flirting made me giddy.

I threw myself into the work, determined I was going to be the best, the *very* best, Central Res clerk in the *world*. David to Goliath, we were going to beat our partners (i.e. deadly rivals) BEA on every route where we challenged them with our little Viscounts against their much bigger Vanguards. They sometimes even flew *jets* short haul – how was that for not playing on a level pitch?

Our secret weapons were Carvairs. So what if we could only accommodate a couple of dozen passengers? We could ferry cars and horses, couldn't we? I couldn't wait for those BAC 1-11s but they didn't arrive until 1965, just as I left.

Even in that rumbling boiler room, we felt our contribution was as good as anyone else's. Certainly I did. Hierarchically, I never felt any sense of 'them' and 'us' and, as far as I was concerned, we were all in it together to get our little airline flying high. We'd fix our competitors. We'd beguile punters with a patina of Irish charm while, at the same time, leaning on their sense of patriotic duty to fly under the logo of the green shamrock. We even used religion as a competitive weapon, putting heavy public emphasis on the annual Blessing of the Fleet and on the subsequent protection afforded *our* passengers who, smugly, could fly in a plane anointed with holy water and emblazoned with a saint's name.

When Central Res moved en bloc out to the new headquarters at the airport, my pleasure in my job grew exponentially as I was transferred within the department to Todays and Tomorrows, a small unit where we controlled only flights departing within the next twenty-four hours. I loved the rostering: early mornings meant free afternoons and evenings when colleagues and I could take the bus out to Dundrum to play tennis at the company sports complex at Knockrabo; late nights meant free days for going to the cinema, or even just lying in bed – to your mother's endless frustration. And by working extra shifts, you could build up time off in lieu for holidays.

I was even collected and driven home from these anti-social shifts in crew cars, green minibuses in the Aer Lingus livery, thereby being treated exactly the same as the lofty air hostesses with their French-pleat hairdos, smooth make-up, vanity cases and gossip about the differing prices of twinsets and olive oils in various Rome markets or of sheets and towels in the bargain basements of New York.

Again, to take such delight in what was, on paper, just a clerkship on the very lowest rung of the airline's administrative ladder might paint me as a truly sad person – but I loved the constantly moving challenge, where the aim was to ensure that every flight took off without a single empty seat and with no one left behind. We had a policy of deliberate over-booking for certain flights, particularly dawn and star flights, knowing from experience that they would attract a quotient of cancellations and no-shows. I loved the way the load factors constantly teetered on this knife edge.

For instance, if, a few hours before take-off, we discovered we had called a particular flight wrongly and too many people were going to turn up at check-in, our task was feverishly to identify soft targets on the passenger list, frequently, I'm sorry to say, lone passengers with the prefix 'Miss' or 'Mrs'. Then we would hit the phones and, as diplomatically as possible, try to sweet-talk a diversion onto another flight. Conversely, when we were fairly sure we were going to be left with empty seats, we would telephone people booked on later flights and offer them the 'gift' of an earlier departure, 'Which of course you are under no obligation to accept, Sir, but in looking through tomorrow morning's flights, I just thought it might be convenient for you. You know, get a head start on the London day?' It was surprising how many people thought this was a great service and were delighted with us for picking them for the privilege.

And as for the great news that someone was being granted a seat off the waiting list, joy was unconfined. Spoiled rotten, they felt.

Even when I rang to offload, although memory could be selective here, I don't remember any abusive run-ins. Moans and groans, yes, but, in general, people were polite and co-operative.

This, of course, was pre-*Liveline*.

My own first flight was to London in a DC3. Wearing my Sunday best, augmented by my good headscarf, white gloves, my gunmetal stilettos and a shiny plastic handbag that I hoped looked like leather, I climbed up the steps into the steeply tailward-sloping cabin of the plane and tottered downhill to my seat.

Seatbelts with a tricky fastening device. A little tray that could be pulled out from the back of the seat in front. A sick bag tucked discreetly there too. All around, a low, confident buzz of conversation amongst men in suits, women in costumes, some wearing pillbox hats like Jackie Kennedy's.

Door thudding shut. Sucky sweets offered from baskets by the hostesses. Propeller outside the window swinging a little, first this way, then that, before bursting into screeching action, whirling faster and faster until the blades are no longer visible, showing as two blurred grey rings. The same thing happens on the other side of the plane. Now we are fully ready.

Chocks away. Bumpy, rocking ride across the apron and out into the field. A brief halt, engines squealing, floor, walls, windows, ears, feet and teeth shuddering.

A sudden hurling backwards against the juddering seat then, suddenly, no tarmac. Blue. Blinding sun.

The genie out of the bottle. A traveller born.

13

A Ronson Cigarette Lighter

When the airline finally installed its huge IBM 1410 mainframe computer, it ran a company-wide aptitude test to select ten people from all grades, including managerial, to be trained as programmers for it. I was chuffed at the honour and glory of being selected as one of this elite. But after the first glow of chuffdom subsided, I began to have doubts.

The room-sized beast was already running on data inputs in its specially air-cooled environment and I had seen the stacks of cards being fed into the grey, clacking input machines.

Uh-oh! Although I knew that programming would be very different from data input, having been so happy, did I now want to spend my days hunched at a desk working not with humans but the binary system? No matter how prestigious it might appear to my friends, colleagues and family, did I really want to get involved with a computer?

The honourable thing to do would have been to resign my place on the course to make way for someone more deserving and more interested. But, having basked in the congratulations of my colleagues and pride of my family, could I go back now and tell them that I had made a mistake? Could I offend those who had given me such an opportunity – and, more crucially, could I bear to disappoint my parents? Although, as usual, they had not said anything directly, it was obvious they were thrilled that their daughter had been deemed clever enough to be taken in on the ground floor of what was clearly going to be the future course of business.

I shilly-shallied and tried to convince myself that, since I did not yet really know what programming entailed, it might not be as soulless as I imagined.

But, on Day One of the course, faced with the endless rows of zeros and ones on the papers in front of me, I saw my future in programming exactly as I had feared. So I did my usual thing and mentally switched off, paying only minimal attention to the hapless tutor who, faced with such incomprehension, must have been baffled as to how on earth I had been selected.

When I fell out of the course, I cantered happily back to Central Res, where, computer or no computer, Todays and Tomorrows would always see the real action and I could half truthfully tell colleagues that I had found programming too boring.

In my spare time, I joined the Aer Lingus Musical & Dramatic Society (ALMDS) auditioning first for *Oklahoma!* I was delighted to land the part of the sexagenarian Aunt Eller and, complete with unconvincing grey wig and deep guttural voice, got to gurn at Dermot Brophy who came on singing 'Oh What a Beautiful Morning' as the hero, Curly. Later on, I even got to lead the company in singing 'The Farmer and the Cowboy' and shoot a real gun up in the air: our producer/director, Commandant Con O'Sullivan, was the man with the firearm access. We played the show in the late lamented Father Mathew Hall and toured to the Waterford Festival of Light Opera, where I got a mention from the adjudicator as being 'very promising'.

Next was *Showboat* where, again, I was cast as someone more than three times my age, Parthy Ann Hawks. This time, I got to sing the duet 'Why Do I Love You?' with the exceptionally talented Ed Brady.

Talent. As it happened, there was serious all-round talent in that society. ALMDS' then musical director, Colman Pearce, is a conductor of 'serious' classical music; our Laurie, Deirdre Greer, became a professional soprano, our Will Parker was played by Denis Rafter, now a professional actor and writer in Spain, and our Ado Annie was the late Máire O'Hanlon, who also turned professional and went on to become one of the stalwarts in the soap *Tolka Row*.

And when I started to get cast in straight plays (Pegeen in *Playboy of the Western World* and The Bride in Lorca's *Blood Wedding*) I met a further cohort of Aer Lingus actors who could have held their place in any professional company and some of whom actually did: Glynis Casson and Terry Martin, for instance.

Along with Carol Cronin, Glynis (daughter of Christopher, grand-daughter of Sir Lewis Casson and Dame Sybil Thorndike) is one of those lifelong friends I garnered from my time at the airline. She came with me on my first continental holiday – to Athens – where she had a terrible time keeping tabs on me.

My abiding image of that trip is looking upwards from the corner of the street where our hotel was situated to see Glynis, the morning breeze lifting her hair, gazing seawards from the balcony of our room as dawn broke over the Aegean. She looked like a character from a Chekhov play.

Although outwardly she appeared as composed as always, she was panicking. Our flight homeward was due to take off in just a few hours and her last act before leaving Athens was to call the police in order to report a missing, very naïve eighteen-year-old who had met some character named Georgio in a park and had promised to be back in the hotel room by midnight. It was now six o'clock in the morning and the poor girl had already called every hospital in Athens. 'What was I going to do?' she asked later. 'I was just going to have to go home without you and tell everyone, "I lost Deirdre…"'

Georgio, who spoke quite a bit of English, had brought me home the previous evening to meet his parents in their first-floor apartment, situated in a narrow alleyway and smelling of cement. I don't know what he told them about me in his rapid Greek, but whatever it was, they seemed thrilled to see me, instantly producing a large mound of a white, gooey substance I'd never seen or tasted before. I promise I'm not exaggerating quantities here; the stuff covered a large dinner plate and, to me, tasted like rancid wallpaper paste.

To add to my misery, I was the only one eating: Georgio and his parents sat watching me while, trying not to gag, I struggled to get it down. Each time I stopped and with sign language tried to indicate to the parents that it was *delicious* but that (patting my stomach then making balloon-like shapes in the air above it) I couldn't eat another *spoonful,* they smiled delightedly and made encouraging, shooing motions with their own hands, indicating that I should eat more. Their son told me they would be insulted if I didn't and, somehow, I managed it. This, it turned out, was my introduction to natural yoghurt.

After his parents had gone to bed, leaving Georgio and me to our own devices, his first intention included an attempt to ply me with ouzo. I fended him off by pointing to the little badge with the bleeding red heart I wore on the lapel of my blouse, then bored him rigid by rhapsodising at length on the history, provenance, ethos, aims, advantages and widespread membership of the Pioneer Total Abstinence Association in Ireland.

He tried to change the subject by putting his arm around me so we could get down to the real business of the night as he saw it. I, however, succeeded in compounding his confusion by whipping out my Child of Mary medal – my 'gong', as my father called it – then started on the history of the Sodality of Our Lady and what membership signified: chastity, for instance.

I embarked then on an explication of why exactly Irish girls took virginity so seriously and how, once we had made vows of dedication to the Sacred Heart by pledging not to drink alcohol and to Our Lady by not giving away the precious gift of our chastity until we got married, we never broke them.

Georgio instantly asked me to marry him. His parents loved me, he said. He himself loved me. He would come to Ireland. We would write to each other. He could easily get work.

But the last straw for him, I think, came when I began in on the early saints of Irish Christendom, starting with Patrick, Bridget and the monks. 'Have you never heard of the Book of Kells?'

He headed this off by sitting up – we were in his bedroom, he bare-chested and lying on the bed, me beside him but sitting and fully clothed – put on his shoes and socks and said it was very late and he was very tired and his parents would be getting up soon for their day's work.

In fairness, he remained polite and, because I had no idea where I was in Athens, he did walk me as far as the corner of the street where Glynis and I temporarily lived. But when we caught sight of her, watchfulness personified, on that balcony, my erstwhile fiancé muttered something in rapid Greek and fled.

Guess he felt he'd had enough entertainment for one night.

Intriguingly, I did get a couple of letters afterwards from him. He was obviously an unusual man.

I didn't answer. While my vocation to the religious life had evaporated, as my parents had shrewdly suspected it would, I was still being pathetically faithful to the evanescent Edward. I was saving myself for him.

So Glynis and I go back a long way and I'm mad about her, about her acerbic wit, her ladylike carriage, her extraordinary self-confidence and tenacity. You would not stand in her way, mind, if she was coming at you with a project she wanted you to help with; 'no' is not a word she likes to hear. And, although I think of her as the embodiment of 'sisters doin' it for themselves', she also acts as the adhesive who keeps together that Aer Lingus gang of so long ago, persisting in offering not only the privilege of early booking for her own forthcoming gigs and shows, but the hospitality of her lovely home opposite Sandymount Strand. She's the one who passes on the bad news if one of us falls ill (the late Ed Brady, Máire O'Hanlon) or of anyone who has triumphed over illness (Marie Bradshaw, a long-time heart-transplant survivor). She's the fulcrum of that group and, without her, I'd be bereft of refreshed access to the laughter and joy of such a carefree period of my life.

To give you a taste of what it was like to be surrounded by that talented bunch at that time, here is part of the programme note she asked me to write for the 2004 production of *The Importance of Being Earnest* – she produced and starred in it as Lady Bracknell in Liberty Hall, with sets by her sister, Bronwen.

Picture it. A beige room in the bowels of the (defunct) Aer Lingus booking office on O'Connell Street, Dublin: peeling, dun-coloured walls, a low ceiling underhung with plumbing ducts; a chipped coffee table, an assortment of battered chairs placed in unusual formation, four lined up in the centre of the room, two spaced some feet apart to one side, the rest scattered around the walls.

Smells: of ashtrays, damp coats, sweat, duty-free perfume (Intimate), tired feet.

Sounds: the incomparable mezzo of Glynis Casson giving it all she's worth: 'A *hand*-bag?'

This was a rehearsal for the same play forty years earlier, with the redoubtable Glynis as Lady B, Terry Martin as Algernon, Frances Harney as Gwendolyn, Agnes Cogan, the late Ed Brady, Denis Rafter, and yours truly as Cecily.

We took ourselves seriously, we had artistic differences, we suffered from first-night nerves. There was a great deal of hugging, even envy and weeping. But there was real talent there: Ed Brady went on to found Take Four, specialising in the more esoteric musicals (*The Fantasticks*, *Mack and Mabel*); Agnes became an RTÉ arts producer; Denis went to Spain; Frances, having eschewed acting for directing, later discovered academic life and, draped with firsts, is sweeping all before her.

I have enjoyed many lives since, but I've never again reached the pure, golden joy of the after-work evenings in that peeling, beige rehearsal room where we transcended youth and shyness by employing the passions of theatre, where any dream was possible of realisation and, we believed, within reach.

I don't think there was a day or night of my life in Aer Lingus when I was unhappy.

On a personal level, I was beginning to suspect (slow learner!) that, since I hadn't heard from him for years, 'my' Edward was no longer mine. I had found out – via Patricia, who else? – that he had joined a foreign air force and was now stationed in Germany. So in one last-ditch attempt to see him, I embarked on the most embarrassing trip of my life.

I tell my mother I am going on a shopping trip to Manchester. What I do not tell her is that I will not get off the plane in Manchester but will stay with it to its eventual destination – Düsseldorf.

I arrive very early at the airport. It is 23 December 1964, two days before Christmas Day. I am nineteen.

Staff fly standby; I find I can't get on the Dublin–Manchester–Düsseldorf flight but manage to get my ticket changed to fly via London. Aer Lingus has an interline agreement, which means that most of the IATA airlines, including Lufthansa, will honour staff standby tickets.

So I get to Heathrow, stand by for almost seven hours as flight after flight to Düsseldorf takes off without me. I am eventually offered a flight to Cologne.

I get to Cologne just as 23 December turns into Christmas Eve. I take a taxi to the station, find a late train bound for Düsseldorf, get there at 4.10 a.m. and book into a hotel just outside the station entrance. I set my travel alarm for 8.30 a.m. but I spend the night reading Conrad's *Lord Jim* until the alarm goes off.

I wait twenty minutes for respectability's sake, then, at 8.50 a.m., I ring the telephone number of the base and ask the orderly who answers if I can speak to 'Edward X'. I hold my breath because I don't even know if he is there or not.

Miracle of miracles, he comes on the line. 'Hello?'

'Hi, Edward [cheerily], long time no hear, remember me? Deirdre Purcell? I work for Aer Lingus now, would you believe and I just happen to be in Düsseldorf for a couple of hours – I was escorting an unaccompanied minor...'

There follows a long, burbling, exhaustively rehearsed explanation as to what that entails. Then, 'Going back this evening, naturally, but just wondering, since I'm here, if you were free for a cup of coffee or anything?'

He sighs. 'Dammit, if only I'd known. I'm actually going into town with colleagues right this minute. There's a car waiting for me, but I have to come straight back. That's such a pity—'

'Ach, no problem. It just occurred to me, doncha know? Since I was here...'

'This is such a pity.'

'No problem. Good luck, anyway. And Happy Christmas, by the way!'

'And a happy Christmas to you too, Deirdre.'

We hang up.

I get out of the hotel bed, check out, take a taxi to the airport and manage to get on a Lufthansa flight Düsseldorf–Heathrow, where I sit all day and evening because, this being Christmas Eve, there is no availability whatsoever London–Dublin on any airline.

I can't ring my parents to tell them I will probably be stuck sleeping on the floor at Heathrow for Christmas: I don't have enough sterling to call direct – and can't even ask a fellow passenger for some in exchange for my last few punts because I have to keep them for my taxi fare to Ballymun. I can't reverse the charges either because the operator would say, 'Hold for a call from London.'

I, you see, am shopping in Manchester.

Christmas Eve clicks over into the first hour of Christmas Day. The last stuffed Aer Lingus flight departs and still there is a disconsolate crowd around the BEA standby desk: Irish staff from various airlines, plus a few 'ordinary' revenue passengers who have either missed earlier flights or are trying their last-minute luck. Then that wonderful, marvellous, charitable, delightful airline, BEA – forerunner of BA – decides at one o'clock in the morning to put on a Vanguard instead of a Viscount for their very, very last Christmas flight to Dublin and we all get on…

Everyone is in bed when I let myself into the house.

At Christmas dinner later that day, my mother asks casually what I'd bought in Manchester. I brush this off equally casually, 'Nothing much. Didn't see anything I liked.'

They don't press it.

Unfortunately, there is an even more toe-squinching postscript to that episode. In my luggage I had carried a gift-wrapped Ronson cigarette lighter. If things had worked out it was to have been a Christmas present for Edward. I had even (cringe) had had it engraved with his initials. And, in the New Year, I actually (cringe, cringe) posted it to him with a cheery message on the accompanying Christmas card, wishing him a Happy Christmas and saying it was a pity we hadn't been able to get together for that cup of coffee.

A few days after I posted the thing, I woke up one morning, realised what a chump I'd been and, painfully, started working on myself to give up the dream. It helped that I had such a great, happy job and I threw myself fully into it.

But the confidence gained in Central Res was not to last long. It was destroyed in short order almost as soon as I set foot in the Abbey Theatre.

14

Clitheroe in Drag

Although I didn't know it at the time, my adulthood commenced in August 1965 when I was twenty. Everything that happened afterwards, moving to America, marriage, subsequent events and jobs, turned on one crucial twenty-four-hour period.

Thoroughly enjoying the work challenges and with the world at my disposal for mere pennies, I was dancing along in Aer Lingus, having a terrific time with interesting friends and making the most of the creative outlet in the ALMDS. Also, having been chosen as one of the 'air hostesses' to walk in the New York St Patrick's Day Parade, I was smitten with America and had cemented an undying love affair with the place, begun and continued for years in the cinemas of Dublin. Determined to get there as often as possible, I had applied to become a real air hostess. I'd done my second interview and had been called for a medical. Things were looking good.

Then one of those ALMDS friends decided he would like to take the first step towards becoming a professional actor. That step was to audition for the Abbey School of Acting, a training body that fed into the permanent company at the theatre.

He and I had played opposite one another as Christy and Pegeen in *The Playboy of the Western World* and also as Bride and Groom in Lorca's *Blood Wedding*. He asked me to be a foil at his audition and, of course, I agreed.

At the time appointed, we duly turned up at the old Queen's Theatre in Pearse Street to which, after a fire in 1951, the Abbey company had decamped for a 'temporary' stay of fifteen years.

Except for the bare white working light hanging above the stage, the old theatre was dark, I remember, the brass rails separating the orchestra pit from the stalls glinting only dimly. It was also cold, draughty, and the mustiness wafting towards us from the ancient carpets and seating, combined with the pungent scent of the size used by the set painters as a primer on cycloramas and stage flats, made me sneeze like a baby.

I think we were daunted while, as per instructions from the man who had introduced himself as the stage manager, Joe Ellis, we waited for something to happen. As the seconds ticked away, we realised that here we were, about to perform on this venerable stage where the famed Abbey Theatre Company now strutted its stuff, but also where generations of internationally known music-hall artistes had entertained Dubliners. (Maybe, I thought, even Dadda's grandfather, who had run a dairy in Cork Street.)

Then, from somewhere within the dark hole of the stalls, a harsh, breathy northern voice instructed us to begin and off we went, with me, for my colleague's sake, putting my heart and soul into the task.

I've always believed in the old adage that good acting involves 'changing the expression in the other actor's eyes': while remaining aware of your own dual presence as self and character, you ditch the ego of self. You interact and respond truthfully, not only to the author's intentions as written for your own role, but to the way your fellow actor is expressing his.

Anyway, I did my best for him.

When we had finished, Earnán De Blaghd – Ernest Blythe, the theatre's oligarch – came to stand in front of the orchestra rail and, little round glasses glinting in the gloom, thanked us, had a short conversation with us in Irish (Scoil Mhuire experience coming in useful there!) and left. My friend and I agreed that his audition had gone well and, with high hopes of his hearing something positive, we parted to take our separate buses home.

I've so often related the fairy-story outcome of that audition that I hesitate to recount it again here, but it was such a crucial pivot that I feel I should. I will strip it to its barest bones, cutting out the histrionics, the dithery, jittery feelings, the consultations with almost everyone I had ever met, even those I hadn't, like the man sitting beside me next morning as I took the bus to work.

That evening, a few hours after my friend's audition, I got a phone call at home from De Blaghd. He was inviting me to join, not the school but the Abbey Theatre Repertory Company.

I would have to join immediately. The following day. Máire Ní Néill, one of the actresses on staff, had been offered a film role and could not be released to take up the offer unless a substitute actress could be found to play the part of Christine Lambert in *Drama at Inish.* The problem was that the play was due to open the following Monday and this was already Wednesday.

In case I didn't understand, Blythe spelled it out; I was being made an offer of a permanent, pensionable position as an actress in the Abbey Theatre. Since I would have to leave my job in Aer Lingus, the theatre would pay me the same salary as I was getting there. I must ring to accept or decline this offer before four o'clock next day. 'The earlier the better,' he added in his gravelly voice, 'and if I'm not able to come to the phone at the time, you can talk to my secretary, Mrs Woods. She'll tell you what the arrangements are for rehearsals and so on...'

Secretary? Rehearsals? The offer was fearsomely real – collapse of stout party on the kitchen floor of 15 Willowpark Grove after I had replaced the black telephone earpiece on its cradle. It had not crossed my mind to seek acting as a profession.

Feverish consultations.

Sleepless night.

Next morning, I rushed up to my supervisor's desk at Central Res to explain the situation. I had decided I'd like to take up the offer but didn't want to walk out on the airline without giving notice.

Tom Carney, tall, red-haired and with a permanently worried expression, was taken aback but sympathetic, 'Let me make a few phone calls.' Within an hour, he had sought me out on the floor of the open-plan office where I was, with limited success, trying to carry out my job as normal. He told me that since this was obviously the opportunity of a lifetime, Aer Lingus would not want to stand in my way. But 'in case things don't work out', the company was offering me a year's leave of absence, starting that day. 'You'll always be welcome back – congratulations!' He stuck out his hand.

In the introduction to this memoir, I have mentioned that awful morning when I awoke and realised I was late for my first rehearsal. That was actually my first rehearsal for *The Shadow of a Gunman*, my first official repertory casting, not the mere replacing of Máire Ní Néill in the *Inish* emergency. I have no memory whatsoever of being 'read in' to *Drama at Inish*.

I certainly do remember two aspects of the performances, however.

The first was of playing opposite the late Donal McCann, who, as Eddie Twohig, was in love with me as Christine, the Dublin sophisticate who continues to reject him.

Although not all that tall, Donal was broad and physically powerful, with a very large head, thick dark hair, short, nicotined fingers so expressively rubbery they seemed boneless, a full mouth that he kept pursed for a lot of the time, and strangely liquid eyes. Even at that stage it was clear to me, panicky newcomer as I was, that in the infancy of his stardom, Donal was a magical stage presence. For instance, voice breaking on one barked, explosive syllable, 'Chris-*tine*!' at the end of an otherwise anodyne sentence, he managed to convey not only to the audience but newly to me each night a heart so full of hurt, wounded pride and, simultaneously, an intention to wreak terrible revenge on me and his patronising relations that, as my character, I couldn't but react appropriately. I could sense the anticipation from the auditorium each time he made an entrance.

For someone who is justly celebrated for his iconic creation of profoundly serious and affecting roles, for instance in Brian Friel's *Faith Healer* and Sebastian Barry's *The Steward of Christendom*, his sense of the ridiculous and instinctive comic timing were exceptional. (However, I must point out that as well as running an inevitable risk of fading to nothing in the glare of his star, there was also a physical hazard in acting opposite Donal; he literally spat with passion – a fact that can be verified by any audience member who sat in the front two rows of the stalls for any of his performances.)

That *Drama at Inish* fielded a great cast: not only Donal, but Eddie Golden, Aideen O'Kelly (Emer's sister), Geraldine Plunkett, Des Cave, Philip O'Flynn, Angela Newman – the list goes on. They were all more than kind. I know they were because I would remember if they weren't.

But even the privilege of making my professional debut opposite Donal McCann, surrounded by such a cast, has been eclipsed by the recollection of the behaviour of someone who had nothing to do with the production.

At that point in the Abbey, there were two main producers, Tomás Mac Anna and the late Prionnsias Mac Diarmada – Frank Dermody – who was the principal teacher at the Abbey School of Acting and reckoned by most theatre people and some critics to be a directorial genius.

Drama at Inish was a Tomás Mac Anna production – and he must have rehearsed me into the show during the three days available before the Monday night opening. By nature, he is efficient, patient and humorous, as I learned in subsequent productions, and he most probably did work with me for *Inish*. But from opening night on, for some reason known only to him, Frank Dermody persecuted me.

Perhaps it was from spite that I hadn't come into the company through the normal channels, i.e. his school; perhaps, although I doubt this, he genuinely wanted to give me a leg-up and to put me straight on all the bad habits he felt I must have picked up as an amateur. For whatever reason, he haunted me.

I really am not exaggerating when I say that on certain nights during that run of *Inish*, which was mercifully short, almost every time I exited at whichever side of the stage, Dermody, who was a small man, smaller even than me, was there to accost me. If I was seated on stage during a hiatus in my own script, I could see him hovering in the wings watching me, always within my eyeline. I could see his tongue flicking venomously like a snake's in and out of his mostly toothless mouth; I could see the gleam of his bald pate in the overspill from the stage lighting.

Worse was to follow. Unfortunately for me, my first casting in my own right was as Minnie Powell in Dermody's repertory production of *The Shadow of a Gunman*. (Yes, that was that debacle, when I overslept on the first morning of the rehearsal set up exclusively for me.)

You can imagine the (justified) torrent of abuse unleashed on me when eventually I made it into the small lounge of the hotel on Westland Row. On my timid opening of the door, Dermody erupted immediately like a small volcano, spitting and yelling at me in front of the rest of the undoubtedly inconvenienced cast, who probably believed I deserved everything I got. During the tirade, my fellow actors pretended to be elsewhere, gazing through the window at the traffic in Westland Row, studying *The Irish Times,* knitting...

Although I can't remember whether she was knitting or crocheting, while she waited for her own scene, Eileen Crowe, widow of F.J. McCormack and a veteran of the Abbey stage, continued to work her wool throughout my increasingly dispirited attempts at Minnie's tenderly evocative first scene with Donal Davoren, played by Pat Laffan. I couldn't get through two consecutive lines, even in some cases a full sentence, without furious interruption and excoriation from my producer. Afterwards, Eileen took me aside and, as a long-ago Minnie herself, kindly gave me some advice on how to play the scene. I really appreciated this and listened hard but was too demoralised and scared to take any of it in.

Somehow, I got through that morning. But later on, during the dress rehearsal at the Queen's, when, as Minnie, I burst through the door of Davoren's tenement room – 'They're all around the house, they must be going to raid the place' – I almost went into orbit with fright at Dermody's reaction. Immediately on seeing me, he took off from his position at the back of the stalls from where he had been watching the play and, roaring like a demented bullock, raced to the front and attempted to leap over the railings in front of the orchestra pit. I thought he was going to attack me and was backing upstage in terror when I realised that for once, his rage wasn't the result of anything I had or had not done. His spittle-bubbling ire was directed this time at the wardrobe department who had dressed me in a voluminous white nightgown.

He was so incoherent it took me a while to understand what he was yelling: that I looked like 'Nora Clitheroe in drag'. (Nora is a character in O'Casey's *The Plough and the Stars;* she goes off her head on learning that her husband has been killed, and for her final scene is usually dressed in a nightdress. I never figured out what he meant by the 'in drag' bit.)

Again, I got through the rest of that rehearsal, and the run, but I was beginning to think I'd been more than a little hasty in leaving my lovely Aer Lingus. The acting profession was turning out to be a long way from what I had imagined it to be.

In an attempt to propitiate Dermody, I joined the classes at his school – although as a staff member of the company there was no onus on me to do so. This proved to be a truly surreal experience. Dermody's 'lectures', if that was what you could call them, included his love of climbing on the piano in the room and falling off it onto the floor. 'See?' he'd say, picking himself up, flapping his hands and repeatedly shrugging his shoulders as if they were little jackhammers. 'Doesn't hurt a bit. Now you do it.' Obediently, one by one, we tried. And every time we fell on the hard floor, it did hurt.

He had us dash headlong at a wall and attempt to run, spider-like, up its vertical surface, an exercise destined, of course, for failure. And he felt we were all deficient not only in skill but in depth of passion. 'Take Christ off the cross!' was his regular shriek when one of us didn't come up to his expectations in the delivery of a couple of lines.

He must have believed in astrology because he asked us all what our signs were, and on learning that I am a Taurus, pursed his little mouth in derision, 'The Lord preserve me from a Taurus woman!'

But most disconcerting of all was his demonstration of the correct way to play a love scene. These days, when we meet from time to time, the actor Niall O'Brien, a fellow pupil from that period, still gets great mileage out of my expression when, one evening, Frank Dermody chose me as the model on whom to demonstrate. He grabbed me by the shoulders. 'Get right in there between the knees,' he said to the class, and shaking me a little as though I were a recalcitrant rabbit, showed everyone just how tightly, far in – and up – between the knees a man should go with his own knee. I stood there, mortified, straddling his grotty trouser leg and trying to avert my eyes from the caked spittle in the corners of his mouth while he repeated the action a couple of times, tucking himself in more snugly.

'And now the kiss.' Suddenly, he stuck his tongue into my mouth.

According to Niall, my face was 'a picture'. Niall's good at understatement.

15

The Business

The upside of being a member of the Abbey School of Acting was that there was safety in numbers, and although for the rest of my time at the theatre I was never totally to overcome my lack of confidence – the damage was done – I no longer felt Dermody was picking on me personally. And being in the same boat as highly talented people like Niall, Frank Grimes, Sabina Coyne (who subsequently became the wife of Michael D. Higgins TD), Niall Buggy and the seventeen-year-old, beautiful Sinéad Cusack, who became my pal, also helped a lot.

The repertory casting system meant that one week, when you checked the latest cast list posted up by Mrs Woods inside the stage door, you could find your name beside the juvenile lead in a play, the following week you mightn't be there at all (and therefore with a paid sabbatical). Then, the following week, you could see your name amongst the spear-carriers. Sinéad and I took advantage of the latter during one run of *The Plough and the Stars* in which we were cast as 'crowd' in Rosie Redmond's pub scene. We both had long hair. Nightly we washed it a few minutes before our scene and, authentically rat-haired, could then urge on the fight between Fluther and the Covey in the happy knowledge that our hair was drying nicely in the heat from the strong stage lights. And since curtain calls were compulsory only for the people who appeared in the last act of any play, we could be across the road in The Plough, all clean and shiny, less than ten minutes after our exits.

That curtain-call rule was amazing: in some large-cast plays, the bows could sometimes be taken by as few as three players. And to further facilitate his even earlier arrival in the pub after his appearance in one particular show, one colleague came up with an ingenious wheeze. He had only a single scene, consisting of a long speech delivered from a doorway. He had been costumed in a sort of toga and his role required him to 'black up'; with arms and legs bare this would have meant a long, tedious session in his dressing room applying make-up and, after his exit, an equally long one to remove it. So he blackened his face and neck – but only the front of his arms and legs. Then, on his cue, he sidled crab-like into an opening in the canvas flat, delivered his speech, then sidled off. (I saw this for myself but there is also anecdotal evidence that since his toga-thingy fastened fussily at the back, instead of going to the bother of doing it up, he customarily held it closed during the scene with one hand behind his back.)

Sinéad's dad, Cyril, had a flat in Hatch Street and many were the nights I spent there with her, illicitly drinking his booze and talking about, not boys now, but men – plus, of course, our art. We toured cinemas in the afternoons and, while I hovered in the background, she would stride confidently up to the window of each box office, announce who she was – or, more specifically, who her father was – and we'd get in for free.

So, gradually, despite my daily worries and – after the highs of Aer Lingus – a terminal slide in my self-confidence as an actor, I nevertheless came to appreciate my situation. There were many compensations.

For instance, there is no feeling akin to that of being suspended in light in the midst of darkness. Although you can't see them, you know that, out there, hundreds of pairs of eyes are focused on your every move; the same numbers of ears are waiting for what you might say next and how you might say it. It is a two-way mental and emotional communication; its manifestation is physical. You feel a warm tide washing through your limbs and veins. You feel light. Airy.

Deeper than the aim for laughter or applause, which if they occur are primarily affirmation that you're getting your timings right, this communication becomes an addiction, what the stand-up comedian Hal Roach has called his drug of choice, more important than anything else. It is a feeling of being in control, of being power-ful. It is why, I think, if they have even once experienced it, film actors yearn for the stage. When things are going well, a house can be controlled with the smallest of gestures, a pause, even with a tiny change in tempo or tone of voice.

The opposite is the case too: waves of boredom and dislike can be felt as keenly as those of rapt attention, and there is no actor's struggle so dreary and disheartening as trying to maintain focus and concentration in front of a fidgeting, throat-clearing, paper-rustling audience.

An audience's inattention can have a lot to do with the quality of the play, of how well actors are cast and performing, of how the play has been directed, of appropriateness and effectiveness of set and costume – but not entirely. Audiences can be innately iffy and actors can tell within minutes of the curtain going up whether tonight's house is intrinsically 'good' or not; this intuition is difficult to describe, other than to say that you can detect the quality of immediate attention or expectation from the moment the play starts.

It is even more mysterious than that, though. It is to detect an instant gelling of players with audience.

All actors, even veteran professionals, are nervous before going on, sometimes desperately so, and the combination of trembling, breathlessness and nausea known as 'stage fright' is common. But once you are on stage and settled into the lines and action, on a good night there is a sense of simultaneous relaxation and exhilaration. For those few minutes or hours, you temporarily overcome the fear of failure – at least I did. And while maintaining your sense of bodily self, you are now a conduit in a ritual, hoping you will transmit the playwright's intentions effectively – with added grace. In the process, temporal concerns about overdrafts, rows with your parents, tiffs and rifts with lovers, toothaches, headaches and any other kind of ache are overcome. Nothing exists except that, in someone else's skin, you are riding on what is coming at you from across the footlights – and we did have footlights in the Queen's. They were sometimes even used. (I mourn their general demise. From the actor's point of view – and even from the audience's – I think they added to the magic.)

I thoroughly enjoyed touring too. I loved the insularity of a touring company, your temporary family with whom you ate and drank and shared cheap hotel rooms and bitched about the venues and the cheapskate management back in Dublin, whose near-sighted meanness deprived you, as the true artists you were, of the type of accommodation you so richly deserved.

During one tour, Joan O'Hara, a greatly accomplished actress (who is at present on a TV screen near you as Eunice in *Fair City*) taught me two useful life lessons, each of which in different ways have stood me in good stead ever since. With Cyril Cusack in the lead, we were playing *Conn the Shaughraun* at the World Theatre Season at the Aldwych Theatre in London. I was sharing a (small) hotel room with Joan during a particularly steamy period of that city-centre summer, and the first lesson I learned from her was that to help keep yourself cool in muggy heat, you do not dry yourself after a shower but walk around wet to let the water evaporate naturally off your skin.

The second, more important lesson was about the vulnerability and openness of even the most celebrated and talented actors. One afternoon, we went together to see a matinée of Tom Stoppard's *Rosencrantz and Guildenstern Are Dead*. I was blown away by the show – and by the performances of the lead pair, John Stride and Edward Petherbridge.

'Let's go backstage and tell them as fellow actors how much we enjoyed it,' Joan suggested at the end, but I was reluctant. I knew that the necks of these men were garlanded with public and critical praise and I was so far out of their league I could not envisage myself as a colleague. 'I don't think I will – we don't know them after all. But you go!'

'They're *actors!* We're actors too!' She would not brook any objection. 'We're colleagues and it's important to tell them how much their work was appreciated by people like us.' So we went backstage and I discovered that her instincts had been spot-on. These two men, who had just given stellar performances in one of the hit shows of the West End and who had only a short tea-break before they had to get ready for the night performance, were genuinely delighted to meet two contemporaries from Ireland. They drank our congratulations like victims of a long drought. 'It's always marvellous to hear from peers.'

That lesson spurred me to review my own attitudes. I began dimly to recognise that the universe didn't start and end with me: that what people thought of me was less important than reaching out. So what if you were rejected? Your motives had been good.

I was, perhaps still am, deeply shy but give the impression of the opposite. Acting, goes the cliché, is the shy person's revenge – and in my experience, the majority of actors are shy. (Patricia Scanlan sussed this trait in me the first time we met. It takes a writer to see beneath the surface.)

But you learn about yourself in the weirdest places and from the most unexpected experiences. That excursion into that London dressing room may have been the start, but it wasn't until some time later, when I read a magazine article in a doctor's waiting room, that the penny dropped. Shyness, said this article, is an indication of self-centredness; while you are worrying about how everyone else will react to you, you are thinking only of yourself.

I set about training myself to be properly interested in other people, not just as incidentals or participants in my own life, but cutting myself out in order to celebrate and empathise with them. Although the process is not complete and probably never will be now, I think I have succeeded to a degree. And although, with some justification, I was at one point accused of being an emotional voyeur, so deeply had I become immersed in someone else's affairs, this determination to deal with shyness served me well in two later lives, those of journalist and author.

A huge bonus of my three-year stint at the Abbey occurred when, early on, I was accepted by a well-established group of the actors and became part of a loosely constituted gang who dandered around the countryside in the couple of bangers they had between them: Vincent Dowling's big green boneshaker and BYI 268, Pat Laffan's black Morris Minor. We were joined on these jaunts occasionally by Tom Murphy, the playwright, and also P.J. Carroll, proprietor of Molloy's pub on Talbot Place, who drove a BMW, no less, and of whom more anon.

In those days, the regime for Abbey actors was rehearsal in the mornings, Monday to Saturday, afternoons off, performances at night. So, during Holy Hour, the period after lunch when the pubs closed, we frequently travelled out to the Wren's Nest in the Strawberry Beds near Lucan, or Myo's in Castleknock, where as 'bona fides' – bona-fide travellers from outside a certain radius of these pubs – we were legally allowed to consume alcohol. It wasn't that we wanted to drink much: to start with, we didn't have the wherewithal and in any case we were usually playing that night. There was a principle involved. Holy Hour was an abomination, a preposterous imposition. Almost a denial of human rights, and certainly not to be tolerated by artists like us.

So, feeling flattered to be included, I could sit on my bar stool, nursing my glass of Phoenix, while immersing myself in all kinds of theatrical lore, including well-told stories of the fit-ups – the touring companies that pounded up and down the country playing single nights, weekends, or sometimes, blessedly, a full summer season, in tents and parish halls, or anywhere with a roof and a potential audience.

Incidentally, when I once asked my mother if we had any theatre connections in the family, she paused for a second's thought. 'Well, your great-grandmother took in theatrical people.' This was in the house on Castle Street. I have no idea how they crammed extra bodies into that house: Mamma couldn't elucidate either, as it was before her time there, but the wide village green in Durrow was a regular stop for all touring shows and carnivals and that house was just a few steps away. Even in those days it was Location! Location! Location!

The actor T.P. McKenna, a former Abbey actor but based in London, usually teamed up with our group when he was at home. At the time, I had taken to horse riding (too late, alas! to have professional ambitions) and was very keen. On one occasion, T.P. asked if he could tag along and maybe give it a go. I took him to my regular stables alongside the Phoenix Park where I was given Fudgy, my usual Arab pony, then persuaded the management to let T.P. up on Snowy, a very large grey. I'd ridden this animal several times and found him to be a docile plodder. I promised I'd mind them, so T.P. and Snowy came out in my charge.

Off we went into the park with a suddenly apprehensive T.P. tottering around in the saddle, while I trotted alongside, trying to demonstrate how he should relax and go with the flow. We were in the park for less than ten minutes when, for some reason, Snowy took exception to something, probably T.P.'s jerky piloting, and bolted, something I'd never known him to do before and for which he had no reputation.

Somehow, T.P., although falling around, managed to hold on and I chased him on Fudgy, who was a really fast pony. But Snowy had the bit literally between his teeth and, before I could get alongside, the inevitable happened: Snowy decided he'd made his point, veered towards a tree and T.P. was felled by a branch, badly injuring his arm and shoulder. Gallantly, apart from a bit of good-natured muttering, I don't think he held it against me – but I did get a postcard, years later, from the set of a film shooting somewhere on the Bosphorus. He wrote that for his role he had to ride a horse. A *nice* horse.

The company took a month's holiday in the summer and, after

my first year, I took myself off to C'an Pastilla in Majorca, suffering major sunburn within the first forty-eight hours – which probably set the seed for a melanoma some twenty-five years later. I'd never been away alone and had worried I'd be lonely but as soon as I'd recovered from the blisters and was back on the beach, I overheard a bunch of Irish accents grumbling from beach towels a few feet away.

They noticed me noticing. We introduced ourselves and we teamed up, sort of, for the rest of their holiday: I ate with them a few times, attended their parties, used the swimming pool at their hotel.

It turned out that the lads (they were all lads) were mainly from the midlands. Places like Mullingar. They were in the resort for a fortnight.

Guess there aren't many Abbey actors who can say they spent most of their holidays with Joe Dolan and the Drifters.

16

Doing the Ton

At the time I met him, the late P.J. Carroll, who became a very dear friend and later godfather to my son Adrian, was a shy bachelor who lived with his mother in an apartment above their pub in Talbot Place. Blue-eyed, ruddy-faced, of middle height and prematurely balding, the best way to describe him is that he was an enthusiast. In all the time I knew him, I never heard him bitch about anyone. He was enthusiastic about his pub and his patrons. He loved golf and was an enthusiastic member of Howth Golf Club. Possessed of a giggle he suppressed by trying to keep his mouth closed when it erupted, he was a deeply cultured man who was enthusiastic about the arts and supported them all.

He ran his pub well, hung its lounge with original art by artists he admired – Gerard Dillon, Arthur Armstrong, John Kelly and George Campbell. (After I got to know him, George asked if he could paint me – but on further enquiry I discovered I'd have to take my clothes off to sit for him. Well, that wasn't going to happen: I hadn't yet thrown off the influence of the Child of Mary medal.)

In fact the first naked person, man or woman, I ever saw in the flesh, as it were, was during one of our actors' danders, along with P.J., into the country.

The plan was to have a picnic at the Meeting of the Waters. It was P.J. (of course, an enthusiast for weather forecasting) who picked the day, and when we had found what we thought was the right place and had emerged into the sunlight from the cars, one of our number instantly threw off every stitch and splashed through the shallows until he found the place where he deemed the waters to have met. He mounted a small sandbank and, turning to face those of us staring at him from the safety of the bank, posed, *a là* the little Belgian Boy statue, a replica of which can now be found in the water-feature section of any garden centre. I pretended to take this vision in my stride.

P.J. loved to be in the company of artists of all descriptions, actors included, and after his pub closed, he hosted a small and select late-night salon. It was in P.J.'s I met luminaries, such as the critic Séamus Kelly (Quidnunc of the 'Irishman's Diary' in *The Irish Times*). But the attraction wasn't really with whom you rubbed shoulders; it was the quality of the encounter. P.J. would light the fire in the inner lounge, throw down a sheepskin rug in front of it, put on some quiet Bach or Mozart on his stereo and we were off.

He introduced us to tuna, a commodity none of us had tasted before: I would go upstairs with him to the kitchen in his apartment and help him make platefuls of sandwiches; it was up there that I got to know him because, downstairs, he was outshone by the much larger personalities of the raconteurs, opinion-throwers and arguefiers. But we had quiet times, too, in that lounge, just listening to music and waiting for the Galway train to go by at ten minutes past one. P.J. always threatened to throw us out when he heard that train, 'Come on, come on, you lot, some of us have to get up in the morning, you know!' He never carried out his threat and we were there sometimes until half past two or three – although once or twice we did find ourselves up on the roof or in the cellar as he thought he heard guards outside.

Molloy's had an early licence, opening at 7.30 a.m. to serve the night-shift workers from the nearby docks and railway depot. P.J. complained about this being onerous, but actually knocked great sport from the people in that bar, where you could barely see your neighbour on the next stool through the thick blue fug of cigarette smoke. He reserved a special fondness for the women who snuck quietly into his snug for a half-pint of shandy and sup of brandy.

He also had great time for his early-morning barman, Paddy. Paddy's forte was lining up the pints and the shorts but, one night, P.J. creased himself telling us about the way Paddy handled a hapless American tourist who had wandered into the bar that morning at about eight o'clock at the height of the rush. This American, obviously in search of an authentic Irish drinking of the green, ordered a crème de menthe frappé.

Poor Paddy couldn't believe his misfortune. 'A crème de menthe wha'?'

In light of the American's insistence, he consulted a dog-eared cocktail recipe book someone had given him and that for years he had kept under the counter for such emergencies. Crème de menthe frappé, it said, was to be served over crushed ice. So, in full view of the American and the fascinated regulars, Paddy picked up the slops towel he had already put to multiple uses that morning keeping his counter clean, threw a handful of ice into it, rolled it up and bashed the hell out of it against the bar. Then he funnelled the result into a glass, poured the liqueur over it and handed it to the gob-smacked American. 'Crème de menthe frappy!' he announced.

P.J. just *loved* that one.

It was P.J. who told me he was going to teach me to drive and took me in his car out towards the Naas Road, newly expanded into Ireland's first dual carriageway. At the top of this jewel of road making, he pulled into the verge, got out of his new BMW, handed me the keys and said, 'Now go!'

I'd never driven any distance, although I had sat behind steering wheels and practised a little in safe, enclosed and unpopulated spaces. But I'd observed other people driving and felt fairly sure I knew the rudiments. So, after a short introductory lesson with clutch and gears, I started off cautiously along our side of the (mercifully empty) roadway. 'Faster, faster!' urged my tutor.

I went faster.

'That's not fast enough. Come on. Faster!'

I looked at the speedometer. I was doing about sixty. I pressed the accelerator and the car jumped immediately to seventy.

'No. Faster. Do the ton. Go on, do the ton. Are you game? There's no one around. Do the ton. Go on.'

I'm afraid I let him down there. I didn't do the ton – at least not deliberately, though I may have done it involuntarily. (He always said I did.) At the time I was too white-knuckled with a combination of excitement and fear to know for sure. I did touch somewhere near ninety because that was the last time I dared glance at the speedometer.

When Naas was looming, I stopped the car at the side of the road. When I got out to change places with him, my knees were so wobbly I could barely stand – but I'd done it and I've loved driving ever since.

Subsequent teachers weren't so lucky with me: on one of our group outings, I scraped one entire side of Vincent Dowling's car in an over-confident attempt to get it through a gateway. Vincent really came up trumps: instead of giving out to me or panicking, he didn't even get out to look at the damage but insisted I keep on driving, 'You've got to get back up on the horse, you can't lose your confidence now.' And he never held it against me. I think.

Groome's Hotel, opposite the Gate, was where we went when we weren't in P.J.'s. And P.J. very occasionally came with us but never stayed long.

Compared to his salon, with its sumptuous atmosphere, round-table discussions and subdued classical music, Groome's late at night was a whole different experience, rambunctious and frequently so crammed it was hard to hear yourself think, let alone have an interesting discussion. On the other hand, it was a great venue for meeting people outside your own small purview, a place where clerics and film stars were punters just like us.

Others have written a lot about Groome's. I was witness to some of the legends that grew up around it: Patti's good-humoured but stern gate-keeping of her establishment; Jim Fitzgerald's dancing on a table; the politicians, including a government minister, nabbed for late-night drinking during a raid by the guards; the arguments; the friendships made and sundered; the affairs started; the fist fights in the laneway outside. For anyone who worked in theatre or the arts, it was an essential part of life. And I am grateful to Patti for letting me in on the same nod she granted to Peter O'Toole, Siobhán McKenna and John Hurt – for giving me the illusion that I belonged to that club.

17

The Next Step

It was P.J. who facilitated the next giant step in my life. He lent me enough money to buy a one-way ticket to America.

The reason for this arose directly from what turned out to be my Abbey acting swansong, an extensive, multi-venue Irish tour of Eugene O'Neill's *Long Day's Journey into Night* in which I played Cathleen, the young maid to the Tyrones. It was the first major tour the Abbey had undertaken in twenty-seven years and we were presenting the play uncut, starting at 6.15 p.m. in most venues, to be out by 11.00 p.m. if we were lucky.

Because expectations were so high, but also because the show was so long, we were granted an unheard-of fourteen weeks of rehearsal. And it showed. Angela Newman's performance as Mary, her interaction with Philip O'Flynn (her husband both in reality and on stage) and her sons, played by Vincent Dowling and Pat Laffan, was spellbinding. This production of this show was probably Frank Dermody's masterpiece.

Whether he knew this in advance, whether I'd toughened, or whether he had mellowed, he had backed off from terrorising me. Anyway, the role of the maid is pretty peripheral, and he spent ninety per cent of the rehearsal time on the other four, all of whose parts were huge and emotionally draining.

For whatever reason, glory of glories, I was free from worry and fear and thoroughly enjoyed that long rehearsal period, watching the deepening and intensifying of all the others' performances. I was, without fully realising it at the time, the serendipitous beneficiary of an acting master class and sometimes became so absorbed in what the others were doing and how they were doing it that I was reluctant to break in with Cathleen's lines in case I should break the spell.

As an addendum to my troubled relationship with Frank Dermody, years later when I was interviewed on radio about one of my novels and was asked about my Abbey days, out it poured, my well-worn recital about being bullied by this man.

Later, I received a letter, forwarded to me from RTÉ. It was from a person who had known him as a child and who had written to me with the intention of ameliorating these bad memories and perhaps helping me to understand why my tormentor had been as he was. Frank Dermody's childhood had been appalling by any standards; my correspondent was explicit in telling me how.

Although I never fully recovered the see-sawing confidence, destroyed in Scoil Mhuire, built up again in Gortnor Abbey and Aer Lingus, to be again demolished, at least partially, by my experiences with him, that letter had the intended softening effect. If I had known what he had been subjected to as a child I would have made allowances. And my sympathy for him grew when I heard later that, after retirement, this talented, tormented man had lived a solitary life in a caravan, with few, if any, visitors, hardly any money or other resources and scant company except for his books. I always meant to visit him but never did. Anyhow, the poor man is dead now and my heart goes out to his memory.

To get back to *Long Day's Journey* – cumulatively, I was on stage for so short a time, the management felt they could ask me to double-job. As well as acting, I was to be in charge of the cast laundry. Wisely, although I grumbled to my friends, I kept my mouth shut within the theatre and said of course I would look after everyone's dirty washing.

One never knows where education will take place and it was through that laundry mandate I discovered the truth about Good Shepherd Laundries, Magdalen homes, and what, shockingly, went on inside them. All of this was a revelation, even though I constantly visited my Aunt Nellie, who for many years lived in Rutland Cottages off Summerhill, just around the corner from one of the largest Magdalen homes in Dublin.

The tour itself succeeded brilliantly. We played theatres and halls – and, once, a crossroads ballroom in a place called Carrickmore on a high hill, the centrepoint of a wide empty landscape in Northern Ireland. One of the great images of my life was created there one evening prior to curtain up.

I had sorted out the laundry and was in costume and make-up, outside the ballroom taking in the 360-degree view. It was getting chilly as dusk was melting into darkness, and I was going inside when something in my peripheral vision caught my attention. I came back out to look and saw, reticulated on the undulating landscape, four lines of vehicles, cars, vans and even a couple of motorbikes coming from all points: four illuminated Chinese dragons converging steadily on where I stood.

We had worried about booking this ballroom as a venue: for almost four and a half hours, our audience would have to sit on rows of hard chairs looking at what was in reality a bandstand. We need not have worried. That night was one of the highlights of the tour. The concentration from and within those spectators was absolute. They were rewarded afterwards – those who chose to stay – because the venue's management had asked us to chat with them after the performance, offering an incentive of one crate of beer and one bottle of whiskey *per actor*! Philip and Angela chose to go back to our hotel in Omagh, but Pat Laffan, Vincent Dowling and I did hold the fort.

It was in Sligo that we had our first social setback. Having been fêted at civic receptions almost everywhere we went, we were, by now, quite blasé about them but were bumped down to earth when we turned up as arranged at the appointed time and building in that city to find the place locked and deserted. We milled around, wondering what to do. Could we have made some kind of diary mistake?

Then, along came the mayor on a bicycle. He greeted us cheerily, removed his bicycle clips and unlocked the place. He showed us into a nice office and, having unlocked a cabinet, poured several large whiskeys and handed them around to the men. Then he turned to me, 'Would you like a Fanta, Miss?'

As it happened, Sligo was also the venue where I felt most sorry for the people on the floor of the hall who were forced to crane their necks to watch us on the tiny stage more than thirteen feet above the floor of the hall. It was like playing in a wall-mounted television.

Sometimes the physical constraints of a venue were difficult for me, as the person least in need of plush changing and makeup facilities. There was one place where my 'dressing room' consisted of a shelf above a tiny hand-basin (with one tap from which a trickle of cold water was the best I could get) in what was really a toilet cubicle with the toilet removed. And because I was on stage so little and there was almost no other space backstage where I could hang out, or read, I just had to lump it. So I did. I washed my hair under that tap – usually giving myself a crick in the neck as a result – and with the use of a hand-mirror put on my stage makeup as well as I could under the feeble light of the bare bulb hanging from the ceiling. I was also very cold, but I did my best not to moan because this would have cut into the concentration of the others, even irritated them. Meanwhile, I thanked God we weren't playing this place for a full week. Oh, the glamour!

The only place we did not attract a full house every night of the week we played there was the Cork Opera House. Phil O'Kelly, who had come to manage the theatre from a successful career selling Renault cars, could not understand why. We couldn't either: we had stuffed venues everywhere else in the country; in the non-theatre venues where people had had to sit on those hard, movable chairs, there had been barely a scrape or any other sound during the full length of the play. So we had arrived in Cork on a high (but not smug – actors are *never* smug) and were very disappointed at the sight of empty seats.

For that appearance at the Opera House, the *Cork Examiner* sent along as a reviewer not a critic, but a cub newsdesk reporter. No disrespect to him, of course, but the choice of him as a reviewer might have been an indication of Cork's lack of interest in what we had to offer. Kevin Healy remembers the show, thought it was OK, reckons he might have said something along those lines in his copy, but for the life of him cannot remember whether or not he mentioned me. Well, he certainly knows me now: when he wakes up every morning he finds me staring at him in anticipation of the cup of coffee he's going to make for me. (Isn't Ireland small?)

I had had such a good time, I was miserable when that tour ended and we were returning to Dublin. But after the last performance, I was knocked for six when the other four presented me with a gold bangle to thank me for doing their laundry. They'd even had it inscribed: 'Deirdre. Long Day's Journey, 1967'. It is one of my greatest treasures.

The other spark of light at the end of the tunnel to Dublin was that we were going to play the show in the home theatre. I got a lift as far as Abbey Street, but, postponing the return to Ballymun, I went across to the Plough in search of company. Sitting up at the counter was Donal McCann with a couple of others. I joined them.

Donal, who was fond of the horses, had had a big win and the cash was burning a hole in his wallet. 'How would you like to go to Deauville to the races?' he asked, as I ordered my first drink.

What would you have done?

I rushed home (inasmuch as one can rush within the schedules of the 19A bus) and, to the consternation of my parents who had been expecting at least an account of my travels, I unpacked, repacked and was in Dublin airport in time to meet Donal for the night flight to Paris. He was going through his Peter O'Toole period at the time: the older actor had taken him under his wing during his visit to Dublin for the production, with Siobhán McKenna, of *Juno and the Paycock*, and McCann now walked like his lanky mentor, talked like him, had even tailored his head movements and disconcerting stares to resemble his hero. (I was present at one of the great Dublin put-downs of all time during a matinée of that *Juno*. Twenty minutes into the show, O'Toole's Captain Boyle, who had started valiantly with his Dubbalin accent, began to let it slip. From behind me came an uninhibited roar, 'Ah, go back and ride yer fuckin' camel!')

Anyhow, at the airport that night, McCann's luggage consisted only of a toothbrush, the head of which peered from the breast pocket of his jacket. It was the way Peter would have travelled.

Well, we never got to Deauville. Instead, we spent the entire winnings eating in the best restaurants of Montmartre and other trendy areas, touring the cafés and bars of the Left Bank, visiting Shakespeare & Co., taking a boat on the Seine, strolling on the Champs-Elysées, eating *soupe d'oignon* in Les Halles, tearing baguettes apart and dunking the pieces in our *grands cafés au lait*.

Donal asked me to marry him during that trip but, knowing I wasn't the first he had asked, nor would I be the last, I said I'd think about it.

And true to form, back on terra firma a couple of days later, he telephoned and asked to meet me in Terenure, his parental stomping ground. There, with the two of us sitting on a park bench near Terenure College, he looking off into space, me waiting and pretending not to know what was coming, he stumbled through a retraction of his offer. Peter would have approved of the sentiment, if not the inelegant delivery.

I don't know why he asked me, really, because I had made it clear in the pub before I agreed to go that our trip together was to be purely platonic. And on the way home in the plane, he did opine, more colourfully than I will report here, that being with Deirdre Purcell in Paris was nearly as good as being with anyone else in Lourdes.

Things returned to normal, or what passed for normal – parties in the flats of Stephen Rea or Seán McCarthy, where we listened to Nina Simone's 'Pirate Jenny' by the light of candles guttering in wax-encrusted Chianti or beer bottles, but drank Pedrotti or Soave, shared mattresses on the floor and thought ourselves incredibly sophisticated. At least I did.

Then, during the Dublin run of *Long Day's Journey,* one of the audience members came backstage to meet the cast. He was a Jesuit, Fr John Trahey, who had recently been installed as head of the

Theatre Department at Loyola University, Chicago. He became friendly with us and then – the shocker – asked me if I would be interested in going to Loyola as his first European Theatre Artist in his inaugural European Theatre Artists' Program. I would act in all the plays in the new state-of-the-art theatre on the campus – thereby setting a standard for the students. In return, he would offer me a full tuition scholarship – with which I could study anything I liked. He would get me a job in the college library so I could support myself in an apartment. He would organise that apartment for me, also my visa – but I would have to sit SATs (the standard entrance exam for universities in the States) in order to get it. And I would have to pay my own fare to America.

I hadn't been to university: now university was being handed to me on a plate. In addition, I knew that I would be guaranteed good parts in unusual plays instead of having to depend on the dispiriting casting system in the Abbey. I could hone my acting skills; I could gain confidence because I would suddenly be a big professional fish in a student pond – and since I would be twenty-three when I arrived and probably several years older than my new confrères, they would probably look up to me on that score too. Loyola, according to Fr Trahey, was a great place. There was a lot I could learn there.

There was another aspect of this offer I could not resist – it was *America*. I hadn't been there since I had paraded along the green line painted on Fifth Avenue. I wanted more, more, more…

So I sat the SATs in the American Embassy and apparently did well. Why wouldn't I? The questions were nearly all multiple choice, a new one on me. For an Irish person, accustomed to the essay questions posed at that time for the Leaving Cert, being asked to pick your choice of answer to each question from a shortlist was manna. They gave you *clues*, the pets! If you didn't instantly know what the answer was, you could winkle it out by applying logic and a process of elimination. For the first time in my life, I enjoyed an exam.

Then the question of money for the fare arose. P.J. offered. I accepted. 'But what'll I do if it doesn't work out and I have to come home?'

'We'll cross that bridge when we come to it. Anyway, it'll mean that you'll have to stay in touch – but I'm not worried. It will work out.' (For the record, I did repay the loan.)

During the last few months of my stint as an Abbey actress, I wasn't an actress at all – although I did a couple of films in which my performances were even more unmemorable than the movies themselves, and that's saying a lot. Since 1966, the company had returned to its brand-new bunker in Abbey Street from the Queen's (where, if memory serves, the last show in the old place was a riveting piece called *Irishwoman of the Year*, with Sinéad in the lead).

For some reason, the installation of the state-of-the-art sound desk in the new theatre was delayed – and when it finally arrived, Tomás Mac Anna asked me to train on it and be its first operator. When I asked, 'Why me?' he replied, with typical bluntness, that (a) they needed someone; (b) he thought I'd be very good at it and anyway I was 'too intelligent to be an actress' – I didn't know quite how to take that. Was this a backhanded compliment or what? (He did subsequently get permission from the Abbey to cast me in one of his outside productions, O'Casey's *Drums of Father Ned* at the Olympia, so he can't have thought I was all bad.)

But since I would be leaving the following September anyhow to go to Loyola, since the new job involved learning a new skill – always a carrot to me – and not least because it would give me a fifty per cent hike in salary, I agreed. The money would come in handy in America.

I love start-up situations and, for a while, I enjoyed working that sound desk after I had completed the training on the vast new array of switches and faders and had bedded in. It felt really good to watch a play through my glass window above the back of the balcony, where no one could see me but I could see everyone. What's more, I found I could use all of my empathy antennae, feeling what the actors were feeling, watching their moves and then, at the right time, letting my fingers do the talking as I stole in or crashed in the sound effects or music as appropriate. It felt like acting without the stress.

What's more, my fear of being cast out of the actors' group because I was now a techie did not materialise. All my friends continued to treat me as if I was one of them. And I was still welcome at P.J.'s.

But I did get bored, and I resigned from the Abbey a couple of months before I was due to go to America. However, I needed to save – so I blagged my way into a job as a messenger for Hackett's, the architectural drawings stationer. The money was £2 a week more than I had been getting in the Abbey and the Situations Vacant ad in the *Evening Herald* had contained the magic words 'company car supplied'. I thought I would enjoy zooming around the architects' offices of Dublin in a Morris Mini. I got the job (I didn't tell my new employers that I would be with them for only six weeks), I did enjoy it and now I was able to *drive* to P.J.'s in the evenings.

I am certainly ill equipped to judge whether or not I was a good actress. The exuberance of my performances in the Aer Lingus Musical Society, where a degree of raw talent was enough to carry me through, had been very quickly eroded. I spent half of my three years at the Abbey during the company's last days at the Queen's when it dwelt in the sad twilight of its glory and, as I had neither the pedigree nor the visual impact of my pal Sinéad, was understandably overlooked for the few juvenile leads that were going. For instance, while she, inevitably, became the *Ban-Phrionnsa* (to Donal's *Prionnsa*) in an Abbey pantomime one Christmas, I was cast as *An Sióg Olc* – the Bad Fairy – one of an unholy trio, the others being Peadar Lamb and Pat Laffan, who were cast as warlocks. (At least, for that part, I got to learn how to play bones – a skill, however, that I am not often called upon to exhibit!) I did get good reviews now and then. Although I was ignored in some shows, I don't remember ever getting a bad one. In general, though, I was not long enough at the Abbey, or given enough to do, for anyone to make a definitive judgement.

One of my favourite parts was not a big one: I absolutely loved playing Bridie, the most uncouth of Tarry Flynn's uncouth sisters in the P.J. O'Connor adaptation of Patrick Kavanagh's novel. Wearing a beret over my uncombed hair, unlaced boots, a shrunken cardigan over a faded summer dress and eyebrows thickly pencilled into a beetling straight line, I tramped on stage at the beginning of the play, carrying two buckets, plonked them down and announced to our mother in a broad Monaghan accent, 'The strawberry's looking the bull!'

Kavanagh, in the last months of his life, was around the place during rehearsals. In the afternoons, he held court in The Bailey on Duke Street, sitting just inside the door to consume liberal quantities of the only drink he could then stomach: 'Put Bicarbonate in it!' was his (peremptory) order when a fresh glass of whiskey was proffered. This cocktail was supplied by the Bailey's proprietor, the late John Ryan, whose patronage of the arts and artists was exemplary.

Donal, who played Tarry, and Pat Laffan, who played his sleeveen friend Eusebius, became friendly with Paddy, and I tagged along now and then as we went south of the Liffey, I suppose to pay homage. While we were all delighted that *Tarry Flynn*, which was very successful, gave the poet some much-needed funds, I found him to be more than somewhat lacking in social grace. 'Are you Bridie?' he barked at me each time, looking me up and down as if I too was a strawberry cow.

'That's right.'

'Hmmph!' he would dismiss me and order another drink while grunting that he had never liked Bridie. 'She became a Reverend Mother, you know…'

I would not have made it as a freelance actor, I am certain of that. I had neither the gumption nor the thickness of skin and neck, necessary tools in the armoury of the freelancer. I could not have badgered cold-eyed, indifferent producers to give me a start or tele-phoned agents to ask them if they would put me on their books. I could not have taken each no as provisional and bounced back to ask again.

My time at the Abbey was over and, although I didn't really know what lay ahead for me, I was going to have a great year in an *American* university in one of the most exciting cities in *America*. It was September 1968. Mayor Daley was taking no nonsense on the streets of my future city, where protestors, many of them students, were trying to disrupt that year's Democratic Convention; students were wielding their power in France, in Kent State, in California… I was going to be part of that; I was going to be a student too. I would walk to the university from my apartment to my campus, two words I knew only from books and movies.

This new twist and everything that would follow from then on had hinged on that crucial twenty-four hours when Ernest Blythe had watched me try my best to help a friend. If I hadn't gone to that audition, I might have stayed in Aer Lingus. I would have enjoyed a modest lifestyle, but would have seen the world. If I had married, my children would have used planes like their friends used buses.

I hope it does not sound big-headed when I say I might have climbed some ladder in the company (on the somewhat shaky premise, evidence to the contrary, that a combination of hard work, dedication and loyalty will be recognised and rewarded). I certainly would have continued being a member of the ALMDS. While many amateur actors are as innately talented as their professional friends, there is a big difference in the work they do and how they get it. In essence, amateurs have the best of both worlds: they enjoy an enormous amount of personal and artistic satisfaction without having to ride out public ridicule or scorn. They don't have to depend on the results of 'open casting' auditions to feed their families. They don't have to compete for parts for which they are summarily dismissed as too old, young, fat, thin, small, tall; they aren't discussed as prize cattle are – turn of leg, perkiness of nose, gracefulness of movement. Frank Dermody had insisted I have a dentist file down my front teeth to make them shorter; he had told me I looked like Bugs Bunny. And in the alleyway outside the stage door of the Queen's, I had unexpectedly encountered Ernest Blythe one evening after a show; he said he'd been meaning to talk to me. 'Your nose is too long and your calves are too strong.' Not knowing how to react to this, I stood rigidly against the wall – I can still remember the feeling of rough stone coldness on my back through the thin jacket I was wearing – while my managing director stooped and felt my legs. Properly. Each in turn. Taking a bit of time over the task. 'Yes. Dancer's legs. I suppose there isn't that much we can do about that, heh, heh!'

This was the man who, legend has it, refused Jackie McGowran a tiny, overdue and well-deserved pay rise. Jackie, later to become a renowned Beckettian, went up to the office timidly to ask for a few bob, using as ammunition the fantastic reviews he had garnered as an Indian judge in some play or other.

From behind his desk, Blythe stared at him through his little round glasses, 'Ach, d'you see, Jackie. We don't have parts for Indian judges every day of the week!'

Professional actors are brave people, and I was privileged to live amongst them for a time.

18

Nellie

In the course of a radio programme some years ago, I was asked what my overriding impression of the 1950s was. I answered honestly that it was one of fear. Fear of hell, punishment, the priest or the bishop, teachers, officialdom, parents' censure – of almost everything. The world seemed frugal and repressed; grown-ups' anger was just a heartbeat away and the rules seemed impenetrable.

Certainly, my own experience of the period between my blithe, princess period and the time I settled in at Gortnor Abbey seemed in memory to be emotionally frigid and fraught.

I am writing this section in the caravan we have on a site in Argelès-sur-Mer, between Perpignan and the Spanish border. Although rain is forecast for the weekend, the sun is shining and the thermometer on the deck outside the open french doors indicates that the temperature is 25 degrees. La Roseraie, smelling of warm dust and mown grass, is almost perfect. When I went outside to drink my first cup of coffee this morning, I startled a hoopoe, which flew off from the roadway, flashing its plumage of black, white and brown. Right now, I can see a golden oriole in one of the trees outside the deck. And when I went to buy my baguette earlier, the mountains of the Albères in the distance were a misty blue.

Dressed in shorts and a T-shirt, I am waiting for my hair, still wet from the shower, to dry, so I can go to the supermarket and look the chic French housewives in the eye. Genetics can be brutally unfair. My father was tall and lean, Declan is even taller and leaner, and – the killer – his hair is thick and wavy.

So he got all of the best bits of both the Butlers and the Purcells, dammit – leaving me to make do with the low height, squareish shape and slow metabolism of Dadda's older sister, Nellie. (And, of course, Dadda's hair.) Against the modern developmental norm where a daughter is at least a couple of inches taller than her mother, at five foot four, I am two inches *shorter* than mine.

You may have noticed references here and there to Nellie. You may not have paid much attention to a person who seems to have been a pleasant incidental in my childhood. A nice but ordinary aunt. Today is 5 May 2006, the twentieth anniversary of her death, and she was anything but an ordinary aunt to me.

She was a woman who seemed to be the most conservative person in the world, who was stubborn, who walked only at her own speed – slowly – ignoring the pace of any companions and all entreaties to keep up, yet who embodied the motto of the Girl Guides – she had been one into her twenties – because she was always ready. Cautiously ready, but nonetheless wide open to new experiences. Television, that window on the world, had been designed for her. She spoke Italian, Spanish and French, garnered through attendances at night classes, and, within the constraints of her limited holidays and budget, was well travelled. Rome, which she visited many times, was her Mecca.

In thinking about her, it turns out that I have to revise my beliefs about those early 1950s as, like sunflowers, episodes continue to pop into my mind and exit through my fingers onto these pages. Nellie was a large part of ensuring that I hadn't had it so bad after all.

I used to tell everyone, usually in response to questions at public readings or questionnaires for newspaper features, that there was only one person who had been seriously of influence in my life: Vincent Browne, my boss at the *Sunday Tribune*.

Professionally, Vincent had a powerful, even overwhelming effect on me but, from an early age, Nellie became important, more so than my parents in many ways, and was probably my primary influence. In the 1950s, she, and the activities she organised, gave me respite from my preponderant state of childhood fearfulness.

If you remember, my two imaginary friends were Little Nellie and Little Sheila, named after my two aunts. Little Nellie, complete with perm and small round glasses, remained as the companion of my bosom for a long time.

My mother used to tell the story of being on a bus from Ballymun going into town when I was about three and a half. We were sitting on the side seat just inside the open platform and the bus conductor came to us to collect our fares as the bus moved away from our stop. Then I noticed that Little Nellie was not with us. I began to shriek, 'She missed the bus! She missed the bus!'

'Who's missed the bus, love?' The conductor looked through the window.

'Little Nellie. She missed the bus!'

My mother tried to calm me down, but I wouldn't have it. I evaded her grasp, stood on the seat and banged frantically at the window, 'Look – look! She's running! She's running!'

Fair dues to that bus conductor. He rang the bell and rushed up to the driver who stopped the bus. Then everyone on it had to wait until Little Nellie caught up and, puffing, joined us on our bench seat. She remained with me until some time after I started school, when she faded quietly away and the real Nellie took over.

Somehow, their family had found the money to send both Nellie and my father to secondary school – her to Warrenmount, him to Synge Street CBS, from which Dadda's proud boast was that his classmates had been the authors Cornelius Ryan and James Plunkett – and to keep them there as far as Leaving Cert. Although Nellie completed hers, Dadda left school two months before sitting his: he had been called as a Clerical Officer to the civil service and the family needed his wage.

Their father, Jack, was a housepainter for Dublin Corporation and, in mentioning this, Nellie and Dadda always added that he had been very proud of his profession, especially since he had earned the right to be called a 'master' painter, which apparently entitled him to mix his own paints.

Unfortunately, neither Declan nor I know all that much about the Purcell side of the family – and, of course, neither asked nor listened properly when we had the opportunity to learn about it. We do know that our Purcell grandmother, who rejoiced in the wonderful name of Rose (Roseanna) McTavish, came originally from Scotland and that Dadda's great-grandfather, with his grandfather after him, ran a dairy in Dublin's Cork Street. We also know that Dadda and Nellie had a third sibling, Paddy, who died of TB when he was only thirty-two, and that their Uncle Willie, after whom Dadda was named, went off with the Dublin Fusiliers and was killed in June 1916 during the Battle of the Somme and is buried at Ypres. We have cousins, Nancy, Frances and Séamus Gartland, in Carrickmacross.

And that's almost it.

From the time I was five or six years old, Nellie took me out every Saturday afternoon. She had astonishing speeds in typing and both Pitman and Gregg shorthand, and worked as secretary to Harry Band, manager in Ireland of the film company, United Artists, with offices in Middle Abbey Street. So she was always up with the play in the matter of films and film stars.

Every Saturday morning, I would take the 13 bus, first from Ballymun and then from Glasnevin, to Beechwood Avenue in Ranelagh where she lived in a bedsitter. We would have our dinner, then go back into town to attend something.

At Christmas, the choice to be made between pantomimes was bewildering; so it became a matter of prioritising in which order we wanted to see them because we went to them all. We went to the visiting shows in the huge Theatre Royal: I particularly remember Roy Rogers and Trigger, mainly because Trigger danced on his hind hooves with a kilt around his middle.

In spring we went to the Spring Show; in August we cheered on our gallant show jumpers at the Horse Show.

At other times, there were movies, an ice show in the Stadium, folk dancing in the Mansion House, Pilar Lopez and her Flamenco Dancers in the Gaiety (was there a José Greco too?), a circus, a concert on a bandstand in the Phoenix Park, a matinée of a visiting ballet company, the feis ceoil or, if there was nothing else, an ordinary feis. Curiously, the only performances we did not attend were those in the straight theatre, and I was fifteen or sixteen when I saw my first play, *This Other Eden* with the Abbey Players at The Queen's.

If there was nothing on that we fancied, we went to the zoo, or to Bray, or up to the Summit in Howth on the clanging tram. We took the bus to Dollymount and went across the wooden bridge, me fearing that, at any minute, we could fall through the cracks into the water beneath, and where sometimes the tide was so far out we couldn't even see it. One year, Nellie took a room in a house in Dollymount for a whole week so she and I could have a holiday there.

Sometimes, we took Mystery Tours. These were all-day outings for which we met early in town. CIÉ ran them. You paid your money in advance for your ticket but you didn't know until the train left the station where it was taking you. It could be Wexford or Galway or even all the way to Killarney. Nellie and I liked that one best. We went on a jaunting car and had a cup of tea in the Great Southern Hotel before we boarded the train home. As we travelled, there was entertainment through a public-address system, with somebody on the train's staff acting as MC. There were proper singers, but also ordinary passengers volunteering to do party pieces when noble calls were announced; there was food, there was a feeling of happy communal adventure in which the staff fully participated.

In extremis, Nellie and I could always fall back on climbing Nelson's Pillar. We went up it a few times but, to tell you the truth, I was never impressed. There seemed to be a lot of pushing and shoving to get to the front of the viewing platform and, anyway, at the time I was not all that interested in looking at an oul' view.

At tea-time, when that Saturday's outing was over, Nellie would give me my pocket money for the week and put me on the bus home with an extra few pence for my fare.

She paid for me to go to the Municipal School of Music in Chatham Street to study the piano. She also paid for my ballet lessons with Cepta Cullen, who ran her school in a studio behind the Country Shop in St Stephen's Green. She paid for my ballet shoes and my class dress of white piqué cotton and stiff black grosgrain belt, lined with petersham. She helped me sew on my shoe ribbons and darn the toes. And when we were doing our shows in the Marian Hall, Milltown, she paid for my tutus, tights, Russian boots and anything else I needed.

It is not hard to discern where I found my lifelong love of performance and performers.

When I left it all to go to Gortnor Abbey, my aunt wrote to me faithfully every week, enclosing a postal order for 2/6d., obviating the need for my parents to send me anything.

Actually, my mother and my aunt did not get on. For a short period, Nellie came to live with us on Dean Swift Road, I don't know why. Perhaps, after her parents died, the artisan dwelling in Long Lane was sold from under her – or maybe it was never theirs to sell and the owners took it back. Anyhow, in she came with her spaniel, Flush, and her cat, Tisha.

I was delighted, of course, but could never understand why, all of a sudden, there were frequent tears from both her and my mother; I remember raised voices between Mamma and Dadda. I remember several big rows when, after my mother had cleaned the kitchen floor, Nellie opened the back door to admit both Flush and Tisha from the muddy garden. They lived in the back garden when she wasn't in but then, rain or shine, newly cleaned floor or no newly cleaned floor, as soon as she came home, Nellie would open the kitchen door to let them in.

This might have been the reason her sojourn in our house did not last long.

When I grew into adulthood, our companionship of earlier years remained secure, and I spent a lot of time with her. While I was in the Abbey, I used her next bedsitter, a high-ceilinged room at the front of a house in Harcourt Street, as a crash pad where she fed me my tea – usually brown bread and a boiled egg – and let me listen to her LPs of light classics and Broadway musicals and didn't mind if I took naps in her bed. She was living in that flat when she won the Golden Goose: a lottery-type affair run by a local grocery chain. The prize was £500 and to her it was as good as a million. We all got a share of it – the cousins in Carrickmacross, me, Dadda…

And, in 1966, when Tomás Mac Anna asked Veronica Murray and me to act as Assistant Stage Managers, i.e. gofers, while he planned his massive 1916 commemorative pageant in Croke Park, the two of us spent days in Nellie's flat using her treadle sewing machine to construct the hundreds of banners and flags he wanted.

That pageant was some logistical feat. Its scale was massive and it employed almost every male actor in Ireland. I remember Ray McAnally, a stickler for verisimilitude, taking five hours to mould his nose and chin into the likeness of Pearse.

So if every child needs someone to spoil them rotten, Nellie was that someone for me.

But when my first marriage broke up in 1977, and she generously gave up her job to live with us and look after my two baby sons, I began dimly to see why Mamma had rebelled against her in Dean Swift Road all those years earlier. Nellie's routines were the only routines allowed. She was obstinate and opinionated, but so was I – and I expect what affected us was the old cliché of two women in the same kitchen. I had no choice but to yield because I was the one who was out working to keep the financial show on the road while she held my fort. I did love her dearly and I know she loved me. Neither of us ever expressed it, though – that wasn't the style in any relationship within our family.

She died in 1986 after a crippling six-month illness. At one point, we found what we thought was a good nursing home for her but then discovered that, because she was contrary and demanding in her illness, the staff was in the habit of disconnecting her call bell at night. We managed to get her transferred to Our Lady's Hospice in Harold's Cross, where she had peace.

And, I hope, happy anticipation. I had arranged for her and her beloved Carrickmacross cousin, Frances Gartland, to go to Lourdes with the Dublin diocesan pilgrimage, which offered specialist care of the sick. She was very excited about it – but she died the day before she was to leave. She had been in the hospice for only three weeks.

Nellie gave and gave and gave to me, but I hope that in the process she gained something too: not only a favourite niece but, later, my two young sons to cherish as if they were her own. They, I know, returned her love, and I hope with all my might that some-how, while she was alive, she felt this was some recompense for all she did for me.

The hospice carers assured me that she went in a few seconds and did not suffer; I comfort myself that at least she died while cradled in wonderful, calm care and in expectation of her holiday with Frances.

19

'Bill. R.I.P.'

Nellie and my father were not close, and I think he was surprised to find that he was the beneficiary of her estate, which, if memory serves, came to just under £2,000.

They were alike in many respects. Both were great readers, curious about the world and avid to learn more. Just as she was a Girl Guide into adulthood, he was a Catholic Boy Scout and, while an underlying adventure-loving, even anarchic streak could be discerned in both of them, in daily life each was methodical and orderly and, on the surface at least, espoused predictability.

My father's personality was complex. His choleric temperament, particularly around mealtimes, was balanced by a deeply sentimental streak. He had a fine tenor voice that, when used with sobbing emphasis at parties, could pull tears from the most stony-hearted, especially when he sang emigrant chestnuts such as 'The Old Bog Road'. His volatility calmed almost instantly and to an astonishing degree, when, in his early fifties, he was diagnosed and treated for diabetes. Being the meticulous civil servant that he was, he followed his diet and insulin regime to the letter.

There seemed to be lots of parties in our house when I was growing up. The Gang of Eight were always at the core, but the guest list could include neighbours, my Aunt Sheila and Uncle Jimmy, my Uncle Jack and his wife, Marcella, the Solo school and their wives and, many times, a contingent from Durrow. Late in life, Joe Brophy, whom we all thought was a confirmed bachelor, went to Glasgow and brought home a Scottish bride. He had sold his cement business to Readymix and had 'done well for himself'; we all took immediately to Mary, a brilliant pianist who could anchor any party and who was, therefore, much in demand. His pride in her was almost palpable.

The very point of those parties seemed to be a re-hearing of well-worn party pieces over and over again and to join in the choruses. Sheila and Mamma duetted 'Whispering Hope', Jack sang 'Abdul Abulbul Emir', Jimmy sang 'I'll Take You Home Again, Kathleen' – from party to party, the musical menu varied as little as the ham and salad sandwiches, ginger nut biscuits or Gateaux Swiss roll. Dadda's 'big' one was 'Love Thee Dearest'. But the song that really got to me (even as a two- or three-year-old, by all reports) was when, by popular demand, he sang 'I'm Sitting on the Stile'. I would sit gazing up at him, tears rolling down my cheeks, while he would sing to my mother, Maureen (Mary) whom he, like the song says, had married on a bright May morning:

> *I'm sitting on the stile Mary*
> *Where we sat side by side.*
> *On a bright May morning long ago*
> *When first you were my bride.*

I'm very lonely now Mary
For the poor make no new friends.
But, oh, they love them better still
The few our father sends.
And you were all I had Mary
My blessing and my pride.
There's nothing else to care for now
Since my poor Mary died.

I'm bidding you a long farewell
My Mary kind and true.
But I'll not forget you darlin'
In the land I'm going to.

Even as an adult, I was inconsolable every time I heard him sing that one.

Yet, for someone who obviously had such dramatic propensities, Dadda's attitude to mine was mixed to say the least. 'Don't come the Sarah Bernhardt here!' and 'Don't forget, whatever Deirdre says about anything, cut it by fifty per cent,' were his frequent and exasperated comments when, as I still do, I exaggerated details of a story or an incident for dramatic effect.

I don't think anything encapsulated his frustration more than my Fifth Year switch at Gortnor Abbey from Commerce to Music as subjects for Leaving Cert. I had taken perhaps four or five off-putting classes in 'typing' on a flat cardboard 'keyboard' spread over my desk, bashing away with my fingers to the tick of a metronome. It was excruciatingly boring and, after a few weeks, I decided I had learned enough. To know the QWERTY keyboard positions was all anyone needed, I told myself. I was now fully equipped with the knowledge and, henceforth, to become an expert touch-typist was just a matter of practice, something I could do at any time in the future.

And, anyway, there was more to life than the practicality of commerce. I had a good ear for music – I had the basics from the Municipal School some years previously and, I told myself, rationalising, I could catch up with those who had already started on the curriculum. So I made the switch.

Knowing my father would be informed in due course by the nuns, and knowing also I would be safe from his rage because I was 150 miles away, I got my licks in first and confessed my crime over a crackling phone line in the draughty, creaking corridor outside Mother Claudine's office.

As I had predicted, he was incandescent but, secure in the knowledge that the deed was already done, I simply let him run himself to a standstill. I knew, of course, that his anger was reasonable: the study of music would give lifelong rewards but I was not going to make a living out of it, on the other hand, a knowledge of shorthand, typing and bookkeeping would give me a head start. Yet, five years later, on the night when I was dithering about making the leap from Aer Lingus into the far more risky acting profession, it was he who swung my decision. What he said to me that night is burned into my brain, a wistful, 'If I'd been given a chance like this when I was your age…'

Dadda finished his public-service life in a bobby's job: that of permanent secretary to the public-service interview panels. These sat not only in Dublin but anywhere there were vacancies for county managers, engineers, medical officers – all kinds of professions and humbler occupations, too. As a result, he got to travel around the country and to stay in hotels, which he loved. And since the panels, drawn as experts from their relevant fields, were not paid for their trouble, his task was to play host at a compensatory lunch.

The main bonus of the job, though, was that he had the opportunity now to learn about aspects of Irish life he had never known before in any detail: municipal sewage, policing, military command structures, even the way the postal service operated. He became a great authority on nearly everything and absolutely adored that job.

He turned down a further promotion to Principal Officer even though his salary would have increased and his pension would have been a lot better. The snag was that he would have to give up his interviewing peregrinations around the country and return to base.

He retired from the public service when he was sixty and took to his new life with gusto. Having hated Fianna Fáil all his life, he converted when Charlie Haughey gave pensioners the free travel, free TV licence, et cetera and, from the time he received these entitlements, he took full advantage of everything. His morning routine involved taking the (free) bus into town, having a (free) pensioners' swim in the Countess Markievicz pool in Townsend Street, going back as far as his Glasnevin bank on the (free) bus where he had a (free) cup of coffee and then taking another (free) bus home where he watched his television, delighting in the knowledge that he hadn't had to pay for the black-and-white component of his TV licence. Then, in the afternoons, he could read his (free) library book.

One afternoon, 22 February 1999, I went in to see him in the Bons Secours Hospital where he was having a check-up. Neither of us was to know that, two hours after I left, he was to fall, and begin a rapid descent towards death.

He liked to do the Simplex crossword in *The Irish Times* and, never before having had the patience for crosswords, I had taken to doing it with him. Although now we were now genuinely good friends, about which I was delighted, I was never totally relaxed in Dadda's company, unlike Declan, and this was a peaceful way to communicate.

Anyhow, crossword completed, for some reason (and for the first time), I asked him to tell me about his childhood. He lit up as he expounded about Long Lane, about being sent as a boy each summer to stay with his Carrickmacross relations while he worked for a few shillings on the farm of the Shirleys who were the landed gentry of the area. He told me about his father and mother, his Uncle Willie who went to war, about the Christian Brothers of Synge Street – for whom he had great respect and who afforded him one of the highlights of his adolescent life: a one-line part as a soldier in *Julius Caesar* at the Gate Theatre, with James Mason in the lead. I already knew about this because, ever after, it had given him the opportunity to send himself up with his own oft-repeated one-liner: 'When I played with James Mason at the Gate…'

He spoke about the sanatorium where his brother had died, about his trips to Lourdes with the Scouts, about hiking in the Wicklow Mountains. Of Mamma and himself cycling all the way from Dublin to Durrow one weekend to attend a dance and cycling all the way back again next day, a round trip of about 130 miles.

I listened properly for the first time. Or thought I did – but because the emotional events of the following few days superseded what he told me, I can remember very little of the detail. What does survive is one image in particular, as evocative as a painting by Constable.

It is high summer on a farm near Carrickmacross. Young Willie Purcell, aged about twelve, a peaked tweed cap shading his head and eyes from the sun, is hand-weeding a field of yellowing grain alongside Major Shirley, who is directing a pair of horses pulling a farm machine. From the Catholic church in the town, the noon Angelus bell rings out. The boy continues weeding. The major pulls his horses to a halt, steps down, gently takes the cap off the boy's head and tells him to say his prayers. He takes off his own straw hat out of respect. The two of them, boy and man, stand side by side in the humming field while the boy bows his head to pray.

Eighty years old in that hospital bed that afternoon, what was most telling about Dadda, and probably many others of his generation, was the wonder he conveyed that a Protestant establishment figure would show such respect for the religious traditions of a Dublin urchin.

His big ambition had always been to go to Ypres to see his Uncle Willie's grave. I had planned, vaguely, to take him there. To that end, Lucy Cronin, daughter of my friend Carol, did some research and found it for us.

We never got there, Dadda and I, but Adrian, my son, now displays a framed photograph of Willie in the hall of his house with the letter from his commanding officer informing Willie's family of his death: a shell exploded above their trench, killing Willie and his lieutenant.

I will go there some day in memory and on behalf of my father and Nellie.

Dadda died in Beaumont Hospital at 9.10 p.m. on 26 February 1999. His prostate cancer, held at bay and brilliantly managed by himself and his consultant urologist for eighteen years since first diagnosis, had finally metastasised further than his poor body could handle.

I remember him lovingly for all the wonderful things: the calm charity of his later life and his sense of public duty. He was a member of the St Vincent de Paul and of the visiting committee at Mountjoy Gaol. Even after his tenure of that committee ceased, he continued to visit for years: 'there's a poor oul' divil in there who murdered his wife'; he brought this man naggins and fags and, eventually, attended his funeral. He was also, briefly, a Knight of Columbanus – until the internal rituals of that organisation got on his nerves.

He loved a party, and his sense of the absurd was infectious: his bent-double giggling, for instance, while watching *Dad's Army* or *Last of the Summer Wine* was a sight to behold. His favourite movie was *Blazing Saddles* and, if at all possible, he would not miss *Keeping Up Appearances,* deeming Patricia Routledge's bizarre Mrs Bucket ('Boo-kay') to be the comic creation of all time.

Although I love and admire that series as much as he did, I now find it difficult to watch the reruns. By strange coincidence, during the last half hour of his death throes, the television set in his ward was blaring with Hyacinth's latest misadventures – until a priest arrived to announce the Rosary around his bedside and some charitable visitor to another bed turned it off. To this day, I can summon a sense memory of the dense silence from the other patients in that ward as everyone knew the end was near.

When Mamma came to see him during his final three days in hospital, Declan and I sat in the corridor outside his room, leaving them as much privacy as dying patients can have in a multi-bed ward at visiting time with children running, giggling and munching sweets and *Coronation Street* at top volume on the television set mounted over the door.

When he saw her arrive, he immediately removed his oxygen mask, 'I'm bunched, Maur!'

'You're not going to leave me alone, are you?' she retorted.

It was she, anguished, who reported this exchange to me after he died. She hated herself for it. I tried sincerely to reassure her that it wouldn't have mattered to him what she said – that he would have known she was deeply afraid and hadn't meant it to come out like that, but there was no comforting her. For what was left of her own life, she regretted that reaction and brooded over it.

The French have a saying that in every relationship there is one who loves and one who allows love. Loving him in her singular way, she had fulfilled the latter role and, that evening, the realisation that he would no longer be there for her crowded in to overwhelm her. Appearances to the contrary, I think she had convinced herself that, albeit a serious setback, this hospitalisation was just the latest in a long line of similar occurrences and he would overcome it as he always had.

He would have completely understood why she wouldn't come to see him for his last hour.

At around teatime on his last afternoon, Declan and I knew he had little time left and drove from the hospital to Ballymun to break the news. Initially, she went upstairs to dress to come back with us, but I'll never forget the subsequent picture of her as, eyes wide with fright, she teetered at the top of the stairs, one foot poised as though to come down, but shaking her head and clutching the banisters, as if it was the only solid object in the world.

She had always refused to treat his illness, in conversation or, more crucially, in her mind, as anything but a step into old age. Now, an undercurrent of fear had finally surfaced. She couldn't handle it, and Declan and I drove back to Beaumont without her while my wonderful sister-in-law, Mary, stayed with her to count down the hours.

When we got back to her later that night to tell her it was all over, she was sitting quietly at the dining-room table with Mary. She barely reacted on being told he was gone. Later, I went upstairs to visit her when she was in bed. She was still calm. 'When you're eighty-one,' she said to me, 'your tears are used up and you've no more left.'

The next day, with the funeral arrangements in place, I was in the house, cleaning up, accepting the kind condolences and gifts of food from neighbours, showing them in to where she sat centre stage in our dining room to receive them.

As it happened, we were alone when the doorbell rang for the umpteenth time and, not bothering to remove my rubber gloves, I answered it, this time to find a priest offering sympathies on behalf of the parish – although he did make it clear that, being new to the area, he hadn't known either of my parents. He was in for an education.

I showed him in, took off the gloves and poured tea for the three of us. He said all the right things. Then, in all innocence, he asked, 'And how long were the two of you married, Maureen?'

'Fifty-seven years!' My mother proudly emphasised each syllable as though she was reliving each long month of each long year.

'Fifty-seven years?' the priest marvelled. 'You know, Maureen, in these modern times, that's the average length of almost four marriages!'

'Indeed it is,' Mamma agreed solemnly. Then, with a faraway look in those extraordinary eyes of hers, she gazed at a spot somewhere above his head. 'Of course, Father, we weren't compatible!'

The poor man had no idea how to react. This was way off the script.

Seeing his confusion she took pity on him, 'But the truth is, Father, he adored me!'

He did too.

Her diary entry for that day shows, in huge, black, doubly underlined capital letters: 'BILL. R.I.P.'. When I came across it I wept bitterly, for her, for me, for him, for Declan, who followed him into 'The Service' and of whom he was so proud. For all four of us.

She knew that the nurses on Dadda's ward had given me the small bundle of his personal effects: his pyjamas and washbag, his spectacles, his watch, his pen, his rings and his ancient leather wallet curved to the contours of his hip. Some days after his death, tentatively, not meeting my eyes, she asked me for the latter, 'I believe he carried around a photo of me.'

I searched that wallet, even turning out the lining, but could not find any photo. She made no comment, nor showed any emotion when I told her.

It was only after she herself had died that I found it. Declan and I were clearing out the boxroom in Ballymun and, from one of Dadda's impeccably neat filing drawers, I retrieved an old plastic AA membership-card holder and there it was, a black and white snapshot, obviously taken by him during their honeymoon in Glengarriff. Two inches by one, it was creased and so long stored it was difficult to peel it away from the plastic.

They had got married during the war years, when tiered cakes were made from cardboard because of sugar rationing and when weddings and wedding breakfasts were held as early as 6.00 a.m. because trains for the honeymoon destinations of Kerry and Cork left early. (They dined out on the story that their particular train had ground to a halt halfway, so that they and their fellow passengers had had to disembark to help the driver and engineer gather turf from a nearby bog to feed the depleted furnace.)

One of my mother's pensive complaints in the years of her ageing had been that, 'No one ever told me I was beautiful.'

In this photograph, her dark hair is falling around her face, she is wearing a swimsuit, as she sits in the prow of an open rowing boat in the waters off Garnish Island. She is beautiful.

20

A Ring on Every Finger

While Declan and I were growing up, Mamma had dutifully kept house, cleaned out the ashes from the fireplace, darned and mended our clothes, knitted our jumpers and cooked for us. Yet I, for one, was in no doubt of how passionately she hated these mundanities. She particularly resented two aspects of her life: the full three-meals-a-day regime without which my father could not have existed and the fact that, as in most traditional marriages of that time, she was financially dependent on him.

All changed for her in mid-life.

Dadda lauded her intelligence and always said that she had been born ahead of her time and should have gone to university with a view to a career. She developed one for herself in her mid-fifties.

She began by taking courses in art, flower arranging, calligraphy, how to throw wobbly and misshapen ceramic pots – anything that would excuse her from the drudgery of being 'just a housewife'. Then she became a founder member and president of the Ballymun Ladies' Club, edited its newsletter *The Ballymun Eagle* (it had its eye on Czarish local events!) and wrote its acerbic gossip column. She joined the local choir and took creative writing classes, as a result of which a few of her whimsical pieces were published in *The Evening Herald*'s 'Petticoat Panel' series; she even broadcast a piece for *Sunday Miscellany*. After I became a writer, I overheard her at the launch of my first novel, telling people that it was from her I got my writing talent.

Having gained confidence, she dyed her dark hair a bright blonde, took a course in professional guiding and spent the next fifteen years bussing tourists around the country, leaving Dadda (agreeably) to sew on his own buttons and make his own coddle on Saturday nights.

She learned to drive their tiny Fiat Bambinos and Suzuki Altos. I dreaded sitting in the passenger seat because she was utterly oblivious to the snarls and bunched fists of road users behind her as she sailed along the crown of the open road at her idea of a safe speed while grandly indicating and expounding on buildings and historical sites along the route. 'Would you look at that?' she would snort, as some poor wretch, patience exhausted, screeched past her on the wrong side of a double white line. 'Where're the guards when you need them?'

Her attempts at parallel parking were legendary, the failures borne out by the successive dents and scratches on the little cars. To be fair, though, she always left an apologetic note under the windscreen wiper of the victim car, and in our mechanic, Martin McGowan, we had a marvellous and very patient fixer-upper. Martin never uttered a word of condemnation or exasperation when Dadda, having paid off the victim-car's owner, turned up at the garage with another request for a small bit of panel beating. 'And would you have a look at the clutch again, Martin?'

Until even she had to admit that her sight was no longer adequate, Mamma was also the one who picked up and transported her ageing pals to the Addison Lodge opposite the Botanic Gardens on Tuesdays for lunch, the Thursday night get-togethers in each other's houses, hospital appointments or to visit 'old people' in nursing homes. 'The poor old things,' she would say, from her vantage point of seventy-five years to their seventy-eight, 'they could do with a bit of cheering up.'

It was Kevin Healy who affectionately dubbed as 'Spots' these *femmes plus d'un certain age.* The epithet was initially bestowed on Mamma alone because we had a dog called Sooty that she continued to call Spot. However, the soubriquet spread within our circle to become a generic shorthand for women like her, spirited dames dressed to impress and up for any adventure but who, as the years advanced, tended to become vague and forgetful. Even my father used the nickname – I know it sounds patronising, but it was never less than loving. My fondest image of her during that period is of her and her cronies, a closely packed bunch of four or five bobbing Spots, roaring off in first gear on their latest outing.

Mamma certainly had a gift for friendship. Her address book is packed with names of women from all over Ireland but also with the Americans, Swedes and Japanese she encountered on her tours and with whom she corresponded for the rest of her life. All over the country, I am still approached by women: 'Are you Deirdre Purcell? I knew your mother…'

Guiding was the undoubted highlight of her life and, even when she became too feeble to walk any faster than a slow shuffle, she never fully came to terms with the evidence that those freewheeling days on the tour buses were over. When she spoke of them, her eyes clouded with yearning.

She continued to try to find a role for herself outside the house and, when I visited her in Ballymun, I'd frequently find her pooching through her squirrelly store of notes, maps, cuttings and her own writing, always in the hope that somehow, maybe with my help, she might again get published. It is a matter of sorrow to me that I never managed this, although I did make some attempts. In an era of modern, thrusting, issue-driven journalism, there was no room for 'Petticoat Panel' or its ilk, and her efforts at writing her memoir were too scrappy to be fashioned into anything meaningful.

In that regard, she was actually quite jealous of Alice Taylor who wrote so successfully of her bucolic childhood: 'I could have written that!'

I did try, mildly, to point out that Alice Taylor actually sat down and wrote when Mamma had been too busy flying around the countryside. No dice. She still thought that given the right opportunity, she could be a contender.

At one level, my father tsk-tsk'd about her gadding but, deep down, he was proud of it, certainly within their gang, and basked in the shadow of such a tall poppy. ('What will she do next?')

I truly believe that she, with her love of being the centre of attention, should have been the one in our family who had the public profile. She would have enjoyed it so much – even in old age, she always entered a crowded room as a real star does, pausing at the threshold to look around for a moment as though considering on whom she should bestow her queenly presence.

I wasn't the only one who noticed this quirk – it has been immortalised in a book.

Our family association with the Romantic Hotel in Sitges, a

coastal town south of Barcelona, goes back to 1963 when I started work in Aer Lingus and brought Mamma there for the first time on a ten per cent ticket. Later, she brought Dadda and, together, they developed a parallel, very joyous life there. My mother had found her element, and although, given his apparently innate conservatism, this might sound odd, my father did too. No sooner were they home from one visit there but he was back in the travel agent's organising the next one, making out it was for her – 'You know how she is about Sitges' – but it was clear that for him it was just as important. In many ways, Sitges became not a home from home but an idealised home for them, where they were both happy.

They made sixty-four visits altogether and, in Dublin, acted as an unofficial PR agency for the town, talking it up so enthusiastically that almost all their friends made visits there too. This was officially recognised when, on their fiftieth joint visit, the mayor and the town's tourism interests honoured them. I am now in possession of the ornate red and gold plaque with which they were presented at a civic reception in the town and which, in Catalan, names them as Forever Friends of Sitges:

MAUREEN i BILL
El Gremi d'Hosteleria
us recordara
sempre
com
AMICS de SITGES

In the early days when we went there first, the Romantic, then called the Tropic, was still in start-up mode. Run by the Sobrer family, Mother, Father, various relations called Jaume and two extraordinary brothers, Goncal and Josep Miquel, it fermented with poets, painters, actors, Catalan activist-separatist intellectuals – and some brave, pioneering gay men, many of them English, who had come out of the closet.

Goncal and Josep Miquel were the front men whose showmanship, nous and charisma turned visitors into habitués. We dined in an ancient walled garden under stars and fairylit trees to the strains of classical music. When dinner was over, the music was changed so that the trees shook to the thumping of the latest international pop songs. Late into the night, we jived, sardanaed and fandangoed, with both brothers acting as ringmasters and picking up reticent strays to pull them into the action.

Goncal created champagne towers, roared energetically through heel-clicking demonstrations of pastiche flamenco, then held court to outline his perfectly serious plans to become president of a free and independent Catalonia. Josep Miquel, younger and less ebullient than his irrepressible brother, devotes an entire chapter to my parents in a wonderful history of his family and his family's hotel. Although he is an academic now, he writes with the observational skill of a novelist.

> This kind of endurance is made of love, to be sure, but not only of love; some wiliness must enter into the picture, some astuteness and the art of preserving individuality. Bill and Maureen have been vacationing in Sitges, and staying at the Romantic, for longer than I can remember, and more often. They are part of the family; they've known me since I was a lad of fifteen; they have grown wild with us and we have grown wise with them. And Bill has taught us all the Irish Gaelic we know: *Go mbeirimid beo ar an am seo arís.*

The phrase has become their Romantic life and ours, 'May we be here again next year.'

The swallows come back to Capistrano, and Bill and Maureen come back to Sitges, except that the swallows returning to the California town may not be the same year after year, while Bill and Maureen are the same. The same slightly dissonant couple who appear again, thank God, again one more year, again to their own separate rooms, again together, again individual. Again, Maureen will cast around the lounge her haughtily benevolent, mildly disdainful, always playful gaze. Again, owlish Bill will go for an energetic early morning swim. Again, they will both complain whenever the weather is less than perfect. And, again, we will all know that they don't really mean it, that they are happy, and that if they complain it's because they want us to know they haven't drowned in the divine ataraxia of their souls.

He 'gets' both of them but without doubt brilliantly catches the nuances of her regal entrances.

There can't be many authors whose mothers and fathers each have a hotel room named after them in an ancient Catalan town. 'Room Bill' and 'Room Maureen' are side by side on the first landing atop a white marble staircase in the Romantic. His is shadowy and windowless; hers blazes with light and has a 400-foot-square tiled and balustraded balcony overlooking the garden. She was in her element in the warm sunshine, ease and quirkiness of that hotel to which, against my father's protests, she always travelled with sixteen, eighteen, even twenty pairs of differently coloured shoes and sandals collected over the years, 'I don't care! I *have* to match all the different outfits.'

She loved colour, spectacle, glitter and sparkle – this is one trait I have inherited – and, within her very limited means, always turned herself out well. Sometimes, I would go to visit her relatively early in the mornings to find her, like her own mother beforehand, already in full gear and war paint. There was a difference, though: whereas Nanna's colours were muted browns, creams and greys, Mamma's were reds, blues and emerald greens.

There was a further difference: she bedizened herself with earrings and costume jewellery, wore a ring on every finger and rounded things off with red nail polish and a jaunty scarf. This was on the principle that she should always be ready for an unexpected visit or outing. 'If you're properly dressed first thing in the morning,' she exhorted, in the vain hope she'd influence me, 'you don't have to worry for the rest of the day, no matter what turns up. Try it. You'll see…'

She despaired of my slapdash approach to clothes, and my preference for convenience-cum-comfort scandalised her. Yes, I am drawn, magpie-like, to gold, silver, sequins and shiny beads – oh, give me diamonds! – but, in early morning, I am usually intent on unravelling something that has knotted itself around my brain during the night or am bent on getting to the keyboard as quickly as I can. Therefore, unless I'm going to a board meeting or to some formal occasion to do with work, I can't be bothered to choose something to wear, but will fling on the first clean outfit I can find. I am most comfortable in my fifteen-year-old jeans and, since I started writing, a succession of postal workers has become accustomed to me answering the door in my dressing gown.

This behaviour was incomprehensible to Mamma; there was even one time when, noticing that I had holes in my shoes, she offered me some of her own. (I have to add that Dadda disapproved of my slovenly habits as well – and, although he doesn't say so, I know Declan, who, with his lean elegance, is always beautifully clad, does too!)

As her age advanced and she was confined more and more to the house – interrupted with frequent hospital stays – my mother grew increasingly irritable with her lot. Her non-acceptance upset me, and now and then I reacted angrily to the barbs she threw at me, even suspecting that Alice Taylor was not the only object of her jealousy. For instance, she invariably offered unwanted criticism of my books or even me, 'I'm only being honest. Don't you want me to be honest?' Or 'You looked very fat on television last night. There's nothing wrong, I hope. Are you OK?'

In retrospect, all of this was merely part of the normal and well-documented mother–daughter to-and-fro, I suppose, but, instead of letting the gibes roll off me, I bridled and became defensive. The underlying tension was that I was living the life she craved: with interesting work, a certain degree of public notoriety and financial independence.

So why couldn't she have it too? She couldn't. That was the truth and I had no power to fix it for her. But I was hit with proof of my own defensiveness each time I went into her bedroom to fetch something for her and saw the virtual shrine she had erected: all my books lined up in chronological order on a shelf, her scrapbook with cuttings about me, the still photo of me, captured from a television programme, that she kept on her 'desk'.

If guiding had been the highlight, it had a dark side too: away from home for extended periods and having her own money for the first time since she got married, Mamma developed a problem with alcohol. She managed it relatively well, and one of my enduring sadnesses is that I frequently fought with her about it, a conflict that proved of no benefit to either of us and served merely to drive her underground. After her death, when clearing out her house, it was unbearably moving to find the half-empty quarter-bottles of Blossom Hill, predictably stored with the bleach under the sink where the Amicardo used to live all those years ago, but also stuffed beneath cushions and in the most unlikely places such as the breadbin.

When they were both in their seventies and he had to acknowledge that her drinking had become a problem, Dadda did not confront it directly. He had always been careful with money, but this trait became more pronounced and I reckon that, in this way, he believed he could keep a handle on the situation. He also told me on numerous occasions he was afraid he would have nothing in reserve for their old age. And he frequently remarked, in her hearing, that he had to husband their resources because, if she became a widow, he wanted to make sure she would be a comfortable one. 'Don't you want to continue going to Sitges?'

Nevertheless, after the financially flush years of guiding, this loss of personal control was tough for her and, predictably, she railed bitterly against what she saw as meanness but which he presented – and no doubt saw – as prudence.

Sometimes, in the latter years, when I was finding it hard to hold my tongue with her, I managed to do so by remembering a remark our brilliant family doctor, the late Brian Daly, once made to me about her. I had been talking to him about my own frustration with her wine intake, although, in fairness, she had taken to mixing it with water. I felt that, if she gave it up completely, her general health would improve a lot. (Her view, of course, was that I was overreacting wildly to what she insisted was merely a small daily tipple to help her cope with life.)

Dr Daly considered his words carefully. He would not breach

confidentiality, but he did want to help me. 'I know she can be difficult,' he said slowly, 'but I've known her for very many decades and I adore her. She's...,' he hesitated again, '...there's a deep sweetness about her.'

There was, too, and it kept her loyal friends bound tightly to her.

My relationship with her, with both of them, was complex. In later life, I was on the board of the Abbey Theatre for twelve years, and on leaving a meeting one evening, I looked into the auditorium to see again a set I had particularly admired. With a shock, I saw the seats were not empty as I had expected. It was pensioners' night, when the tickets were free or reduced in price, and there they were, my parents, alone and silent in two seats near the front of the cavernous, dimly lit space, each staring straight ahead, waiting for a performance that was not due to start for more than an hour. I guessed that they had come in early to nab one of the metered on-street parking spaces on the quays, free after six thirty but bound to be snapped up nearer to theatre time.

I never found out how Dadda managed to get them into the auditorium before it was officially open. I didn't want to know, really – and can now only presume that, since they were regulars at the Abbey, elderly and not in very good health, kindness had prevailed amongst the front-of-house staff who would have known them.

That evening, I watched them from the back of the theatre for maybe five minutes. She cleared her throat once, a small sad sound, lost in the vastness. Other than that, neither spoke or moved.

To my eternal shame, I could not face what I perceived to be their mutual melancholy and so, without so much as a hello, I stole away.

21
America!

Early in September 1968, Mamma said off-handedly that, since she had to go into town in any case, she might as well come with me in the taxi for the first leg of my journey to America. We sat in strangled silence from Ballymun as far as O'Connell Street where the taxi had to stop in the heavy traffic in front of the Gresham Hotel. My mother suddenly grabbed my arm. 'I think you're a great girl,' she said, then burst into tears, jumped out of the taxi and ran off down O'Connell Street.

Mol an óige agus tiochfaidh sí... Give praise to the young and they will come to you.

My parents, God bless them, probably each subscribed to this theory. Theoretically. And so, theoretically, did our teacher in Scoil Mhuire. In practice, though, in the minds of virtually all of the adults I had known while growing up, Ireland's young were not to be given 'notions', and except for once from each of the three – my mother taking her turn with that outburst in the taxi – I cannot remember overt praise.

Our teacher's encomium occurred when I was in Second Class and she asked, incidentally and in English, if anyone could tell her what the number plate on a car was called. Instantly, I put up my hand, the only girl to do so. 'The registration number,' I said.

'My God,' she said, 'you're a topper.'

My father's was oblique and came in 1958. In the days when post was delivered before breakfast, I was still in bed when I heard the clatter of the letterbox down in the hall, then Dadda padding to pick up whatever had come in. A few seconds later, the house resounded with his voice, breaking with pleasure and pride, as he yelled, 'Deirdre's got a full scholarship to Gortnor Abbey!'

Perhaps my parents' presence at my opening nights and book launches, my mother's collecting of my press cuttings, the 'shrine' of my books in her bedroom should have been enough for me but, as the taxi jolted back into motion that day after Mamma ran off, my tears were for what might have been.

The first few days of my migration to Chicago in September 1968, shot through with tiredness and a seesaw of homesickness and elation, have compressed themselves into a jumble of impressions. I remember being disappointed that I had missed, by just a couple of days, all the downtown excitement of the Democratic Convention and the response of Mayor Daley's heavies. I would have liked to have seen that!

I remember the film of muggy heat that clung to my skin as Fr Trahey introduced me to my two new room-mates in our apartment on Winthrop Avenue, just a few hundred yards from the entrance gates to the Loyola campus. Kathy O'Donnell, from Cincinnati, was an English major; Peggy Lescher was a trainee nurse – Loyola encompassed a well-regarded medical school.

I remember being introduced to the Dewey Decimal System in

the university library where I would work part-time to fund my rent and food, and where I was startled at the shortness of the American twenty-minute lunch break. I also remember how aghast my room-mates were at my habit of eating banana sandwiches, a concoction new to them.

I was fascinated at seeing people doing very odd things on the campus: for instance, wearing a fireman's helmet or an enormous bell or a sack and nothing else. Once I almost tripped over one student who, on hands and knees, was using her nose to push a peanut along a roadway. These people, I discovered, were Pledges: first-year students who were performing the induction rituals required by the campus fraternities and sororities. If successful, with their new brothers or sisters, they then had use of the exclusive frat houses and, more significantly, after college they had, like Masons or Knights, access to a business network.

I also remember realising with horror how inappropriate my own clothes were. The unofficial uniform for girls in that conservative college was 'preppy' – knee-length skirts, brogues and neat sweaters. I had arrived with only the micro-minis that at the time were the norm in Dublin, certainly amongst actresses. In addition, the wooden Dr Scholl clogs and black fishnet tights I wore to complement them were a source of astonishment everywhere I went. Although I was acutely embarrassed, I could not afford to replace this wardrobe, so I squared my shoulders and swanned. I was a person apart, after all: I was Fr Trahey's first European Theatre Artist and I had an Abbey Theatre pedigree. No one there was in a position to argue with *that*.

Two incidents during those first few days proved to be very significant. On the very first afternoon that I walked through the gates into the campus, I was hailed by a young man on which, as he strode towards me, everything flapped: shoulder-length hair, long mackintosh fastened only with one button at the neck, fringes on his calf-length brown moccasins. 'Hi,' he said. 'I'm Rob Weckler. Are you the Irish actress?'

Maybe the miniskirt and clogs had been the giveaways. 'I am,' I said.

'Would you like a cup of coffee?'

I was taken aback by the suddenness of this. But then I thought, Hey! They do things differently here. I have to get used to this openness and I'd better start integrating. Anyhow, although he looked terribly young, he was six feet tall and very good-looking. 'Thank you,' I said, 'that would be lovely.' As we walked towards the coffee shop, he filled me in about himself and his family, and informed me he was going to be a fellow student in the Theatre Department.

A few days later, I was accosted in a corridor outside a classroom by a tiny dynamo with huge blue eyes, a wide smile and curly hair. 'Hi,' she said. 'You're Deirdre? I'm C.Sue Braun. I'm twenty-three too.'

Thus were born two relationships. Rob and I married fourteen months later. C.Sue became a lifelong friend.

What I did not know when the latter buttonholed me was that up to the moment Rob stepped, literally, into my path, she had been his girlfriend. 'But I thought,' she explained a couple of weeks later, 'that since Rob was so much into you, y'know, you must be somethin' really special? So I thought, Gee, I should become this person's friend. And since we're the same age, we'd have a lot in common.'

This was some shock. It is not often that a woman dumped for someone else accepts it gracefully and then, with no malice intended, takes the initiative to become friends with her successor. It is so unusual that, at the time, I found it hard to believe and wondered what her motives were.

Rob had indeed been popping up everywhere I went. He had told me over one of the numerous cups of coffee we had together that he would marry me – a pronouncement I had laughed off disbelievingly but, I hoped, kindly: he was only nineteen, for goodness sake. While I thoroughly enjoyed his humorous and entertaining company, his mimicry, his fund of anecdotes and warm, open, have-a-go-at-anything personality, that was as far as it went. I was Experienced. I was a person with two livelihoods already under my belt, three if you count the Civil Service Commission. Against his American Boy, I fancied myself that sophisticated creature, European Woman.

In the course of our meetings, he had never mentioned that he'd had a girlfriend, but when, after C.Sue's revelation, I challenged him, he confirmed it. My suspicions of her motivation in courting my friendship had been unworthy. Her giving him up had been stylish.

So I settled in, signing up for courses in psychology and classical theatre – and, of course, was cast in and performed in the plays. As I had expected, I got terrific parts: Clytemnestra in *Iphigenia in Aulis*, Rosie Probert and Polly Garter in *Under Milk Wood* (with Rob as Captain Cat). Liberated from the Abbey cosh, I had recovered confidence. The Loyola theatre studies students were competitive and very talented, had plans to become professionals after graduation and, therefore, took their acting and theatre craft seriously. Playing with and against them put me on my mettle and, once again, I knew I was good. I was even daring to have fun again: back in the ALMDS mode, I thoroughly enjoyed the rehearsal processes and, particularly, performing in the new and magnificently equipped Kathleen

Mullady Theater, where the acoustics were sharp and allowed intimate communication with the audience.

Actually, I enjoyed everything about my new life. It was thrilling to be living the American way as the leaves of the trees reddened and fell. I loved taking showers instead of baths. I loved watching drive-in movies in Rob's ancient but stately black Pontiac – the type I'd seen only in gangster movies (and in which we did an illegal U-turn on Lake Shore Drive, which led me to bailing him out of a cell in a downtown police station. What seemed to concern him most afterwards was not the humiliation but the outrage of having his belt and shoelaces confiscated).

I loved the informal dining: Campbell's tomato soup and a banana sandwich for the twenty-minute lunch with my room-mates in our apartment. I learned about the amazing – and cheap – take-away facility where you just lifted the phone and twenty minutes later dinner arrived. I took seriously to pepperoni pizza. On street corners, I ordered hot dogs with the works – onions, piccalilli, ketchup and mustard – and in Rob's house could, eventually, even tolerate liverwurst sandwiches.

I took to being a consumer with dedication. Although I had very little money, this was not a new experience and, in America, what little I had seemed to go a very long way. There was always a sale on somewhere and stuff, i.e. the detritus of domestic living, seemed so cheap I couldn't resist it. I responded to coloured leaflets that fell out of the Sunday edition of the *Chicago Tribune*: whereby for $18.00, within days I could and did accept free delivery of not only a comforter – a padded quilt – for my bed, but a bonus set of four copper-bottomed cooking pans and, because I had ordered before a certain date, two added gifts of a transistor radio and a watch. Couldn't believe it. I felt like Ali Baba.

And when I discovered *catalogues*...

Instead of going on a year-long waiting list, you could get a telephone installed within hours of ordering it and when you got it you could pay for your usage through 'packages' – all local calls were free and others, including international direct-dial, were at a vastly reduced rate.

You could get 'transfer' tickets between buses on different routes, all of which had crossover points at specific junctions. And the El – the elevated downtown railway that connected with other trains – was real, proper public transport that you could use to go anywhere in the city. Yay!

I learned about Americans, very quickly discovering that, while we Europeans might be sniffy about their politics and patronising about their tendency to be insular and naïve about the outside world, the flipside of this is directness and an eagerness to learn about new people and ideas. And, of course, the outstanding trait with all Americans is unstinting and superb hospitality.

I got my first taste of yams and pumpkin pie at Thanksgiving, when, with a couple of other strays, I was invited to the home of my Theatre Department colleague, Carole Ocwieja (whose father was an undertaker with an unusual sense of humour: the table centrepiece was a baby's coffin holding a paper turkey). And, at Christmas, Kathy O'Donnell invited me to become one of her family in Cincinnati.

Rob had acted in community theatre with a lady, in all senses of that word, named Joan Spatafora, who kept the front door of her house permanently open to us, and who, with her husband, Jack, have remained dear friends of us both.

In fact, everyone was inviting me everywhere: there were parties and visiting, sleepovers, plays and concerts – the dazzling Art Institute, Navy Pier, the Aquarium, the Museum of Science and Industry with its real U-Boat parked outside; I was even taken to the Chicago Opera House. I loved everything.

I also took part in Loyola's student demo. While the rest of the student world boiled with lippy and militant anger, we decided to show our displeasure by boycotting our canteen and parading around the campus bearing home-made banners. One I particularly remember bore the legend 'Father Maguire: Go To Your Room!' Father Maguire was the head of the university.

It was a daily thrill to wake up in proximity to the movie-set suburbs of Chicago's Gold Coast, a long stretch beside the shores of Lake Michigan, with opulent gated estates and private mansions. That autumn, however, the air had been polluted along the north shore by the arrival of the dead alewives: this was, apparently, a regular occurrence but was particularly bad that year. Alewives are tiny fish, the size of small sardines, that every so often die by the billion and, smelling to high heaven, wash up on the lakeshore. Everyone was moaning about the stink but to tell you the truth, acquainted as I was with the Liffey, I didn't think it was all that bad.

And although I heard on all sides how Christmas had become too commercialised, to me everything about it that first year in America was fairyland. The north-shore mansions outdid one another in the glory of their holiday raiment; Lake Michigan itself froze, the solidified wavelets at its edge glittering like tiny mountain ranges under the white winter sun. Marshall Fields, the huge and classy department store on State Street, had taken literally the admonition to deck its halls: with an enormous Christmas tree at its heart, everything in the shop seemed to shine, shimmer or spin – or, if it did not, it was tipped with artificial snow or icicles.

My Christmas gift from Rob was a pair of Nestor Johnson ice skates, apparently the best of breed. The custom in Chicago in winter was for the fire department to turn hoses on certain downtown parks to create huge open-air ice rinks and, after a few fraidy-cat starts in Grant Park, the early ballet training and roller-skating stood to me and I did manage to stay upright. The bonus afterwards was retirement to the fringe of booths selling hot chocolate, hot dogs and roasted chestnuts.

My proper introduction to America proved to be enchanting: acceptance and respect, romance, artistic satisfaction, a marvellous physical environment. I also found a surrogate family in Rob's house where I was received with open arms – but a degree of wariness.

This was not because I immediately became involved in a long-running and virtually permanent political argument with Wally, Rob's dad, who, while continuing to insist he was proud to be a registered Democrat and had always voted that way, was, in my upstart opinion, by nature and leaning a right-wing Catholic Republican. I would guess, in hindsight, that from the start, the senior Wecklers figured correctly that a match between their eldest son and me was not a match made in heaven.

So, they might have nodded sagely to one another when Rob and I broke up the following summer after the academic year. But since I kept contact with the Theatre Department in Loyola, largely because Vincent Dowling, my former Abbey colleague, was now in residence as a visiting producer/director and had cast me as Miss Frost in *The Ginger Man* opposite Rob's brother, Tom, we did run into one another occasionally.

Meanwhile, to save for my fare home and to repay my loan to P.J., I started looking for a job. I got it in O'Connor Travel, an 'ethnic' travel agency run by a Roscommon man, Jack O'Connor.

Although the company was licensed to issue regular airline tickets and did so, the bulk of the income came from the highly successful organisation of a single product: a summer-season charter service to and from Shannon for the Celtic Heritage Society.

Jack was not only entrepreneurial, he was shrewd. Although his business could have afforded a plush office with all the trimmings, he furnished his with old desks, chairs and equipment, including an antediluvian wind-up adding machine. He made sure the posters on his walls were a little tatty too. Irish people like to give a leg-up to 'one of our own', but if they think the same party is getting too successful, i.e. uppity and a bit too big for the oul' boots, they're not slow in pulling him down a peg, even taking their business elsewhere.

He asked me at my interview if I could type. I had caught sight of one of those huge golfball IBM thingies around the place and I was ready for this, thinking back to my stint on the fake keyboard at Gortnor Abbey. I took the punt. 'Oh, yes,' I said, 'but not yet on an electric keyboard. It would take me a little while to get used to that.'

I'm sure Jack saw through me but perhaps because I knew my way around the airline business, even if my previous experience had been on the ground floor, he hired me anyway, and a new phase of my life began, this time in a two-person office.

The luck fairy, or whatever guardian angel I had been lucky enough to secure at birth, had worked her magic again and, once more, I thoroughly enjoyed my job. Every morning, I joined Working America in tumbling out of bed at five forty-five. I took two buses to downtown Chicago, disembarked, found a space in the rush-hour walking-train on the pavement, already hot underfoot, to arrive at 30 La Salle Street by eight.

I was delighted with my new employer's predilection for working on gut instinct, which is the way I like to work too. This, maybe, was astrology rearing its head again because, just as I had shared a birthday with Nanna, I shared one with this new person too. I was only the minion, but since there were just the two of us it was important that, professionally, we were on the same wavelength.

I loved watching him wrestle with the challenge of setting up the charter flights: the buzz of the negotiations with airlines where he went right down to the wire with Pan Am or Aer Lingus to get the best financial deal in the hiring of the planes.

Meanwhile, I did my best to swell the numbers of passenger names I filled in on the booking sheets. I loved doing deals with customers. The fare was $210 round trip for adults, with fifty per cent off for children, but we always negotiated package deals for families – some of whom might, with parents, an in-law or two and as many as ten children under fifteen, number up to twenty.

I loved the challenge of ensuring that no flight took off with an empty seat, being sent to Shannon from time to time to represent the agency at that end for the return trip, and being left in charge of the office when Jack was away on business or taking his annual trip home to Ireland. I loved being at O'Hare on the night of a departure, sorting out tickets and mix-ups, trying to calm down the check-in staff as some of the 'infants' we had booked to travel free by sitting on their parents' laps turned out on physical inspection to be almost of shaving age! I am exaggerating, of course, but there were truly some hairy infants on those flights. On one occasion, the captain of the aircraft refused to take off because thirty-two infants had turned up – way over the legal safety limit. It was a matter of seatbelts, amongst other considerations. We had to offload some and that, believe me, was some test.

Most of all, I loved the feeling of satisfaction as our laden CHS charters, trailing smoke, lumbered into the sky over O'Hare with another group of satisfied customers.

And, quite quickly, I came to terms with the huge IBM golfball typewriter on my desk. It was very, *very* loud, so I practised surreptitiously when Jack was out of the office; if at the beginning he had noticed my stumbling attempts to master the thing when he was present, he had been tactful enough not to say so. Thank God for Tippex.

He was an exceptionally generous and trusting boss; I wrote my own wages cheques – he just signed them. I can't remember now what I was earning but I do know that, while it was not wildly out of kilter with the going rate for an equivalent job, it was the kind of money I could never have hoped for in Ireland; within the first few months, I was well on my way to having saved enough to pay P.J. back. Plus, I no longer had to worry about the cost of returning home as Jack would put me on the last charter of the summer, so that financial albatross was off my neck. It even looked as though I might be going home with money in the bank. An unheard-of position for me.

From time to time, the daytime temperature that first Chicago summer climbed as high as 120° Fahrenheit but although I found this difficult enough to cope with, it was the humidity, sometimes at a hundred per cent, that bothered me. It meant that sitting in the home-going buses felt like swimming upstream through used bathwater. (Naïvely, I had believed that a hundred per cent humidity had to be actual rainfall, but that is not the case. Even a shower, although a relief while I was standing under its cool stream, was ineffectual in my non-air-conditioned apartment because to take two steps out of the cubicle meant that the sweat popped out again.)

Nevertheless, the job itself was terrific, my boss was a dream to work for and, climatically, I would have put up with a lot worse to work at O'Connor Travel. I found that being a cog in the wheel of a successful small enterprise is truly fulfilling and exciting. Of course, I had all the fun and satisfaction without the responsibility of paying the rent.

As usual in my life, however, things did not stay the same. By the end of that summer, the last Celtic Heritage Society charter had taken off without me: Rob and I had got together again.

It happened quite simply: as a result of my playing Miss Frost in *The Ginger Man* at Loyola, I had gone with Tom to the family home for a visit. Rob was unexpectedly there and we got talking on the screened porch outside his parents' kitchen.

That was still within the first year after my arrival in the States. A couple of months later, Jack O'Connor had offered to keep me on at the agency and Rob and I were engaged to be married in Ireland on 19 January 1970, a month after his twenty-first birthday.

22

A Modest Affair

Six weeks before our wedding, I went home to Ireland to prepare for it and to try and settle everyone's nerves. Although they did their best to conceal their misgivings, I think that, along with the Wecklers, my own parents were appalled at the precipitate nature of this undertaking. In fairness, however, they rowed in with lists and plans. Sadly, the Wecklers decided they couldn't make the trip.

Money was tight, of course, so we settled on a modest affair in the Maples Hotel, a small establishment on Iona Road in Glasnevin. I was not going to go to the trouble and expense of getting myself a frothy wedding dress when I had, in my opinion, a perfectly respectable cream-coloured thing with a divided skirt that I'd worn only about three times in the States, so nobody in Ireland – except Rob, of course – would have seen it before. It was empire line, with a flowing, Greek-goddess look to it, so I also took with me from Loyola the thick hairpiece I'd worn on stage as Clytemnestra. By adding a pair of Greekish sandals that would be comfortable for the day, I felt

I would look grand, even co-ordinated. Moreover, I would have covered more than adequately the traditions of 'old and borrowed'.

For 'new', I went to Hickey's in Henry Street and bought six yards of creamy ribbon lace and a half-yard of wide gold upholstery trim. I hemmed the lace edges, gathering one end of it into the upholstery trim and voilà! Headpiece, veil and train.

The guest list was more than one-sided: it was almost exclusively drawn from my family and friends. Not only were Wally and Betty Weckler absent, none of Rob's five siblings, his relatives or close friends was able to make the transatlantic trip – with the exception of Jack and Joan Spatafora and a Theatre Department colleague, Jerry Rossetti, who was, I am sure, surprised to find himself selected as best man. The plan was that, since Jerry had never been out of America before, he would come with us on part of our honeymoon. We were to 'tour' Ireland in a hired car. Bizarrely, Declan came along too.

Our wedding day was as cold, wet and as stormy as it is possible to be in an Irish January. Although I remember little of it, and no one has been cruel enough to remind me, I drank too much sherry at the reception, too much wine at the meal, too much champagne with the cake. And I wept throughout my wedding night with my new husband.

This behaviour was most uncharacteristic, if I do say so myself. I generally tend towards the more stoical end of the emotional spectrum and, up to that time, had never behaved like that. It is too easy to blame the drink, although it undoubtedly had a powerful effect on my inhibitions.

For sure, I was deep down furious with Rob for one thing: he had promised to find us somewhere to live during the six weeks I had been in Ireland organising the wedding, but he had arrived having not done so. I had been looking forward to descriptions, even photographs. Instead, he had asked his mother to find us a place before we got back.

In retrospect, I believe I had seized on this failure as an anvil on which to pound my unease about the marriage; and I know now that he, too, had realised that we were making a mistake.

Each of us, however, lacked the courage to call it off. I certainly did, from pride, stubbornness and a desire not to inconvenience all those people who had bought wedding outfits and, crucially, had travelled to be with us for the great day. I could not let my parents lose face in front of their friends, having argued with them, and after all they had already spent. Sounds daft but it is true and I had no right to blame anything on my young husband. It was not his fault that I, the older one, who should have taken the lead, had been so gutless.

And poor Jerry Rossetti, whose first visit to Europe this was, suffered too. The weather did not improve for our highly populated honeymoon: if anything, for most of the time it was even worse. The Cliffs of Moher in a Force 8 or 9? Salthill deserted? Connemara invisible? And in that mid-winter season – long before the advent of luxury spas and enticing all-year tourism offers – the choice of food on offer in the B&Bs was stark: hard eggs or soft eggs with your rashers and sausages.

The lowest point was on Achill Island, where, one afternoon parked at a seaweed-strewn beach, we rocked morosely on the springs of our hired car under an unremitting assault of wind, flying rain and clumps of spume as large as tennis balls. It was almost dark, although our watches said the time was just after half past three.

Rob cleared some of the condensation from the windscreen. Then he and Jerry, raising their voices to be heard above the racket, agreed that if in the next guesthouse they were again offered a mixed grill as the only food option, they would kill themselves.

Thank God for Tayto, Cadbury's chocolate and Coca-Cola. Jerry, I think, was very glad to leave us and fly to Italy, where he had relatives.

As the plane took off at the end of our honeymoon and Ireland receded under the clouds, I was again in tears – but long before we touched down at O'Hare, I had forced myself to buck up. We would put the last two weeks behind us. I would commit myself totally to this marriage. I would be the best wife I could be because, after all, I did genuinely love Rob, who was so eminently lovable. He was young, but he would mature. We would make a go of it – and not just to please everyone or to show we had not made a mistake. We would *really make a go of it* for no one's sake but our own.

So, although I found it very difficult to conceal my disappointment when I saw the poky little studio his mother had secured for us – and I am sure she thought me an ungrateful brat – within days, I was busy turning it into a home. We adopted a white cat, Adam, from a rescue centre and I got to work constructing furniture from orange boxes, cable drums, foam and scraps of fabric. I went back to work in O'Connor Travel. Rob went back to his job as a mailman.

It was difficult for him to find a slot on the career spectrum. He was a very talented actor and singer but had worked mainly in community theatres, and, as was the case all over the world, the acting profession was precarious and he wasn't inclined to take the risk of 'turning pro'. Especially now that he was married.

In the past, he had tried various jobs, purely for money. At one point, he had been working for a dry-goods store, cutting fabrics for 'picky people', as he described it. Then one day, his boss had come to him and presented him with his very own scissors. Rob had found himself hugging to himself this accolade, 'My own scissors! My own scissors!'

He came to his senses and quit straight away.

For a brief period, he had worked for Sir Whoopee, an ice-cream emporium near Loyola campus, where he had to wear a silly uniform and put up with the taunts of co-eds. Then a particularly obnoxious manager had upbraided him in front of customers for his sloppiness in the construction of a sundae. 'That's not the Sir Whoopee method,' he had scolded, grabbing the offending thing out of Rob's hands to demonstrate the way it should be done.

'Really?' Rob had grabbed it back. 'Well, let me show you the Rob Weckler method!' and, taking a can of synthetic cream, he splurged its entire contents not only over the ice cream but over half of the counter-top as well. He finished the construction with a large handful of maraschino cherries; he was fired on the spot.

He went back to the post office. Although the early mornings did not suit him, the work did. After the sorting, the faster he worked the route in his little jeep, the earlier he finished and the rest of the day was his own. The money was steady, and with my money from O'Connor Travel, we were doing well. In a relatively short time, we were able to move to Magnolia Avenue and a much bigger, light-filled apartment with a wooden floor and a huge bay window; we began to entertain friends.

We also spent a lot of time in Rob's parents' house and in that of the ever patient and loving Spataforas, who had remodelled their own house and, by giving us a lot of their now surplus furniture, had enabled us happily to dump the orange boxes. We went to movies and ate out in neighbourhood restaurants, got takeaway pizzas to eat with beers in front of the network news and, like most Americans, went to bed early to be ready for the next day.

We saved like mad for the house we were going to buy in Ireland and, to that end, I got an additional job as a cocktail waitress in Pat's Pub, four nights a week, 9.00 p.m. to 2.00, 3.00 or sometimes 3.30 a.m.

This was where I learned the Bunny Bob – whereby, rather than bending over the table in my short skirt to serve customers or clean their table, I bent my knees in a 'closed' ballet plié; most importantly, I raked in the cash. As was customary in the service industry in the States, the basic hourly rate was poor but the tips were marvellous and I frequently woke Rob as, heavily laden with coins, I jingled through our front door in the early hours. For instance, on Christmas Eve that year, I brought home almost $200 in tips – a fortune in 1970.

We began to have visitors from Ireland: my friend Carol Cronin and her husband Roger; Declan; even Dadda and Nellie who, incongruously, we took bowling. I can still see Nellie's solid little figure, in her cardigan and tweed skirt, ambling up to the line at the same pace she ambled everywhere, bending to release the heavy ball and turning back without waiting to see where it went.

We moved again, to a terrific duplex on more than an acre of grounds in the suburb of Northbrook, where Rob's family home was. We got a second cat and a second car. And, in addition to Rob's job and my two, we both took on the task of managing and performing in a season of weekend dinner-theatre in a suburban restaurant a few miles away. Dinner-theatre is a peculiarly American institution: you perform, usually on the flat floor, to the acoustic accompaniment of diners munching their way through their meal. We also worked for a children's theatre 'impresario', Lew Musil, 'touring' to adjacent suburbs on Saturday mornings. Lew's scripts were virtually non-existent and, in any case, we would have had no time to learn them, so we made things up as we went along. Poor kids.

So now, with our different shift patterns during the week, our weekend commitments and my commuting downtown to the agency, we saw one another only fleetingly. I was managing on an average of less than four hours' sleep a night, but it did not seem adversely to affect me all that much. I was living the American Way, had plenty of disposable income, my Irish debts had been paid off and our house-buying stash was building nicely in the bank.

My mother came to visit for three weeks. I took time off to take her round the shopping malls – where she bought Dadda a watch – and to see the sights. We sat outside the duplex in the sunshine. We did and discussed ordinary domestic things, had the sort of conversations I knew other mothers and daughters had; it was the longest period we had spent together and, bit by bit, we relaxed in one another's company. I treasure that memory because we were never to approximate it again.

1973 was a crucial year for me. I was pregnant, and thoroughly enjoying my self-given permission to throw dietary caution to the winds. I was due to give birth on 10 July.

In September of that year, I would be eligible to become an American citizen, but, despite my enjoyment of the American way of life, I was hell-bent on *not* settling in Chicago. So the plan was to move to Ireland in September, when the baby would be six or seven weeks old.

I do accept it was very stupid to cut out the automatic citizenship option. Three more weeks would not have made much difference – but I was afraid that the glittering prize, so hard-won by so many immigrant aspirants, might seduce me to stay where I was permanently. I took literally the ironclad theory amongst the Irish community that if you spent more than five years in the States, you would never be happy back in Ireland.

In O'Connor Travel, we had some evidence to back this up. Families would book one-way to 'the old country' at the beginning of summer. After big celebratory 'going home' parties, with bag, baggage and household goods packed into the hold of the aircraft, they would set off from O'Hare in high spirits, cracking jokes about getting out just in time before the heat. Then, in September, we would get a sad call asking if we could organise a one-way flight back. The reasons given were on the surface to do with the poor Irish economy, lack of jobs, housing unlike the standard these families had become used to. But, sometimes, I could detect that the true reason for the rebound was the inability to step away from a competitive and can-do economy into a slower, laissez-faire one. When exposed to the Irish way of doing things for real, people who in Chicago had made affectionate fun of the inability of Irish tradesmen to fulfil promises or to turn up on time, no longer found it amusing. They chafed at long waiting lists for telephone connections. Refrigerators were too small. And having congratulated themselves on escaping Chicago's summer heat, they had somehow forgotten that Irish summers could be grey, cold and depressing. They missed predictable weekend barbecues and watching the sunset from their porch swings or decks. Finally, when set against the community and pastoral basis on which their stateside churches operated, many found the still-rigid hierarchical ethos of Catholicism in Ireland stifling.

So they crept back quietly, somewhat embarrassed, but with relief, which was particularly evident in the kids of high-school age because, instead of the prospect of an all-encompassing drive towards Leaving Cert, they could now romp back to their co-ed high schools with Driver Education, loose dress codes and a modular system of class choice. And, of course, to all their friends and peers.

However, I think there was also something more fundamental

than any of these factors, essentially just details. During the years those Irish had lived in the States, working and saving for the return to the old country, that goal had sustained them. I understood that because I too missed Ireland in a way I have never been able properly to explain since. But observing them after their return, I saw that the adults in these families were now rootless, never now to be fully settled on either side of the Atlantic. I was determined not to let that happen to me, so I took the five-year admonition seriously. Moreover, Rob, bored with his post-office job, was willing to try Ireland.

We had identified a vested cottage – a small, ex-council house – in Ardcath, County Meath, that we could afford to buy, even at the crippling mortgage rates then applying. (Our American friends were appalled not only at the eighteen per cent rate being charged but at the notion that it was variable and could go even higher: 'How can you plan your life?' They bought mortgages in the same way they bought any fixed-price commodity in any store.)

We had seen the cottage on a visit to Ireland and had set the purchase process in train. On almost two acres of garden, it was set into the brow of a gentle hill overlooking the rolling countryside sweeping towards Bellewstown racecourse.

That cool green landscape now called to me because, for weeks that summer, the daytime temperature rose to 120° Fahrenheit and higher – again with 100 per cent humidity – and cooled only a little during the awful sweaty nights. It was also the year of the fourteen-year locusts. These were the real deal and, despite the best efforts of the highway department and their industrial-sized sprayers, they darkened the sky in billion-strong swarms before descending on trees and bushes to strip them bare. If, while driving, you encountered one of these buzzing clouds, you had to stop; even so, the sensation was like being thrust into a massive meat grinder.

When locusts die, their desiccated bodies dry in brittle, ankle-deep drifts and, during the three weeks of their infestation, these drifts created a brown, fuzzy moat around our duplex. They died in heaps on the windowsills, even on the windscreen wipers and air vents of the cars. I learned to park mine as close as possible to the front door so that I had the shortest possible distance through which to crunch.

My due date came and went: I got bigger and bigger and still my baby made no move. I had to give up work, was excruciatingly uncomfortable and spent a lot of time wallowing in cold baths.

Eventually, Betty, my mother-in-law, took matters into her own hands. On Thursday, 19 July, she gave me a large glass of cherry brandy, then took me out in her VW minibus into a section of Northbrook still under development. We bounced and shuddered along the unpaved roads, up and down, in and out of potholes, raising clouds of dust and endangering her suspension. 'Right,' she said, after about twenty minutes, 'that oughta do it!' Next day I went into labour and that evening, Adrian, my son, was born.

I was very ill for the first three weeks of his life and was unable to do very much for him. Rob, to give him his due, took over and proved to be an intuitively skilled father.

Meanwhile, we were making arrangements for the big move. Our neighbour would give a home to the cats; Jack O'Connor had sorted the transfer of the Spataforas' houseful of furniture to be loaded into the belly of our flight; and we had found someone to drive our 'good' car, a VW Beetle, to New York, from where it would be shipped to Liverpool.

Apart from closing accounts and paying final utility bills, there was only one further matter to be organised: a client of O'Connor Travel had asked Jack for help in taking the gift of a large gold tabernacle to a congregation of nuns in Ireland.

The job fell to me. To the bemusement of the Customs officials at Shannon, who, after some head scratching, let me, my husband and our baby through with it and all our furniture.

I would love to have been a fly on the wall that evening in whatever pub they frequented.

23

RTÉ

The house in Ardcath was not ready – we had arranged for some refurbishment and the building of a kitchen extension, a process that was dragging on endlessly – so we had to stay with my parents in Dublin for a few months. With Adrian beside us in his carrycot, we slept on a bed-settee in the dining room.

The arrangement was fraught, for all the obvious reasons. It was a small house with just one tiny bathroom and with us, our accoutrements and our baby equipment tying up the interconnecting reception rooms, the only communal living area remaining was the kitchen, a compact space in which there wasn't even room for a decent-sized table. We had cluttered up the bathroom too, with our nappy buckets and other baby things, presenting physical obstacles to Dadda as he tried to get out to work each morning.

We had decided that, because of the baby, one of us would have to have a steady income and reckoned that this should be me so that Rob could be free to find his feet as an actor in Dublin; we had enough savings to carry us through, we thought, at least until we moved into our house in Ardcath. I would start job-hunting then. Our savings, though, were running low much faster than we had expected and money was becoming a serious issue. So, in addition to the undercurrents of tension because of our invasion of my family's limited space, there was an unspoken strain between Rob and Dadda, who continued to be civil but who obviously disapproved of what he considered to be Rob's lackadaisical approach to finding work to support his family.

Rob was sending out CVs seeking auditions but was having no success. And, with the house in Ardcath still not ready, at the beginning of November, he took a production-line job in Irish Meat Packers, where he was assigned to the early shift.

And so, before six each morning, we stumbled through the cold, rainy darkness into the Beetle for the long trip to Celbridge. If Adrian was awake, we had to bring him too in his carrycot. If he was still sleeping as we crept out, I had a very anxious couple of hours ahead of me in the car: although she never said anything, I knew my mother resented having to get up to tend him.

Eventually, I succumbed to my own stress and took the poor kid with us every day whether he was sleeping or waking. The bonus packs of fresh steak Rob brought home for the table did not really compensate for all of this.

It was with relief all round that our little family of three finally moved into our new house early in 1974. We had a lot of things to get used to. A group water scheme was promised but not yet in prospect, so our basic supply was from a rainwater tank on the roof (we boiled it for drinking) or we walked 100 yards or so down from our gate to fill bottles at a fresh spring.

These inconveniences did not bother us much – I even made

light of the Great Sheep Raid, an abrupt introduction to the reality of country living.

One morning, with Rob absent in Dublin, I unsuspectingly opened the front door and three full-grown sheep barged past me into the house – their sodden, filthy wool wreaking havoc on our newly painted walls and brand-new carpets. I chased them into a corner of the living room but they resisted every attempt to shift them back towards the door, always moving to another corner. Like some sort of demented figures in an automated clock, I'd drive them from one corner and they'd move to the other – back and forth, back and forth and, by the time I did get them out, our house looked like it had been visited by a hurricane. Have you ever seen three wet, unsheared sheep scramble onto and then over the back of a regency-upholstered couch? At least I had had the presence of mind during their initial charge to close the door of our bedroom, which was just to the right of the front door. I had never realised that sheep were so BIG!

Overall, though, it was great to have our own place at last. I happily placed the Spatafora furniture into its new home, where it fitted neatly, and let my husband loose on Rob's Sandwich Center, a separate and self-explanatory area of the kitchen I had created around the fridge solely for his use. I introduced him to the concept of back boilers, coal, slack, newspaper spills, kindling and peat briquettes, none of which he had encountered before.

I began to buy newspapers to search for jobs for which I thought I might be qualified but, dispiritingly, found that all my previous experience never seemed to fit any work on offer – of which, in any event, there was little. And what there was existed a distance away. It would not have paid me to travel into Dublin for five and a half days a week to work in a shop.

I was still in touch with my former theatrical colleagues and was offered an opportunity to stage manage a tour of *Peg O' My Heart*. I had never before been a stage manager, but we needed the money, which was better than an actor would receive; actors received only a stipend for rehearsals. I was offered a flat union fee – and gratefully accepted. Anyhow, the bonus was that I would learn new skills – as usual, an enticing prospect. There was a sting in the tail, however: the producer, the twinkly eyed Chris O'Neill, put on the poor-producer act and charmed me into bringing the Spatafora furniture with me for the set. (It did survive the tour almost unscathed and it is a measure of Rob's agreeable personality that he raised no objections to the prospect of himself and Adrian having to survive in living quarters stripped virtually bare for the duration.)

The money I earned on that tour was useful but, very soon, we were skint again. I was trying to summon up courage to approach Aer Lingus (after all, although six and a half years was stretching it more than a bit, I had been told I would be welcome back 'any time'), when I spotted an ad for announcers in Radio Éireann. The recruitment competition was to be held by audition and I reckoned that my acting experience would help me.

It did, and so, alongside Marian Finucane, Catherine Hogan and three young men who did not continue with broadcasting, I started my training course in the summer of that year with the late Una Sheehy. Una was a lady, a kind but strict tutor and a consummate professional who could detect the slightest deviation from the correct pronunciation of any Finnish, German, Polish or Russian composer's name, not to speak of place, foreign or Irish – including Dublin. Having been born and bred in the city, I was fairly confident, when reading my training scripts into the microphone for her, that I knew the score with that, at least.

Wrong.

'In Dublin today—'

'STOP! Try it again.'

'In Dublin today—'

No, Deirdre. It's that *u* sound. It's too narrow. Try it again…'

I have a good ear but it took a half-hour of wasting the class's time before I could detect the difference between 'Dublin' as I said it and the way she insisted it be pronounced, at the connecting point between Dehblin, Dauhblin and Dahblin. (She was also insistent on marking scripts with due attention being paid first to sense and then to punctuation.)

I got through the course, and, with great trepidation as a part-time probationer with no guarantee of employment, I approached my first official live broadcast in the old GPO Studios in Henry Street. The announcers' booth was musty, claustrophobic, smelled of mice and cigarette smoke and was entered via a double door of bank-vault thickness, guarded by a fully armed soldier. This was in case subversives rushed us. (I did think, though, that on our side of the barrier, the ordinary bolt – a small golden one of the type found usually on the inside of a bathroom door – did not afford much protection if our armed guardian were to be overpowered!)

Our training had been geared to the eventuality of taking over the station if a programme broke down, if the news did not materialise when we called it in, or if contact was lost with an outside broadcast. We had been coached not only in how to use filler material – promotions for upcoming programmes to be read from prepared scripts – but also in how to line up an appropriate LP track on the turntable beside us, stylus poised. Because appropriateness was all: you'd never read a 'promo' for *The Maureen Potter Show* if the Mass went silent. You'd play céilí music for a breakdown during a GAA match or *Nuacht*, light classical during discussion or literary pro-grammes, 'serious' classical during a Mass, concert or recital. And *never* songs: it was a mortal sin to use a song or an aria because we might have to speak over it. This, it was felt, grated on the ear of the listener, who would not clearly understand either set of words.

For sure, breakdowns drew on our powers of ad-libbing but in those days we were not allowed to deviate by as much as a comma from the script provided by the Presentation Department for official announcements.

So, with all of this roiling in my brain, I embarked on my first night as a professional broadcaster. I sat in front of the modest array of switches and dials, under the watchful, not-giving-an-inch gaze of my supervisor for the night, Treasa Davison.

There was a huge, white-faced clock within my eyeline and as the second hand swept away the minutes, my stomach tossed and tumbled as though I was about to be the first to land from the boats at Dunkirk. This was monumental. This performance would deter-mine the rest of my life. Rob, my family, all my friends and relations awaited this announcement; the whole nation was agog.

The signature tune of the on-air programme wound up. In the brief silence that followed, I picked up my script. My heart joined my stomach in the dance.

The second hand reached its apogee.

The sound operator gave me a terse hand signal through the glass of the control booth.

Treasa nodded, giving me the 'Go-go-go!'

I clicked on my green button and quavered, 'The time now is eight o'clock.'

My ancestors would have been proud.

After a decent interval of trials, I was placed on the panel of casual announcers, those who were written in to the roster for a couple of shifts each fortnight and who filled in during emergencies. For this reason, my work patterns were only partly predictable and, as in the case of freelance actors – or, indeed, writers or journalists – I had to be always available to rush in to Henry Street on receipt of a phone call.

This was a nervy way to live. We were always hoping that Rob might be called for an audition – an event he could not predict or turn down any more than I could turn down a request to report for an early-morning or late-night shift in Radio Éireann. Suppose we were both called to work together? Who'd mind Adrian? There was a time when one, sometimes both, of us seemed permanently to be on the road, commuting to Dublin, whizzing up and down the Ashbourne Road with our poor baby strapped into the back of the car and this gives rise to another example of the power of sense memory.

To make best use of time, I frequently liquidised Adrian's solid food and, having enlarged the hole in the teat to enormous proportions, put it into his bottle so he could eat on the move during our commute. Many years later, when we were driving up the Ashbourne Road, Adrian, who was eight or nine at the time, wondered dreamily why he always felt 'very peaceful' when travelling on this road…

By now, my Aunt Nellie had moved to Rutland Cottages. Summerhill is right in the heart of the inner city and, far from Ardcath as she was, if she was available, she became our emergency childminder on weeknights and the customary one on weekends.

Somehow, we stumbled through, even if, once or twice, since I couldn't bring a baby into an on-air studio, Rob had to bring Adrian to auditions with him.

But then an additional and seemingly insurmountable problem with these living arrangements arose. The petrol pumps dried up. The country was hit by an oil crisis and, for us, if fuel could be found at any price, the cost of commuting from Ardcath to Dublin had tripled and then almost quadrupled from what it had been when we first came to live in the area. We could no longer afford it.

Reluctantly, we rented out Ardcath and moved to a basement flat in Monkstown – my first experience of southside living.

The pluses attached to this were that the Presentation Department had moved, at last, to its large and pristine new studio in Donnybrook and was easy to get to from where we now lived. Although still a casual, I had become a regular on the announcers' roster and could count on a set number of shifts. In addition, Rob was beginning to get work, particularly in musicals with Noel Pearson – *Joseph and the Amazing Technicolour Dreamcoat*, *Jacques Brel is Alive and Well and Living in Paris*, *The Fantasticks*, *Jesus Christ Superstar*. Rehearsals and shows were mostly in Dublin and Monkstown had a regular bus service.

But although the flat was adequate, after the airy heights of Meath, I found its semi-subterranean gloom very depressing. In addition, although I continued to go to work, I was crippled out of the blue with a very painful affliction of almost every joint in my body. I couldn't eat because moving my jaws was excruciating and I began rapidly to lose weight. I visited specialists recommended by various GPs: one said I would have to have three vertebrae removed; a second offered that I had a form of scoliosis and should take time off work, lie on the floor for a couple of weeks and get myself a back brace.

Rob was away on tour with *Jacques Brel* at the time and, with Adrian to mind and no paid sick leave, neither of these unattractive scenarios was an option. So I took painkillers and forced myself to get about using borrowed crutches and sticks.

In desperation, and with Adrian being taken by a kind actress friend for a morning, I went back to Glasnevin to visit our old family GP, Brian Daly. He examined me carefully and consulted books he had in his surgery. Then he lit his pipe and, drawing deeply on it, paced his floor, thinking for what seemed to me a very long time. Finally, he said that, in his opinion, I had developed an acute form of rheumatoid arthritis. He wrote a note outlining this observation and referred me urgently to a consultant he felt would know what to do.

But events took their own pace and, early the following morning, with Adrian, who was just nineteen months old, calling for rescue from his cot, I couldn't walk at all and my jaws were so painful and stiff, I could not even talk to him. Somehow, I rolled from the bed onto the floor and inched on all fours to his room, where, unable to stand, I managed to talk him into climbing over the cot side and out, using my back as a step.

The telephone was in the hallway outside his room. I pulled the whole apparatus on to the floor beside me to dial my parents. They came up trumps: immediately they got into their car to drive across the city. Mamma took Adrian home with her in a taxi while Dadda carried me bodily into their car, drove me to the Mater Hospital and carried me inside. Within an hour of being seen, I was admitted to a geriatric ward.

The events of the next few days remain locked in confusion. I retain images of lying in bed, exposed to discussions amongst grave men with curious groups of students in tow. I remember drips and blood transfusions, my hands being immersed in soothing hot wax, a hydrotherapy pool...

I remember someone mentioning multiple sclerosis but I was so ill I didn't care what definitions they came up with: I just wanted the pain to go away and, gradually, as treatments were tried, it began to subside a little and I was able to sit up, even drink.

Then the day came when I got out of bed and went into the corridor to be there when Mamma brought Adrian in to see me. I will never forget the sight and sound of him running towards me, arms outstretched, little feet drumming on the hard floor. Mamma had done a great job: he looked pink, well fed and bright-eyed.

By the time Rob got back from the tour, the firm diagnosis was as Brian Daly had predicted: acute rheumatoid arthritis. The prognosis was uncertain. It could be a once off. It could recur. It could even become chronic in the future. For the time being, I was grateful for the mercy of incremental easing of movement and that the pain was now manageable.

And then, one evening, with the sunset blazing outside the windows of my ward, a nurse came into my cubicle bearing a pink slip. 'Good news,' she said.

I was pregnant.

24

Fracture

I was kept in hospital for almost seven weeks and, by the time I was discharged, the improvement in my mobility had continued so that I could get about again with the aid of two walking sticks.

Rob's work pattern remained sporadic and unpredictable and there were long, frustrating lacunae when it seemed he would never work again – but we were philosophical about this: it is the lot of the freelancer. And, after the best part of two years in Ireland, we had hopes that his name was becoming known in musical and theatrical circles. He signed on with a model agency: exactly six feet tall and with perfect proportions, he was ideal for the catwalk. At one point, he was cast in a television ad.

Then RTÉ Radio, the new name for Radio Éireann, offered me a formal contract as an announcer; this was a godsend because I could now build a store of time in lieu – extra time worked for future time off. At that time, there were no statutory entitlements to maternity benefit, certainly no paid maternity leave from RTÉ for contract workers, and I had worried constantly about how we would manage the childminding. Now, I worked every extra shift and half-shift I could get in order to have at least some paid days off to have my baby.

At five minutes to midnight on 8 October 1975, I read the shipping forecast, enunciating as clearly as I could. This was a task I had always loved because of my mental image of quiet engine rooms and wheelhouses as mariners and fishermen strained to listen to my voice conveying vital information through crackling receivers. Physically, I felt grand. The aches and pains had diminished dramatically, but I had no appetite at all: with my first pregnancy I had gained a horrifying four stone, but with this one I had actually lost two and weighed, even with the baby, under seven stone. I was nine months pregnant, according to the best guess of my doctor; because of the earlier illness, no one could be precise about the actual due date.

Yet, although I was blessedly insulated from outright fear by my pregnancy hormones, there was still an underlying niggle: it had been explained to me that with pregnancy the body releases natural analgesic substances, including cortisone, that deal with pain, so I was not to take it as read that I was cured. The condition could recur after the birth. And, even though our material prospects were now so much brighter because of the steady money my new contract was bringing in, I was also beginning to worry about something else. Serious cracks were showing in Rob's and my relationship: small issues were becoming big issues; big issues were simmering.

Anyhow, as the hands of my studio clock came up to midnight, I said goodnight to the nation, wished everyone listening an '*oíche mhaith,* wherever you are', played the national anthem, turned out the light and went home.

Simon was born at nine twenty the following morning and I ascended into post-natal elation.

This condition is the exact opposite of post-natal depression. I couldn't believe my luck. I was exhilarated, sleepless, giggling uncontrollably at the strangest things, full of energy. When I left hospital, I even asked Rob not to drive us home but to take me into Clerys, O'Connell Street, where there was a sale on. Inside, Rob held three-day-old Simon while I trawled feverishly through the bargains on offer in the baby department.

Even after that, we didn't go straight home but went to collect Adrian from the friends who were minding him and stayed on for a couple of hours for chats and cups of tea. Amazingly, when we did eventually get back to the flat, I was still hopping around like a mechanical toy.

It was just as well I was in such good form because I had managed to store up a total of only eleven paid days in lieu and so, less than a fortnight after signing off on that night before Simon was born, I was back on duty at the Presentation Desk, luckily with no sign of a recurrence of the arthritis.

I remained as energetic as a whirlwind for the first few months of Simon's life, through his christening and into the dark days of winter and another Christmas – when I decided that a basement in Monkstown was not for us. In any event, our lease was due to end, while simultaneously our tenant in Ardcath had decided not to renew. I saw this confluence as an omen.

The excessive and wearing commuting notwithstanding, I had been very happy in Ardcath. I had loved waking to fresh air, to the view through the bedroom window, to the sound of birdsong and the breeze in the young copper beeches outside. But much as I had enjoyed that house, so happily furnished and decorated, with two babies, my work concentrated on the southside of Dublin, and the likelihood that any jobs Rob was offered would be there too, moving out of the city again didn't seem to be a sensible option.

My pal Patricia, now married to her Frank, had mentioned a house, backing on to theirs, which was for sale in Claremont Court, Glasnevin. It is a high, acutely angled townhouse shoehorned into a long, narrow site in a terrace of its fellows and is as far removed from our detached cottage on its sloping, fertile acres as it's possible to be. Needs must, however, and, anyhow, still on the crest of my post-natal high, I saw a move as yet another adventure. And I was sure I could find space for the much-travelled Spatafora furniture.

Rob evinced no opinions about letting Ardcath go or even about the move – he seemed sanguine about the whole thing – so we made the decision, although I was doubtful if, in the depths of winter and with the high cost of transport, we would find a buyer for our rural cottage.

Then something extraordinary happened. When I approached the estate agent who was handling the sale of the Glasnevin house, he asked me, as estate agents will, if I had a house to sell. I told him about Ardcath and he did a double-take: his client was searching for a home in the Ardcath area.

The chances of that must have been close to a million to one but, as a result, we were able to perform a straight swap of the two houses, with a small financial adjustment, on our part. We moved in the spring of 1976. The luck fairy was with me again.

Maybe.

Because Rob and I were to spend just over a year together in Claremont Court.

In May 1977, our two sons were healthy and thriving. Rob was playing the part of the American protagonist in Noel Pearson's production of *Cabaret* in the Gaiety Theatre and I had just taken up a new job as a newsreader for RTÉ on both radio and television.

RTÉ, then and now, is the kind of organisation in which it is always possible – and even encouraged – for employees to move onwards, upwards and even sideways between departments. John McColgan, the *Riverdance* impresario, is always cited as a great example to aspirants: he had entered the company as a humble postboy and had ended up as a television producer with a top management role.

I had become bored with my announcer's job in Presentation. Conditions were undoubtedly good – we had decent accommodation, free car parking and a subsidised canteen. The pay, equivalent to that on the lower clerical rungs of the public service, was not great but it was reasonable for what we did. But the day-to-day work consisted merely of sitting in front of the control desk for hour after hour, trying to remain constantly alert while reading.

'The time now is...'

'And here is the news, read by...'

'That programme was presented by...'

'The producer was...'

'And now – *Céilí House*. Presented as usual by...'

If anything changed from one week to the next, we did not even have to fill in the dots on the sheets in front of us because this too was done for us upstairs by the Presentation clerical staff.

One of our part-timers, a teacher, used the shifts to catch up on correcting her class homework; many of us took to knitting (not, alas I – I never did develop the necessary patience). And over a couple of years of announcing, one of my colleagues even constructed, backed and lined a 2,500-piece patchwork quilt, each tiny diamond pain-stakingly hand-sewn into her own fabulously intricate design.

It was not advisable to read while on duty. While physically possible, for me the danger was that I would become so absorbed that I could miss a programme juncture or even a total breakdown.

On the other hand, maybe I was being too sedulous. Announcers develop an almost paranormal reaction to even a second's unscheduled silence during a broadcast. There is a famous story about Una Sheehy who was on duty one Sunday afternoon during the transmission of a GAA match. Apparently, having handed over to Mícheál O'Hehir, she had settled down to fill in her crossword.

After a short while, she realised that while the atmospherics were coming through to her monitor, there was nothing to be heard from O'Hehir – his ribbon mike had gone blank. Immediately, she leaped into action, apologised formally to the listeners for the breakdown, reassured them that service would be resumed as soon as possible, and opened the fader on her standby disc to play a jolly jig from a céilí band.

At Croke Park, where new-fangled transistor radios had become all the rage so that spectators in the stands could hear RTÉ's commentary as well as watch the action, the music blasted out all over the stadium. They had been having a one-minute silence of mourning prior to kick-off.

There was occasional relief from the workaday tedium when we announcers were assigned to present live or recorded concerts – again from prepared scripts. I did present some of these, but rarely, and, I suspect, on the basis of Buggins' Turn because very quickly the wheat was separated from the chaff. My pal Catherine Hogan was the obvious choice for recitals: not only does she have a wonderfully mellifluous voice, her degree is in music. Ray Lynott was another natural.

In a sense, although the surroundings were more plush and the tasks far more congenial, after a couple of years I began to feel like I was back in that brown room of the Civil Service Commission where I was 'allowed' to do a very limited range of work.

Yet I truly do not mean to disparage the job. I was very grateful for it. These days it is a great career; senior announcers have been set free from the narrow work span of my own time: they now present and produce their own programmes, write their own scripts, develop promotional material. They are technically adept too, editing electronically in suites that resemble control rooms of mini-Cape Canaverals.

And, to be fair, in keeping with their policy of encouraging individual development, the powers-that-be did try me out on *Morning Call*, a gentle early-morning music/chat show, with Liam Devally as my producer. Liam, a former announcer and a professional tenor, blazed in to RTÉ, blazed out again, became a barrister and then a judge, a position from which he is now retired. He is highly entertaining; I remember him principally for the laughs and chats during our breakfast break in the middle of the programme at eight o'clock. While the news was being read from the newsroom, we – producer, presenter, sound operator and disc operator – congregated in the control room to drink a cup of tea.

Even he, however, could not make a light-hearted on-air chit-chatterer out of me. It is an inborn talent not respected enough by the public – who believe that because it seems so effortless, it requires no talent at all; the truth is that the skill, as typified these days by Maxi, Ray D'Arcy, Ian Dempsey and Ronan Collins, cannot be taught. You have it or you don't. It has a lot to do with a sunny personality, a humorous (not satirical or cynical) attitude to the world and self-confidence without self-importance.

Many newsreaders had also passed through the Pres One studio,

Pat Kenny, Maurice O'Doherty and Don Cockburn amongst them and, sensing that I was getting restless, my boss Lorna Madigan thought she detected that even though (shock!) I was a woman; I might make a good newsreader too.

I was flattered. Although I knew I had some of the prerequisites: a good broadcasting voice, ability to read scripts without fluffing, practice in how to act calmly in an emergency, I felt instinctively that a lot more was required of a good newsreader. It's hard to be precise. A lot has to do with demeanour: an ability to garner trust by exuding a blend of competence and gravitas. This, in my opinion, should be mixed with a quiet sense of drama but leavened when necessary with neighbourly gossip.

A further plus would be an ability to read a story ten times as if each airing is the first.

Could I measure up to all of that?

There was another thing: secretly, I was doubtful about my appearance. I felt I could be a good newsreader on radio but television was a different matter, and RTÉ News required its presenters to read on both media. I had never considered myself good-looking – certainly not handsome enough to appear on television.

Years earlier, when I was just eleven years old, I was in Patricia's house in Ballymun. We were up in her bedroom, and she was primping and kiss-curling her hair in front of her wardrobe mirror. I, as usual, was rabbiting on mournfully about my own limp, beige locks. I got carried away and, gazing with disgust at my faceful of freckles, declared passionately that compared with her, I was pure ugly...

'Stop it,' she ordered, through a mouthful of hair clips.

I wouldn't stop it, of course, so she insisted we go downstairs to get her mother's adjudication. She marched me into her kitchen, where Stella was doing something at the cooker. She stood me in front of a little mirror hung by the back door and made me look into it. 'Now, Mammy,' she said, 'will you c'mere and look at Deirdre. Isn't she pretty? She really thinks she's not. You tell her, Mammy.'

Stella wiped her hands on a tea towel and came over to us. She stood at my shoulder, contemplating my reflection in the flyspecked mirror. She thought a little, screwing up her face. 'We-ell,' she said at last. Then, hesitantly, 'She's – er – *pleasant*-looking.'

The poor woman could not have predicted the lifelong effect that had on me.

Twenty years later, though, the luck fairy smiled on me again and after auditions and training – which included a charming lecture from Charles Mitchel on 'How to Deal with Public Acclaim!' – I got the gig as a part-time newsreader. I knew that if I didn't dirty my bib there was now a probability that the job would become a staff one and I could transfer, permanently and pensionably, to the newsroom.

In the meantime, I would get paid per shift, which was a very welcome boost to my income. With even an occasional input from Rob's stage earnings, we would not have to worry about money for the first time since we had come to live in Ireland. We would have enough to pay the mortgage and to employ babysitters when we were both working at night.

On paper, everything looked upbeat, but those relationship cracks were still widening – so seriously that, as far as Rob was concerned, there was no drawing the edges together again.

The fracture occurred on a Saturday morning when he announced that, as of that day, he was leaving me – and he did.

He had not come home the previous night. I hadn't slept but had kept a bizarre vigil by the living-room window. The dawn that morning had been exquisite. Summer can be cruel.

On the night of that Saturday, dazed, I was on duty reading the television news. By another of those coincidences that transcend fiction, there was an arts package in the running order. It included a video clip of one of my husband's shows. I got through the bulletin but I really don't know how. I guess the old acting gene – the show must go on – kicked in. And the following day, I had to appear at a public function to present prizes. My father drove me.

On the Monday, Una Sheehy, who had watched over my broadcasting progress like a guardian angel, came to see me. She was deeply sympathetic about my personal predicament and urged me to take time off. I couldn't, of course. I had to continue to earn: my children and I had to eat and keep a roof over our heads.

I can see from this distance that I was reacting not with any intellectual coherence but viscerally: an animal protecting the den. Because, despite sensing danger and knowing that our marriage was not what it should be, I was shocked when reality bit. Perhaps I should have anticipated this development but, being the type I am, no matter what difficulties I experience, I hang in there, Pollyanna-like, always believing that, if I work hard enough, I will ameliorate them.

Apart from my personal distress, I had genuine and very serious practical difficulties. To a great extent, childminding had been dove-tailed around our work commitments – of which, over the years in Ireland, Rob had had relatively few, so most of it had fallen to him.

For the next couple of weeks, I existed in a state of anxiety. I was panicked at work, unable to fend off the anxiety that invaded my sleep when I did manage to doze, which was seldom. I found myself performing trivial tasks at weird times of day and night – frantically scrubbing at a stain on a skirting board, mowing grass already so short the earth was showing through. I muddled through with the help of friends and babysitters, the understanding of colleagues who swapped shifts with me, and the reluctant co-operation of Rob who came back to Claremont Court to babysit when I couldn't find anyone else – not an ideal arrangement for either of us. The more I searched for a permanent solution, however, the more I could see I would not be able to afford the going rate for permanent childcare. Patricia's telephone line burned as I poured my troubles into her ear. At all hours, she came to sit with me and listen again.

Then Nellie stepped in. She said she would give up her job – having been made redundant by United Artists she had been working with an insurance broker – and move in with me.

I calmed down. Rob and I even managed to say goodbye to one another in a manner that, although fraught, was relatively civilised before he flew back to the US. It was three weeks after he had made his announcement; Adrian was three years and ten months old, Simon was one and a half. They had been very close to their father and now, overnight, they had to get used to his absolute absence and to a complete regime change. Nellie became their surrogate mother and homemaker while I fulfilled the outside role of hunter-gatherer. To a very large degree, this had been my function since we had come to live in Ireland, but, for financial reasons, I needed to work a lot harder now. As well as my main newsreading shifts, I continued to take casual shifts as a radio announcer whenever they were available.

There is no point in spelling out my personal distress here. Marriage break-up is an appalling hurt and has been well documented – and no matter how sunny your basic personality, it permanently closes off at least some part of your heart's trust. For a long time, you cannot recognise who you are and there is at least one point where, no matter what has transpired or how ill-treated you feel, there is the temptation to subsume all rational thinking and do anything at all, even against your own interests, in an attempt to repair the damage.

I have talked to others about this aspect of things and it is common. In my case, thank God, just a few feet away, I had my staunch pal Patricia to lean on. She used not only her professional skills but also her personal instincts to help me over this particular hump.

Strangely, although I have been asked about this, I didn't feel ashamed or stigmatised, even though, at that time, single parenthood was not the relatively normal state it is today. I'd done my very best and, although I was sadder and wiser, I was still the same person I'd always been.

I did worry about Adrian and Simon, though, because, within their school and their peer groups, they were now in a tiny minority of children from 'a broken home'. There was little I could do about it, however, except confide in their teachers, which I did. Inside, though, I bled hard for them. What was ahead for them was not going to be easy and was definitely not what I had dreamed for them.

Despite our personal mismatch and the problems and issues between us, I can now see how unhappy Rob was in Ireland. He is an intrinsically kind and open-hearted person who had come to Ireland because he saw it as a big adventure, and also because he was willing to accommodate my drive to get home. His introduction to his new country was to sleep on a bed-settee in his in-laws' house. And at a time when most of his American contemporaries were still at college, or were picking up transitory jobs in grocery or convenience stores simply to fund dates and beer, his lot was to commute to a production line in a meat factory where he and his new colleagues shared no common experience.

I don't think he ever came to terms with the cultural differences between our two countries.

He referred disparagingly to Irish people as being sunk in what he termed 'Celtic gloom' and although, on principle, I argued indignantly with him about this, having myself lived in the thrusting, positive atmosphere of Chicago, I could see his point. He came here during a grey period of Irish history; at that time it was impossible to be in company, or even at a shop counter, without having to listen to someone complaining about the weather, the government, the price of something, the unfairness of everything. Ireland was a kip, according to its natives, and the only hope for any kind of decent life was to get out of it as quickly as possible.

There were also the physical disparities. He had moved from lazy, hazy baseball summers (he was a Chicago Cubs fan) and the glitter of snowy Super Bowl winters to land within the furious and, to him, incomprehensible county allegiances of Gaelic games. He truly hated the damp Irish climate: the deep dark winters, the unpredictable, frequently louring summers. Instead of flicking on central heating or air-conditioning, he had to make endless piles of newspaper spills, shovel slack, and huddle for warmth over Super Ser gas heaters while the rain pelted down outside during what passed for high summer.

Most of all, I think, he found it hard to come to terms with an environment that was infused with begrudgery, grievance and, to him, the stilted protocols and bogus politeness – i.e. hypocrisy – of Irish life.

And, of course, he was out of love with me.

25

Five, Four, Three, Two, One…

For me, the most exciting part of reading a live television news bulletin was always the countdown into it. I hear everything is automated these days but, in the 1970s, I was accompanied in the news studio by a floor manager, two camera operators, one behind each camera, an autocue person hand-feeding her typed script through the machine and, discreetly in the background, someone from the make-up department, restorative powder puff at the ready.

Taking instructions through a headset from the news director in the gallery, the floor manager stood beside the gaping lens of Camera One directly in front of me and beat out his words with hand signals.

'Five!

'Four!

'Three!

'Two!

'One—

'And we're on!' He swept the air across his chest.

The signature tune swelled, the opening graphics rolled across the two monitors set to both sides of the reader's desk and then, on the hood of Camera One, a bubble of red light snapped on. The floor manager stabbed the air in my direction and then, with a slight smile – or none, depending on the gravity of the first story – I looked directly into the maw of the lens. 'Good evening!'

It is a dramatic few seconds, directly equivalent to the opening of a stage play.

And there are definite parallels with acting. Indeed, at the beginning of my stint as a newsreader, my colleagues and I were members not of the NUJ, the National Union of Journalists, but of Equity, the actors' union. This had changed before I left RTÉ. Some time around 1981, after a long set of union–management negotiations, the role of newsreaders was amended: henceforth they would be allowed to have an input into their scripts and do some interviewing. While retaining our Equity membership, we were inducted as a body into the journalists' union as well.

Up to that time, though, we had not been allowed unilaterally to change a word of the text supplied to us by the subeditors. In practice, we did amend sentences or paragraphs that we would find clumsy to read aloud, but, as the clock ticked towards transmission, we had to do it in hurried and almost submissive consultation with the writers. They were the journalistic experts. We were the Equity mouthpieces.

Nowadays, the visuals are digital and are edited by reporters in the field while in the newsroom itself, servers quietly pass preparatory bulletin information from one desktop computer to another with an aura of purposeful tranquillity.

What I remember most is the cacophony of the last half hour coming up to news time when camera crews and reporters were rushing in bearing aluminium cans of film for editing. The din in that newsroom, long, narrow, littered with tottering stacks of files, piles of new and old newspapers, used coffee cups and personal detritus, was deafening. Subeditors, correspondents and autocue operators banged hard on banks of typewriters, telex machines spewed continuous reports from the wire services, telephones rang and the Banda machine churned out scripts. The unfortunate copytaker on duty usually had difficulty hearing what stringers – freelance contributors – were dictating from storm-racked phoneboxes in deepest rural Ireland while the editor, news director and production assistant had to yell at each other to make themselves heard. A television monitor mounted high on one wall usually added to the brouhaha.

In the middle of all this sat the newsreader, trying to stay cool while checking scripts against the bulletin's running order and the autocue tapes. Each of us had a different way of handling them: I marked mine heavily for sense, underlining key words, adding slashes, dashes, parentheses and musical pause marks – when I was finished with them, my tapes looked as though they had been used by a bunch of square-dancing mice.

Even autocue is handled electronically now, but the principle remains the same: on a glass screen, the words of a script scroll upwards at a pace that suits the presenter. To the viewer, it should appear as though a news story is being imparted directly – and for the first time – as though a trusted messenger has just personally discovered it and is aware of its import. There is a catch, however. If delivery is too smooth, particularly as one story leads to the next, it will prompt vague, even subconscious disbelief: *This is all too pat!*

It looks as if she learned it off by heart – she couldn't remember all of that, surely? Maybe she's making some of it up? This is why the skilled reader does occasionally look down at a paper script – perhaps at the beginning of every couple of paragraphs – and moves the pages between stories. (Not to be confused with scrabbling for the right page, or place in it, when the autocue goes AWOL, or the running order changes unexpectedly.) It should seem as though the reader is so familiar with the story that all she has to do is to keep track of it.

Oddly, although I was, of course, nervous at the beginning of my life as a newsreader, contrary to the general supposition amongst the public – 'You must get really nervous when you think of the millions of people watching you' – I was not at all conscious of the size of the audience I was addressing. The atmosphere within the studio was intimate, quiet and comforting: I was in safe hands, well minded by my colleagues in the room. If anything untoward happened – a late script, a breaking story, sound or film breaking down or a blank screen following a report I had called in – I knew I would be calmly advised in my earpiece about what story to jump to next. A lot of people were taking care of individual slices of the pie: my part of the job was to present it whole.

During training, we had been advised to visualise an individual viewer. My target was a family, sitting attentively on a living-room couch, and my task was to tell them clearly what had happened that day at home and abroad. Tone was very important: viewers trust newsreaders, but that trust has to be earned. If I was reporting the details of a tragedy like the Stardust disaster, I kept in mind that the families affected could be watching and, while delivering the story as factually as I could, tried not to add to their distress by appearing too detached. Yet no matter how harrowing the images, how appalling the corruption, or how unfair the action, viewers do not want to see emotionalism either; there is a fine line to be trodden between impartiality and humanity.

Take, say, Britain's sinking of the Argentinian ship the *Belgrano* during the Falklands War. While revealing the facts as known and the number of deaths so far reported, my job was to convey that I had an intellectual grasp of what had happened and to make comprehensible what a huge and dreadful event it was. At the time, there was an outcry in Ireland apportioning blame for the incident; but I could not show, even by the twitch of an eyebrow, what my own opinion was. This was a political story with connotations for the diplomacy between our nearest neighbour and us. The tone had to be absolutely level.

Nothing prevented people from reading between the lines, of course, especially when domestic political stories entered the arena. I measured achievement of professional impartiality by the content of letters I received from supporters of both Fianna Fáil and Fine Gael, each side accusing me of being the other's lackey. Fianna Fáilers frequently detected a softening of tone, even a glint in my eye, when I mentioned Fine Gael; Fine Gaelers said I smirked if I was reading a story favourable to their rivals. 'We know what foot you kick with – it's written all over your face!' was the general tenor of letters from both camps; the writers usually went on to threaten a report to my 'superiors'. If the writer was from a party in government, that party was going to 'get' the 'whole shower of you in RTÉ'; if the party was in opposition, the rider was that 'manners would be put on us' when their pals got back into power.

We had to be equally careful when reading news on radio, of course: people read all kinds of things into your tone, pacing, even your pauses. And in that relatively less constricted atmosphere, there were different hazards, certainly for me. My imagination works visually and there was one occasion, when I was reading a story about a man in England being arrested for throwing an egg at Queen Elizabeth II, although the egg had not actually hit its target. For some reason, even though I had prepared the story, while I was reading it aloud, the fact that he had missed suddenly struck me as hilarious. In my mind's eye, I saw this little man lovingly selecting his egg, nurturing it, carrying it carefully with him and standing patiently on the sidelines, waiting for the Queen to pass. And then, when his big moment came, he missed. I saw the expression on his face and began to giggle uncontrollably. I apologised to the listeners, of course, but it was to no avail. I couldn't stop and I was helpless for the rest of the bulletin and the weather forecast.

For a time, I was the only woman staff newsreader, which prompted a lot of comment about my appearance and clothes.

And here I do have a beef. A man can wear the same dark suit night after night on live television: he changes the hue of a shirt or pattern of his tie – and *ecco*! Sartorial excellence! He is slicked with foundation and a dusting of powder, pulls a comb through his short-back-and-sides and everyone thinks he's Cary Grant.

I know from correspondence that a woman, on the other hand, is expected to have a vast wardrobe, mainly, it has to be said, by other women. She has to appear with faultless make-up and a fresh, gleaming hairdo or she will get letters referring to her in terms like 'lazy, greasy-faced cow'. I can attest to that.

I could not afford to buy a fraction of what seemed to be expected and, at one point, I did try, half-heartedly, to suggest we all, men and women, wear a uniform. This did not go down well. Then my friend Carol introduced me to her friend and neighbour Anne Sherry. Anne, a brilliant and creative tailor in her own right, worked for the designer Richard Lewis. Incredibly, she volunteered to make me a raft of tops and blouses that I could wear over my jeans. She insisted she would get a great kick out of seeing her work on television. I accepted her offer gratefully and I remain in her debt.

But I didn't want to sponge on her generosity and goodness for ever, so I started to agitate for a proper clothing allowance. I got nowhere with a direct approach to management, so I enlisted the help of the union.

After negotiations, the union did win an annual clothing allowance for me.

But for all the men too.

Including all subeditors.

Including the subeditors on the early-morning radio shift.

We all got an additional £120 per year added to our salaries. It was therefore taxed at the top rate. It gave me just under a pound a week to spend on my clothes and my hairdresser. And, presumably, enabled each early-morning radio sub to amble down to the shops every couple of months to replace his jumper with a nice new one. Each for all and all for one.

Newsreaders attract admirers and stalkers. For years, Charles Mitchel conducted a personal correspondence with many amongst the former group, one of whom, he told us, meticulously dressed up every evening to watch him. My own admirers tended to come from the farming community – and, yes, some did have marriage in mind.

I faced only one really scary situation. It started with a series of complimentary but rather anodyne letters. These became gradually more frequent, much longer and, occasionally, included vague threats – ostensibly because I wasn't replying. The handwriting became larger and wilder, letters of individual words more disconnected.

In the last one, the threat was specific: razor blades and how they were to be used on various parts of me was outlined in graphic detail. This letter had been hand-delivered at the security post, less than 100 yards from where I worked. I handed it to the gardaí. The letters stopped coming. I never followed up why – but, years later, I was told during a social gathering that on seeing the scrawl, the guards had known instantly who was responsible.

Legends grew up about us. For instance, I was frequently asked to convey my admiration to Michael Murphy for his courage in reading so well from his wheelchair. I was pulled aside at a social function and told that my interlocutor had huge empathy with the difficulties engendered by the affair I was having with a (named) prominent golfer – a person I had never met. I also heard that my love child by Charlie Haughey was being brought up alongside another of Charlie's love children in a foster family in County Clare, one he had fathered with a second 'lady' newsreader. *And wasn't it lovely for the two little half-brothers to be growing up together?*

By 1979, I was restless again. I had become friendly with the group of elite journalists who worked in a tightly knit unit of radio news, headed by the charismatic Mike Burns. Known as News Features, it produced programmes such as *News at One Thirty*, *News at Six Thirty*, *World Report* and *This Week* and included Seán Duignan, Brendan Keenan, Dick Hogan, Cian Ó hÉigeartaigh, Kevin Healy, Gerald Barry, Ella Shanahan, Jacqueline Hayden and Yvonne (now Judge) Murphy.

It was Mike who suggested I should switch from newsreading to journalism at a time when there happened to be a public advertisement running. I hadn't considered applying, but he and the others in News Features encouraged me and, at the last minute, I banged in an application. The competition was by audition, written report, interview and camera test (doing that test felt strange on a day I was about to go on air to read the television news!) and, again, I got the gig.

A hitch developed. The NUJ blacked my appointment, on the basis that I had received no training as a journalist, and there ensued fourteen long, miserable weeks, when I reported for work every day, sat at a desk, but was barred from doing any work, even answering a telephone. It was eventually sorted out by negotiation, as these things usually are.

My main work as a journalist in the newsroom turned out to be on *Countrywide*, the forerunner of the early-evening television programme *Nationwide*, so successfully running now. Today, entire programme segments can be filmed, voiced and edited in the field, then transmitted back to headquarters with a single touch of a button. That was far from the situation in *Countrywide*'s era, when film was a physical roll, in a can, that had to be driven or flown back to an editing suite and voiced over in a dedicated studio. Our programme, with its reports on local heroes, festivals, events and curiosities, such as two-headed calves and six-legged lambs, always languished at the end of the queue when camera crews were being shared out; we were also in danger of having the crew snatched back if a major story broke during the day. As a result, many of our reports were filmed with a Bolex – a good, but very old-fashioned camera not equipped for sound. It was frustrating, of course, but we just had to make do and get on with it.

It was in the early 1980s that RTÉ decided to change the role of its newsreaders on television (but not on radio) along the lines of the American model with two presenters for the bulletin, one male, one female, and, henceforth, they would be journalists as well as mere readers. Again, I was encouraged to switch – and, seeing this as a brand-new challenge, I did, and became the on-screen partner of the serene Don Cockburn, a gentleman and true professional.

Then, my luck fairy stretched and dusted herself off. Roughly around this time, Cian Ó hÉigeartaigh left RTÉ to become features editor of *The Sunday Tribune,* a new newspaper being set up by a man named Hugh McLoughlin. Cian knew I had been an actor in a previous life and asked me if I would write a series of actor profiles for the new publication. I hesitated: I had no experience at all in written journalism and, given the RTÉ profile, failure would be very public and would leave me – and my employer – open to derision.

However, I agreed to give it a go. The first interview was with Donal McCann and came out all right, so I chanced the next one, and the next.

I did six in all before the paper ran into trouble and ceased publication. The *Irish Press*, in the person of its editor, Michael Keane, then asked me if I would continue writing these profiles for his paper – and if I would broaden the subjects to include more than the acting profession. So, with Nellie looking after the home front, I spent a very busy year, the extra money from the writing at last giving me a handle to deal properly with the debts still hanging over me from the marriage break-up. I could even see the possibility of paying off my mortgage early!

Some time around the end of 1982, the management in the RTÉ newsroom decided to abandon its two-presenter approach to the television bulletins. From my point of view, the promised journalistic side of the job had hardly kicked in and, although I thoroughly enjoyed Don's wise and drily humorous company, to me, a change in that direction would have been welcome.

This time, we gathered, our reincarnation would arise from the ashes of the old one as a sort of star *über*-presenter; we were all in a tizzy as to what would happen next and to whom.

The choice had not been announced when I got an astonishing phone call. Vincent Browne had bought the title of the defunct

Sunday Tribune and was relaunching it. Apparently, while on a plane, he had read an *Irish Press* interview I had done with the supermarket owner, Feargal Quinn. Would I come and have a chat?

This 'chat' was surreal. It took place at night in an office at *Magill* magazine on Merrion Row, in a poky, windowed attic, redolent of ageing paper – and beer fumes because of its situation above O'Donoghue's pub. Vincent Browne, whom I had never met before, looked tired and stressed (even his hair, standing on end, seemed frazzled).

He was sitting behind a desk. In front of him were several stacks of envelopes and, throughout the time I was there, he continued to write addresses on these and to stuff them with invitations to the launch of the newspaper. Although, at one stage, he mumbled an apology and said he hoped I understood that he had to get on with doing it, he seemed utterly uninterested in me and left virtually all of the talking to the man sitting beside him. This was Brian Trench, the prospective news editor for the resurrected entity.

I was bewildered – and, for a time, Brian Trench and I talked at cross-purposes. Given the Feargal Quinn reference, I had assumed that I had come there to be asked if I would write the occasional interview for the new *Tribune* and I had not yet decided how I felt about it. I liked writing for the *Press* and was loyal to it and to Michael Keane: I had been given great editorial freedom and was getting good feedback. I was not naïve enough to believe I could do similar work for both papers, so I was in 'wait-and-see' mode.

Yet my work for the *Irish Press* didn't feature in the way Brian Trench conducted our 'chat': he seemed to be inviting me to set out my stall. The penny dropped. This was a job interview, the tenor of which was, 'Now then, *you* tell *us* what you can do for us?'

'But...but...' I was flabbergasted at this development. I had never for a moment considered leaving RTÉ. Yes, I was ready for fresh challenges, but I had assumed I would find them within the organisation. I admired the skills, intelligence and wide knowledge of my colleagues in the newsroom and in the wider, technical areas, right down to the make-up department: on a busy day when nerves were jangled and the workload was huge, the gentle and expert ministering in that quiet place was as soothing and refreshing as a good massage. And when a big story was running, it was very exciting to be part of an 'all hands to the pump' ethos.

What's more, I liked the organisation. For instance, I had seen that, when it was dealing with staff in any kind of personal trouble, its attitude was humanitarian, so I had never shared the cynicism, dissatisfaction and grumbling about 'this place' that sometimes surfaced around me. I guess that my attitude to all subsequent work and conditions had been firmly set during those six brown months in my first job.

But now it was made clear to me that, since the launch of the new *Sunday Tribune* was imminent and the roster of named journalists had to be completed before the press releases went out, if they did decide to hire me, I would have no time to dither about my decision. There were shades of my move from Aer Lingus to the Abbey. I was in a state of shock when I left Merrion Row that night.

There was another consideration: my staff job in RTÉ was secure and pensionable. *The Sunday Tribune* had failed before; there was no guarantee that it would not fail again. Whatever about my own security, with two young children and a mortgage, did I have the moral right to do this?

By this time, Kevin Healy – he of RTÉ News Features – was now my partner. No longer an on-air broadcaster, he had become editor of his unit and was then further promoted to become a managing editor in the newsroom. His marriage had broken up in the same year as my own (and, ironically, we discovered that we had each married within ten days of one another) and in April 1979, he had moved into my house in Claremont Court. This truncation is deliberate. Whereas my first husband is now happily settled with his third wife in northern Illinois, where it is certain that no one except himself and his family will have heard of me, Kevin has a former wife and three children from their marriage. They do not deserve to be placed in a public spotlight and it won't be inflicted on them.

Kevin encouraged the move to the *Tribune*; Nellie, who had an obvious stake because she would have to adapt to the changes in the childminding schedule, said she'd go along with whatever I decided, and my parents, who had no say in the matter but who liked to be kept in the loop, gave mixed signals. My mother could not understand why I would give up what she saw as stardom under the bright lights of television; my father was perplexed ('What will she do next?'), but both, although alarmed at the extent of the risk, said tentatively it would probably work out all right.

I was given no time to weigh all this up before I was offered the job. I accepted: as ever, I could not resist the lure of something new while hoping fervently that if it did not work out, I had sufficient experience in the world of work to get something else. I would immediately, that same day, have to hand in my resignation to RTÉ – and beg for a waiver of the notice period.

That night I was watching for an opportunity to knock on the office door of Rory O'Connor, my newsroom boss, when he trumped me by calling me in. And, before I could blurt my own request, he told me that RTÉ had decided to award me the main newscasting position.

26

Transition Year

I surveyed the serious faces around the table at the editorial meeting of *The Sunday Tribune* and quailed. Picture Vincent Browne sitting alongside Gerald Barry, a colleague of mine who had made the jump from News Features in RTÉ and who was – and remains – a brilliant political pundit. There was Brian Trench, who now runs the Communications Department at Dublin City University, who was to be our news editor. There were Fintan O'Toole, Eamon Dunphy, Gene Kerrigan, sportswriters Paddy Agnew and David Walsh, the late and very highly regarded Mary Holland of *The Observer*, the economist Paul Tansey and Emily O'Reilly, now the Ombudsman.

'Women's issues' were to be covered by Deirdre McQuillan, currently the fashion editor of *The Irish Times*, she had been head-hunted away from the Abbey Theatre where she had been its dynamic PRO. If you examine that line-up, what you see is a gathering of stellar columnists, commentators and opinion-makers. Plus, they all had university degrees to back up their opinions.

I do not suffer from a shortage of personal opinions about public matters, or from a dearth of creative ideas – far from it – but, as I listened to the discussion about what we should and should not be covering and how we should be doing it, I was all too aware that in such company, my interventions would sound namby-pamby. Notwithstanding the passion of arguments about the way to handle individual stories, there was an underlying world-view consensus and I didn't, at that stage, have enough self-confidence to assert my own views, which did differ in some respects.

Most star journalists have a killer instinct: the human fate of the protagonists in their investigative stories can be immaterial because the story is the important thing. My inner killer is not dormant – he doesn't exist. As I have said elsewhere, I am afflicted with the-other-side-of-the-story empathy and find it impossible to quash this tendency. If, at some point, someone is on the receiving end of a pummelling from commentators – Michael Flatley, Judge Hugh O'Flaherty and, latterly, Bertie Ahern – my instinct is to jump in with a counter-balancing voice. I cannot seem to join a chorus of condemnation or mockery.

And I have always been fascinated by gutsy, over-the-top personalities who seem to attract particular scorn. Take Adele King – Twink – she has suffered from this snideness just because of the way she is. For me, though, the impact she makes was never more evident than when I saw her in the small Turkish town of Cesmé. I was there on behalf of *The Sunday Tribune* to cover a song contest she was to present, and was with Louis Walsh, Kevin Hough of RTÉ and Eddie Rowley, the music journalist with the *Sunday World*.

One early afternoon, we four adjuncts were wilting at an open-air café; it was anvil-hot, almost too hot to summon up any conversation – the sky was white. I became aware of a commotion behind me. I looked over my shoulder and there she came, wearing comprehensive war paint and a micro miniskirt, blonde hair-extensions in full sail, a white-booted mother ship with a flotilla of slavering Turks bobbing in her wake. To me, that kind of chutzpah is admirable.

I also think I am the only journalist in Ireland, possibly in Europe, who enjoyed interviewing the much-derided novelist Jeffrey Archer, and who did not give him a hard time in print. He was loquacious, personable, impeccably groomed – cuffs showing below the jacket sleeve at exactly the right length – and I found his assurance and unabashed self-belief to be highly entertaining. We talked – well, he talked, I listened – over lunch in Kite's Restaurant in Donnybrook, and he enjoyed the experience so much (he told me so) that he kept his limo ticking over outside for an hour longer than scheduled, thus discommoding the next interviewer on his publicity timetable. He didn't give a sugar about that; neither did he care in the slightest what I might or might not write about him or even about the book of short stories we had met to discuss. He was the brash epitome of self-belief and of 'living in the moment' and I found this curiously refreshing.

But that type of lengthy interview, on what was to become known as 'The People Page' was, again, to be my speciality much later into my tenure at the *Tribune*; at the start, my difficulties in trying to fit in to this new milieu were obvious. All of Vincent's instincts and journalistic drives have to do with his interest in politics, sport and, above all, digging into scandals and the underbelly of Irish society. He simply could not understand how anyone could be attracted to reading anything else, or to writing it.

He did accept that amongst the newspaper's potential readership there was a fluffy element that might enjoy what he disparagingly called 'lifestyle' features. He also knew that, for commercial reasons, he should accommodate them. But he had no grasp of how to serve up this froth, no personal interest in doing so and no enthusiasm for suggestions. His own intellect more than matched the brain-power with which he had surrounded himself and, even if some of the others, Gerald Barry, for instance, did rate stories outside the politics/sport/scandal axis, our editor's dogged, mercurial and – when he wanted something badly enough – persuasive personality was all-conquering. Vincent confused human-interest stories with gossip unless they were about personal hardship and societal deprivation.

So having hired me, he didn't know what to do with me and, for a while, I didn't know what to do with me either. My only experience in written journalism had been those 'big' interviews and profiles but no one, it seemed, was interested in that skill now.

For the first year, perhaps even longer, I had no natural domicile at the newspaper and was writing only bits and pieces in the 'soft' areas, a few paragraphs here, a few there: the Cahirmee Horse Fair at Buttevant; a whale carcass washed up at Bonmahon in County Waterford; a spin around the Mondello Race Track in a Formula Three Ford.

I became the universal substitute, to be sent on to the pitch when necessary. Vincent had bowed to the legitimate demands of the sales and advertising department to include the despised lifestyle element in the paper and, before the advent of the formidable Helen Lucy Burke, I was even, briefly, a restaurant critic. I don't think I traduced the reputations of the restaurants I reviewed, God love them, at least I hope not. Because if ever there was someone who should *not* be a restaurant critic, that person is me. Like most people, I like food, but I do not consider it to be a religious experience. I'm hungry, I eat, end of story. If the food is terrific, it's merely a bonus.

Sometimes, the substitutions turned out to be wonderful, though. On one occasion when Donal Byrne, our motoring correspondent, was unavailable for the launch of a sporty Ford Escort, I was sent in his place, and what a revelatory trip that proved to be.

Our group of hacks, fewer than two dozen, was flown to Málaga in a full-sized commercial Boeing. In the five-star Puente Romana Hotel, we were each given a marble suite where we found thoughtful Ford gifts on our pillows. And then, after a five-star dinner and a wonderful breakfast the following morning, we were sent off in the crisp sunshine from the forecourt of the hotel by mechanics who had fine-tuned the selection of cars to pinpoint responsiveness. Mine was a souped-up Cabriolet in which, with another journalist, I had an entire day of top-down driving, of flinging the thing around the sinuous road curves in the mountainous hinterland behind the sparkling coastline, of pulling in to admire the heart-stopping beauty of Ronda, one of the 'white villages' of that region, perched on the rim of its gorge. Somewhere there exists a snapshot of me sitting waist-deep in a sunny field starred with ox-eye daisies; it typifies the enjoyment of that glorious outing. I hope the piece I wrote did justice to the wonderful car too!

So square-peggery does have its occasional compensations but, in general, I continued to flounder.

I certainly did not blame anyone except myself for these doldrums: my constant companion, the cursed little person who, deep in the base of my brain, runs a continuous commentary on my character and my performance, was becoming tiresomely vociferous: *You're not pulling your weight in this company. Do something about it.*

He didn't have to keep nagging. I knew it was up to me to break the impasse – it was a matter of finding a way. Not for a moment did I regret making the move from RTÉ: it's not my style. Take responsibility for the action and move on. I was going to make this work, come hell or high water.

So, in an effort to find some sort of productive niche for myself, I went back to basics, played to what I perceived to be my journalistic strengths and took my first tentative steps in this direction by inter viewing the tenor Nicolai Gedda. Other personal interviews followed, Vincent himself suggesting one with Joan FitzGerald, the wife of Garret, then Taoiseach.

The breakthrough happened in October 1984. It was fundamentally life-changing and occurred almost by accident.

In common with the rest of the world, I was riveted by the first appalling sight of the Ethiopian famine of that year as shown to us on television by the BBC through the seminal reports of its correspondent, Michael Buerk.

Tony Ryan of GPA, Guinness Peat Aviation, who had been one of the founding investors in the revamped *Sunday Tribune*, had been as affected as everyone else who saw those pictures and he had responded immediately with the offer of one of his planes to fly relief supplies. This report was carried on RTÉ's *Nine O'Clock News* as a rider to the ongoing story of the famine.

Reflexively, I jumped to the telephone and rang Vincent. 'We should be on that plane.'

'Good idea. I'll set it up with Tony Ryan. You'll have to get vaccinations and so on—'

'Ah, no,' I actually laughed in disbelief, 'that's not the reason I rang, Vincent. I wasn't talking about *me* going—'

'Why not?' He cut across me.

I was stumped. It had not occurred to me that this would happen. I had rung only to suggest that the *Tribune* should get the story – and had assumed that if the trip could be arranged, one of the stars would go. It was a huge story: it should be given huge treatment.

But Vincent was quietly adamant. 'When's the flight going?'

According to the news bulletin, it was already loading and due to leave within thirty-six hours…

As I replaced the receiver, I knew that this was my turn to step up to the plate. My transition year was over and, if I had any journalistic or descriptive talents at all, now was the opportunity to test them.

But, more importantly, those poor, damned people did not deserve what was happening to them. The responsibility was enormous – and I have to admit that I was deeply fearful for all kinds of reasons. First of all, would I let those people down? Would I let the paper down? I had never done anything like this or on such a scale; I had never seen a dead body, much less what Michael Buerk's pictures showed.

I also had a personal responsibility to my two little boys, even greater than any professional obligation. They would be fine with Nellie looking after them, but suppose I caught some awful disease and died out there? What would happen to them? Was it ethical of me to place myself into that type of danger? Would Kevin believe this was irresponsible?

In the course of his own reporting work, Kevin had covered some very upsetting stories, both in Ireland and abroad. He had served for a long time as a reporter in Northern Ireland at the height of the Troubles, where he had literally dodged bullets. He had wangled his way into Bobby Sands' wake. He had covered the Stardust disaster, the massacre of the Israeli athletes at the Munich Olympics, the Aldo Moro murder in Italy, and was a key broadcaster during the Monasterevin siege where Dr Tiede Herrema was being held captive by Eddie Gallagher. He had dashed through the night to report on the conflagration at San Carlos de la Rapida, where most of the holiday-makers at a Spanish campsite had been incinerated in a flash fire caused by the lunch-time crash of a truck laden with bottled gas. During the rollover, some of the gas had leaked, the vapours had flowed across dozens of lit barbecues and virtually the entire site had exploded. He says that, to this day, the odour of that charred place and its victims remains in his nostrils. He was out the night I was deciding what to do, but he would certainly have advice about covering a huge story.

It was coming up to Hallowe'en and the shops around Glasnevin were full of seasonal goodies. Having learned of what I was about to do, Adrian and Simon, who were eleven and nine years old respectively, gave me a large plastic bag full of raisins and nuts to take with me. They had seen the television pictures and they were worried that I, too, would starve.

For a time the next day, it appeared that I would not be able to go. As soon as the flight had been publicly announced, journalists – including a crew from RTÉ – had scrambled for the limited number of places, but this was an aid flight, to be packed with medicines, food and blankets. The more human bodies on board, the less aid.

I had a sneaking sense of relief. I had made the gesture, shown willing. It was not my fault if now there was no space for me. The doctor who had done some of the vaccinations and given me a prescription for the malaria medication had told me gravely that I was taking an 'unnecessary risk' with my health since there would not be time to give me all the vaccinations or for the malaria protection to become active. I would have to forgo protection against hepatitis and tetanus.

I had telephoned a neighbour of my brother's, a man who had spent many years in Ethiopia, to ask for his advice. Patiently, P.J. Byrne had explained that I must not be shocked at the sight of running sewage on the main streets of Addis Ababa, or think it strange that men and women urinated and defecated into them in full public view. If I saw a stick on the ground, I was not to pick it up because it was probably a snake. If a snake bit me, I was to run after it, kill it and bring the body to the nearest hospital for analysis. This might be a problem, however, because there was probably no hospital within running distance and, anyhow, if the snake was deadly, I had seven steps to stagger before I fell.

Others warned me about scorpions – 'always knock your shoes out before putting them on' – deadly spiders and TB. And, although I had been vaccinated against cholera, typhoid and yellow fever, I was still to watch out for a list of their symptoms. Then there were dysentery, amoebae (intestinal parasites), 'ordinary' worms, head and body lice…

Somehow, a seat was found for me on the plane and, to brief me, Vincent took me for a coffee to the Georgian Fayre opposite the *Tribune* premises on a corner of Baggot Street. For more than an hour, he filled me in on the history and politics of Ethiopia, the war between it and Eritrea to the north, the legacy of Haile Selassie, the current policies of the regime then in power, the Dergue. He widened the scope of his monologue to include the role of the UN, America and Russia, the general plight of the nations in the Horn of Africa…

As the coffee-shop staff clattered around us, cleaning up biscuit and pastry crumbs, I struggled to make sense of it all and, in an effort to commit the unfamiliar terms, systems and names to memory, concentrated desperately. This wasn't easy, not only because of the density of the information but because, frequently, someone from our own staff would stop by to discuss something or to seek an urgent decision.

Then, Vincent did a typical Vincent thing. He stopped talking and, obviously deep in thought, gazed through the plate-glass window towards the scruffy wall at the side of our own building.

I braced myself for more names and even deeper analysis, but after a few seconds he looked directly at me and imparted what turned out to be the best journalistic advice I've ever received and by which, professionally, I have tried to live: 'Now forget all that,' he said. 'Forget everything I've just said. Go there and keep your eyes and ears open.'

27

Speaking the Words

'Hell is not other people,' I wrote, 'or even a poet's vision. It is real and its innermost circle is the intensive feeding shed at Korem Camp in Tigre province, Ethiopia.'

I took Vincent Browne's advice literally. Except for recording the names of people and places, from the time we left Addis Ababa in two jeeps to travel north into the famine areas, I took virtually no notes – to the surprise, perhaps consternation, of Father Jack Finucane of Concern who was acting as guide to our group. We were there specifically to report on what was happening to the wider world and I'd say he thought I was an imposter. He confirmed later that he had been a little worried.

But I knew from the first minute that what I saw, heard, felt, touched and tasted during that trip would not leave me for the rest of my life. In this context, writing, conducting interviews, would be a distraction; I had to be free to walk in the shoes of people who had nothing.

They have nothing – it is a phrase glibly trotted out, but 'nothing' in the context of the 1984 Ethiopian famine was literal. No food. No shelter. No cooking utensils. Nothing except the filthy rags dangling over fingers and skinny shins, nothing to carry except people. Nothing to touch except the wasted frames of your children and no water to cleanse the thick film of dust from their mouths, eyes and noses.

If I'd been busily writing, I probably would not have properly registered the immensity of the horizon-to-horizon dustbowl through which we jolted for hour after hour, or its monochromatic brownness: the fertile earth of this place, once called the breadbasket of Africa, had crumbled to a powder as fine as flour. I would not have noticed, when we stopped for a break, that the only sound disturbing the profound silence was the ticking from the cooling engine blocks of the jeeps. Although we had heard crickets before we moved into the famine regions, nothing moved there except ourselves and the roaming dust devils, tornado-like genies with no bottles to contain them. No birds. No wildlife. Everything had been eaten or had died of starvation.

It was after dark when we arrived at a recently erected camp called Harbo, the gates of which, in our headlights, seemed oddly placed behind an uneven, tussocky bank of earth. But, as we stopped, this hillock, like Birnam Wood, seemed to be moving. It emitted a continuous, low-pitched hum. Thousands of people were crammed together in the cold, moonless dark while they waited for the gates of the feeding sheds to open at dawn.

What notes might have captured the panicked expression in an individual's eyes as the throngs were finally let in the next morning, to be corralled for assessment as to who would be admitted for intensive feeding and who would not yet be considered malnourished enough? Or the emptiness in the eyes of the stick-wielding guards, who were probably hungry too, as they whacked at the heads and shoulders of men, women or children who had the temerity to step out of line next morning when the gates opened and the weighing commenced.

The thud of wood on bone would not need recording.

> The guards are local men. They are as gentle as they can be while maintaining order amongst the herds. Once a mother with four children moved out of her corral. The guard brandished his stick and caught one of the little ones on the side of the face, cutting it open. The child stopped, blankly looking at the blood as it dripped onto his hands. The mother began to cry quietly.
>
> The guard, too, was upset. Again and again, he came back to look at the child's bloody face. Another guard moved the little group back into the crowd.

With two other Concern nurses, the heroic Moira Conroy, a woman with formidable project-managing skills and the professional detachment to make the hard choices as to whom to admit and whom to refuse, had organised this camp in three working days. She had discovered that one child had measles, another infectious hepatitis; if their isolation had been too late, half of the children there would die.

On the day she opened her gates, there were already 1,000 waiting outside. On the second day, there were 5,000 and there were 9,000 today. She explained that, without the guards, none but the healthiest would get food, blankets or any kind of medical attention.

The weighing is done on a sort of meat hook. The older ones are lifted onto it and are told by one of the helpers to clutch tightly. One or two are too weak and they fall off. The babies are put into canvas slings suspended from the hook. They cry feebly if they have the strength.

They are measured full length on a wooden cradle. One boy of about twelve years old, whose shin would fit inside a circle made by my index finger and thumb, has to be lifted onto it. His eyes are wide with fright. A pulse beats furiously at the base of his throat.

These days, with satellite television and news crews with twenty-four-hour commitments continuously roving the world from disaster to disaster, we have become accustomed, even inured, to seeing fly-encrusted eyes and walking skeletons on our screens. We were not used to it in 1984; certainly I wasn't.

A man approaches me. He has a small child with him. He makes the sign for hunger – slowly patting his breast (you are white, you must be able to do something). There are vertical lines on his sunken belly. This man was once a citizen with a well-fed stomach. Now, in rags, with not a single possession, he comes up to a foreign white journalist begging for a biscuit.

Farmers, merchants and professionals must be herded like cattle and controlled like cattle, because, at the sight of a food truck or a bale of blankets, they surge forward. Like cattle, they stampede. So the men with sticks bang the ground and they jump backwards if they are able.

If I had been a film-maker at that camp, I would have searched for a few shots to counterpoint the bleakness, the suffering, and all that brownness – and then, in all their incongruity, I found them.

Every person registered for feeding was given a personal blanket from donated bales. When one bale from America was opened, it erupted gaily in a multicoloured profusion of handcrafted quilts, magnificent examples of the quilters' art. The contrast between Harbo Camp, where progress was measured by whether or not the open latrines had been dug, and the homes of the people who lovingly made those quilts, could not have been more stark.

Even in the most desperate of circumstances, however, individuality will out; when Foxford rugs were being distributed from the Irish bales, one woman gave hers back. She was dissatisfied. She had wanted a red one.

> In the compound, outside a shelter, a little group is being filmed by RTÉ. They are a father, a mother and three children. Marama, one of the daughters, is five years old. She looks about two. Yesterday, when she came in, Moira Conroy tried for hours to get her to take some food, but without success. Now Marama lies under a piece of sacking, her eyes like milky opals and only half open. Her father is wiping away the froth as it bubbles from her mouth. Marama dies quietly, making no sound. Her eyes close gently, that is all.

We were filming and taking pictures. Well-motivated as I was, knowing that without journalists like Michael Buerk – and now us – the world would have continued to ignore the plight of these people, I nevertheless felt our presence to be horribly intrusive on an occasion of private grief. As Marama's mother, squatting beside her, rocked back and forth, the tiny girl's father watched us politely, waiting for us to finish. I couldn't bear it and had backed off before he picked up her corpse and walked away with it.

The scene was being replicated all over this camp.

Next was Korem Camp, run by an unofficial co-operative comprising Concern, Save the Children, the Ethiopian Red Cross and World Vision. This was the planet after the apocalypse. The total numbers, those who had gained entrance and those outside waiting, exceeded 100,000. Think of Croke Park packed to the rafters, with 20,000 at the stiles pushing to get in. The difference was that in Korem everyone was starving and owned nothing.

Thousands more were arriving by the day.

That day, the queue for the water pump was about 300 yards long. It took four or five hours to get to the top of the queue. The containers were diverse. Some had only sardine cans.

The situation was improving, though: the administrator showed us the register. The improvement meant that only forty-two people had died by ten that morning.

And then the intensive feeding shed. There is no adjective suitable for it in the English language. This is the ultimate degradation. Five children sit on a bed staring at a dish of fafa. They are too apathetic to eat.

A dying boy twitches on the floor. In the last throes of life there is no bed for him. His lips have already drawn back from his teeth, like those of a cadaver discovered in a bog.

A volunteer is trying to force liquid in between the teeth of a beautiful young woman. She succeeds in getting a little in, but heaving, the woman rejects it and vomits over the floor. Three minutes later, she dies. The count is now forty-four.

On the return trip from Korem, we found a corpse by the roadside and stopped. He wasn't dead, not yet. We took him to Alamata, a camp run by the Daughters of Charity.

He was a tall, beautiful man in his twenties. The attendant who lifted him out of our jeep at the camp was about 5'4" and slight. He put the stricken man across his shoulder in a fireman's lift. The man's bewildered eyes looked back at me as he was borne away. He may have been a farmer. He may have had a family. No one knew.

Back in Addis Ababa, our group ran into the smugly fat Robert Maxwell who, attended by lackeys, was holding court in the lobby of the Hilton Hotel. His *Daily Mirror* had run in an aid flight of its own and he, waving, was pictured on his own front page as he emerged from it. He had come personally to Addis to hail and pro-claim the generosity of *Mirror* readers and, wearing immaculate shirts and sharp tailoring, to dispense wisdom to the run-ragged aid agencies as to what should now be done.

We were billeted in the Hilton too. I stayed up all the first night, working on my little portable typewriter what I had seen. Next morning, I dictated my report down a scratchy telephone line to a tape recorder in Vincent Browne's office. It took almost an hour. I held out until almost the end, but just as one can get through a reading at the funeral of a beloved friend until the last line, by the time I had finished, I was hoarse and in tears. I had not wept at all during the days on the road, or even while I was writing, but somehow, hearing myself speaking the words brought the horrors into sharp focus and undid me.

Vincent came on the line. As I had continued to dictate, he had brought Gerry Barry and some others into his office to listen. They were all anxious about me, he said, appalled at what I had been through: he told me I should not come straight home; instead, I should go to the Maldives or the Seychelles to recuperate at the newspaper's expense – 'Take a week. Take two weeks.'

I thanked him for his offer but declined it. We argued a little but I knew that, as a mere observer, what I had 'been through' was piffle compared to the plight of hundreds of thousands, perhaps millions, of people facing unnecessary death because of the inaction, corruption, and warmongering of their government and the self-regarding politics of the rest of the world. A luxurious holiday would have seemed inappropriate, almost obscene. Anyhow, I was feeling ill. Having survived stepping inadvertently into a puddle of diarrhoea in one of the camps, those internal parasites had finally got me via the food in the capital. I wanted to get home to my family.

Pat Langan, the photographer for *The Irish Times*, and I were given a lift back from Addis Ababa to Ireland in an Aer Turas cargo plane. There were no seats and it was a propeller aircraft so the journey was a very long one but, with cushions, Pat and I made nests in the cavernous interior on the floor just behind the pilots' seats. During that flight, we discussed how we could help in some practical way with what we had just experienced.

The result was *The Dark Hunger* – less a book than a rant – put together from conception to bookshelf in less than eleven days: my text, Pat's photographs, layout and subediting by Andy Barclay, the chief subeditor of the *Tribune,* who pulled all-nighters with me to get the job done. Vincent Browne organised it. The Taoiseach, Garret FitzGerald, launched it. The full cover price of £5 was for Concern and it sold out.

That trip changed for ever my perceptions of my own world, where, on our arrival home from Ethiopia, there was a strike in prospect: a group of workers were not satisfied with the level of 'disturbance money' they were being offered to move 400 yards from dilapidated premises to plush new ones.

To put this in perspective, I remembered our second visit to Harbo Camp, five days after its inception and two days after we had first visited. Our arrival on that fifth day had coincided with that of five orphans. Their father had died the previous day while walking his family through the dustbowl. Their mother had died three hours ago, almost within reach of the camp. The children weren't clear how long they had walked; the estimate by others in the camp was perhaps the guts of a week. The oldest, who was nine, had carried the baby for those last three hours while shepherding his three other siblings. At nine years of age, this child had made the decision to leave his mother where she lay.

To maintain my sanity in the face of the contrasts between what was perceived as hardship in Ireland versus the actual living conditions in huge tracts of Africa, I held on to the evidence of what had been achieved at Harbo by just three women in an Irish organisation. Although the bush telegraph was very active – and although along-side our five orphans, the weaker on the backs of the stronger continued to arrive in great numbers – inside, everything was calm and organised. The people had been separated and housed in group shelters according to their local village structures in the charge of an appointed leader. Everyone had been fed twice on the fourth day and they would be fed twice again that day. Moira Conroy and two other Concern nurses had achieved this.

And every time the thought or sight of the continuing suffering in Ethiopia threatened to plunge me into despair, I held even more tightly to the following image: a corral of toddlers, 1,000 strong, all under six years old. They had survived and recovered. They were waiting for their Liga.

> ... they sit in a tightly packed, patient and bubbling rectangle. They cheer and wave as you approach. One two year old crawls out, eager to give her personal greeting, and is hauled back by another tot, who could not be more than three. You wave, they wave. You take their photograph, they cheer. You thank them and clap your hands, they clap their hands. Thereafter, anyone who takes their photograph gets a round of applause.

28

'The People Page'

Some time during that trip, word filtered through that I had received the first 'Woman Journalist of the Year' award, sponsored by the ESB.

I was obviously delighted when I was told about it, but I was watching children die and avoiding paddling pools of diarrhoea, so I didn't fully grasp what an honour I had been given. I certainly didn't dwell on it.

This sense of dislocation persisted in the days immediately after I returned to Ireland when, still in a lather of indignation about famine in a world where food was dumped and governments spent trillions on armaments, I was intent only on proselytising for Africa and Concern through *The Dark Hunger*. It was not until it dawned on me that I had been judged by a panel of high-profile journalists, people like Colm Tóibín and Michael Mills of the *Irish Press*, whom I greatly respected, that the accolade began to sink in.

Vincent Browne rates work rather than awards, but he was complimentary and, although I have no way of knowing whether it did or not, I believe the honour did help, at least peripherally, in securing my 'People Page' slot at the paper and with which I became identified. It probably did not hurt that the award was given for the Joan FitzGerald piece that Vincent had suggested. (A couple of years later, I was very glad that his faith in allowing me freedom with that page was rewarded when I was given the gender-neutral 'Journalist of the Year' award for it.) 'The People Page' usually consisted of a long interview, up to 3,000 words, with a well-known person; the accompanying portrait was most often photographed by the marvellous John Carlos.

I devoted one six-month period exclusively to covering the Kerry Babies Tribunal, held at first in Tralee and then in Dublin Castle. Somewhat to my surprise, the late Judge Lynch agreed to allow me sit outside the public gallery in an open space between it, the legal benches and the witness box. I had made the case that, to show readers the full picture of what was going on, I needed to give them not only an accurate account of the legal proceedings, but of the attitudes of gardaí, witnesses, legal teams and the public present – and to do that well, I needed to *see* the reactions of all those people. I hadn't really expected him to accede to such an unusual request, but he did and, throughout, I found myself sitting in slightly isolated splendour in *my* chair.

Every prominent journalist in Ireland reported on that tribunal from time to time. On one occasion, Marian Finucane and I were having our tea in the local hotel. We were chatting away when a waitress came up and, blushing, asked us if we would mind talking to a local man (staring at us from another table) who wanted to ask us what we thought of a man being deprived of his heritage. From politeness, we agreed – and, as the waitress went off to give the man the good news, steeled ourselves for an onslaught of grievances.

But then she came back again. 'He wants to know which one of ye is Olivia O'Leary?'

Occasionally, 'The People Page' was used for feature pieces. For instance, the marriage of Prince Andrew and Sarah Ferguson – for which, irritatingly, protocol required that to enter Westminster Abbey and take my allocated place on the specially built gallery above the altar, I had to wear a hat. I have to say that, although my report on the event was necessarily about having a close-up view of the ceremony, Princess Diana's green, polka-dotted dress and the Royal Family (who, like any family at a wedding, bobbed and gossiped, smiled soppily and even wiped away a tear), I was far more impressed with the company I kept in our eyrie: Maeve Binchy, Jilly Cooper, Lynda Lee Potter, Marge Proops *et al.* And the music was magical.

My report from Bangladesh for that page could not have been more different. To cover that year's floods, the worst in decades, I travelled again with Concern; the organisation maintains a permanent, Sisyphean presence there.

I had thought I had seen the nadir of human experience in Ethiopia, but I am still at a loss accurately to describe what I felt about my experiences in Bangladesh. Culturally rich and enormously vibrant, yet, at the time I went there, it was officially the poorest place on earth. Periodic flooding of enormous tracts of its land mass is a fact of life in that country because of its situation on the low-lying delta (and floodplain) of three rivers, the Ganges, Brahmaputra and Meghna, plus their numerous tributaries. The loss of life and livelihood caused by these inundations is seen, even by those affected, as a consequence to be expected – but also as an opportunity: *'The recent floods also brought a boom in boat and bridge building. Local entrepreneurs charged tolls in some instances. Farmers became instant fishermen.'*

Mamma in her domain: the balcony of 'Room Maureen' in the Romantic Hotel, Sitges.

Mamma's seventy-fifth birthday, Addison Lodge, Glasnevin. One of the very few photographs of all four of us together.

Rob.

Miss Frost.

Walking up the aisle, Our Lady of Victories Church,
Ballymun, 19 January 1970.

Three actresses – all looking in different directions as actresses will.
The Bride, with Sinéad Cusack and Aideen O'Kelly.

An announcer.

Adrian, Simon and I, Glasnevin, 1976.

My partner, Don Cockburn, and I
in the newsroom.

Kevin Healy at his desk
in the newsroom.

Pat Langan, the Taoiseach Garret FitzGerald, myself and Vincent Browne at
the launch of *The Dark Hunger*, 1984.

With the marvellous John Carlos.   Have bags will travel.

A nice evening in Connemara. Gary Hart and friend.

On the road again, Montana, 1995.

'You'll Never Walk Alone'.

Happy Birthday to me!

Top: Old friends, Tramore, 1960. Above: Dublin Registry Office, 2001.

Or, during the four hours it took to free a Concern Land Rover from mud: *'a thriving industry grew up around it. Vendors erected makeshift tea stalls to refresh spectators. Relays of rickshaws ferried them in and out to the scene…'*

Notwithstanding these flurries of positivity, I wrote about the underlying devastation in terse sentences, which, I can see now, barely conceal the consternation, mixed with rage, I felt about the permanent poverty, deprivation and the unimaginable overcrowding. A country only fifty per cent larger than the state of Wisconsin in the US, Bangladesh had to support a population of more than 120 million when I was there. (The World Health Organisation has estimated that it had risen to 146 million by 2005. Population density is now more than 1,000 people per square kilometre. It is still growing.)

Worst off were the Bihari people, a relatively small group, who consider themselves Pakistani and speak Urdu rather than Bangla. They were trapped in Bangladesh at independence in 1971, cut off from what they consider to be their homeland.

> In Halishahar camp, there are two latrines for about
> 330 people. The latrines are useless because they are
> overflowing. At Sardar Bahadur, the steps into the
> former school are slimy with ordure and there are faeces
> on the courtyard. Some have been living this way for
> sixteen years. They say they are very hungry.

So I wrote as factually and in the most restrained manner that I could manage, about the deliberately maimed beggars, the use and almost casual abuse of women, who were beaten by their menfolk in full sight of the passing crowds on the streets of Dhaka who gave them barely a glance. And in order not to get myself verbally into trouble while I was there, I had to force myself constantly not to see this country in light of my bourgeois western values. I was constantly reminding myself that this was a place with different norms of acceptable behaviour, culturally, religiously and caste-based. Concern had great difficulty, for instance, in finding a teacher willing to work in a school that the volunteers were trying to set up in a low-caste Hindu sweepers' colony. And I tried to keep my mouth shut about the cafés full of men drinking coffee while, at many of the capital's searingly hot street corners, women with children on their backs spent their days breaking bricks with small hammers.

Concern's work in Bangladesh ('Better to light a candle, etc...') concentrated on educational initiatives, co-ops and health centres. Culturally and politically aware, the organisation trod delicately and slowly and, where possible, concentrated on women. Each small success, where women earned their own money for the first time – say, in an embroidery co-operative – meant that, in the words of one volunteer, 'There is no way these women will go back to being the second-class citizens they were.'

If this all sounds discouraging, it is only fair to point out that there is now a smidgen of hope. Herculean efforts have been made to improve the situation, by international governments, aid agencies and the country's own rulers. Although, according to a report from the USAID organisation, half of the population subsists on the equivalent of US$1 a day, the general economy is now growing very fast – the projection for 2006 was six-and-a-half per cent. Literacy rates have improved, there is a birth-control programme in place and direct foreign investment in industry, particularly in garment making, is growing exponentially.

Bangladesh does enjoy one priceless asset: its people. Subjected to living conditions that would not be tolerated for one day by even the most deprived of our own communities, the combination of resilience, resourcefulness, entrepreneurial drive and coruscating hope that seems to drive the personalities of these 'poorest of the poor' is extraordinary.

Even the professional beggars in this largely Muslim country, where alms-giving is a duty, could make a relatively decent living and guarded their patches with ferocity. Two Concern volunteers tried, at one point, to 'help' a deformed polio sufferer who lay half-in and half-out of a stinking gutter. They 'helped' him physically to climb out of it, to find themselves roundly abused and chased away, leaving him to crawl back in and resume earning his livelihood.

Yet poverty is relative to the circumstances of your surroundings, I suppose. The women I met when I went visiting with 'The Vincent' in Dublin at the end of the 1980s had solid roofs over their heads, but they were far more depressed than any Bangladeshi individual I had encountered, and felt far more hopeless. In many ways, I found this even more dispiriting to write about because of the dead expressions in those women's eyes.

> Her baby, who is not yet two years of age, sits under the kitchen table. She has nine children, all less than eleven years old. The Vincent lady has four blankets for her, which is really not enough because she has had to take the curtains off the windows to put on the beds. Her kids were OK this morning, they got cornflakes. But this was only Friday. 'Come Tuesday and you're worrying because there's nothing for the breakfast on Wednesday.' But the girl next door is very good, she gets her money on a Tuesday and she will always lend a few slices of bread on a Tuesday night.

And it was mostly women who were having to cope: in thrall to money-lenders and pedlars who toured the estates with cars and vans filled with saucepans, towels and kitchen necessities for 'just' £2 per week at an authorised interest rate of up to 150 per cent – or more. From accommodating butchers, they bought a few neck bones at tenpence each and ham hocks, at three for the pound, which, along with a packet of oxtail soup and potatoes, would make a stew to feed up to a dozen people for Sunday dinner. They broke up furniture to burn in their fireplaces because they owed the coalman too much and he had put his foot down – and then had nowhere to sit except on the bare linoleum floors. One woman spent every penny she had on bus fares to take her injured child to an A&E and was brusquely turned away and told to go to Temple Street because her child was too young to be treated. But then she had no money for the bus fare from Beaumont to Temple Street.

Following publication of this piece, which was printed at Christmastime, goods and financial donations poured in to both The Society of St Vincent de Paul and to our own offices in Baggot Street. So my work, which I did for its own sake, had resulted in decent consequences. Or so I thought. Alongside the money and the soft toys came some letters, personally to me, that aimed to let me know in trenchant language how gullible I was; how the wool had been pulled over my eyes and those of 'the Vincent'; that 'these people' were spongers who had never had it so good and who hid stuff when the Vincent was due.

In the course of my work for 'The People Page', I met some really good people; the Finucane priests, brothers Aengus and Jack, who individually or together could have run a multinational corporation for their own enrichment but who, instead, devoted their skills and talents to Concern for the benefit of the oppressed and poor of the

Third World; the eccentric but brilliant psychiatrist Professor Ivor Browne; Alice Leahy of Trust, the 'no conditions' charity for the homeless; Sister Stan of Focus, another who could run the world but who chose the 'better part'.

And Gordon Wilson, whose noble attitude towards those who had killed his daughter in the Enniskillen bombing became one of the few lights shining through the darkness of that awful time in the North of Ireland.

The process of writing for 'The People Page' was in two parts. The first involved transcribing every single word of the tape-recorded encounter, a physically wearisome process that took sometimes up to three days, depending on how much time the interviewee had given me.

It does sound excessive, but while I was actually talking to someone, I was engaged in keeping things going, in extracting information, and not only about current ventures or whatever image the interviewee was bent on projecting. I was trying to construct an impression of the whole person without being intrusive or aggressive. So during that plodding transcription, tape after tape, a sense of the person beneath the conversation emerged between the gaps. The pauses and hesitations became as telling as the words, in many cases far more so.

So when I came to write the actual piece from the transcription, I had a head start on where to begin and, having listened so carefully, how to illustrate the personality with the tone and pace of the words.

Having met him just once, and quite briefly, this method allowed me to see, for instance, that the politician in the streetwise Monsignor Horan of County Mayo was more than equal to the priest. He was on the runway to greet John Carlos and me when in a light plane we flew to Knock to claim the distinction for the *Sunday Tribune* of being the first quasi-commercial flight to land there. Up to that time, it been used as a sort of speedway; for a small financial consideration, local buses had been allowed to whizz 'runway tourists' up and down its considerable length. Unfortunately, it seemed hardly any time had passed before I was flying there again with members of the Monsignor's parish, this time with his body in the hold of the Aer Lingus jet bringing him home from Lourdes.

And, of course, I did interview actual politicians, almost all of whom I liked. When I drilled down past the constituency-serving, seat-keeping, power-jockeying propaganda, there was a lot of evidence that, alongside the Big Fish syndrome, what had attracted them to politics in the first place was a genuine desire to help improve the lot of society in general: Ken Livingstone, Barry Desmond, Garret FitzGerald, Michael D. Higgins, Gemma Hussey, the late Brian Lenihan. I realise that, because of the fetid regard in which politicians are held today, I am open to the charge that my Pollyanna tendency is getting the better of me here, but I would robustly defend this theory. I am convinced that, as a nation, if we don't stop ridiculing and castigating individual politicians, as opposed to political policies, which are fair game, we will succeed in frightening off the genuine altruists. And then we will truly have the government we deserve.

29

The Good, the Great and the Gigglers

I am frequently asked who the most impressive person I interviewed during this period was and I always hesitate, because, in some sense, choosing one seems to relegate all the others, each of whom was genuinely special to me at the time.

My first interviewee for *The Sunday Tribune* made an impression on me that he could not have foreseen. Just as I was shocked by Emer O'Kelly's revelation of how she saw me as the direct opposite of how I saw myself, I was taken aback by the honesty of Nicolai Gedda, the world-famous tenor, who confessed that, despite what everyone else said, the reviews he got for the records he made, or how many audiences rose to applaud him during a lifetime dedicated to his art, he felt he was a failure.

This was not the only surprise. The interview was held on an afternoon prior to an evening recital in the National Concert Hall;

I had found out that he was staying in the Shelbourne Hotel and had rung speculatively just after lunch-time.

I had little hope of his agreeing to see me; after all, the interview was not going to be published until the following Sunday when it would have no bearing on ticket sales. To my surprise, when I asked for him, the hotel operator put me straight through to his room. He had answered the phone himself and immediately agreed to meet me within the hour. And when, after the interview, I asked this globally renowned artist why, when he should be resting, he had been so obliging, he floored me with his response. Looking surprised, he said, 'But it would be rude to refuse!'

Two lessons then, both of which have stood to me in public and private life ever since: courtesy is prime, and it is unwise to equate public and private perceptions.

I enjoyed almost all of the interviews, hugely so in some cases: Mike Murphy, with his wicked and very creative sense of humour springs immediately to mind, as does the late singer Frank Patterson, whose sunny confidence and childlike delight in his own achievements and those of his family were marvellous to behold. The pianist John O'Conor, Brush Sheils, T.P. McKenna, the Spillane footballers, whom I met while covering the Kerry team's three-in-a-row football success, during which I was told, quite seriously, by an official in the Croke Park tunnel what a privilege it was for a lady journalist to be let in there. I really liked the actor Gabriel Byrne, Cathal O'Shannon, Pat Kenny, whose public persona hides an inner sweetness and decency, Daniel O'Donnell, Bishop Walton Empey – the list goes on and includes anyone with a great laugh. In my mind, I have grouped them under the heading 'The Gigglers'.

The Greats include (inevitably) Bono, who met me in the Blue Light pub. He was already hugely famous, but, at that time, just for his music. And although there is no need to add my tuppence worth to the canon of encomia about him and his subsequent work for the world, I truly felt that day that I was in the presence of someone extraordinary. I told him I thought he could be a superb actor; I still think that.

I was never enamoured of the group interviews, where perhaps a dozen of us were ferried in, under a PR minder's supervision, to talk to Barbara Bush about 'women' and about visiting Ireland, or to Charlton Heston about his forthcoming movie. The promotions trail has to be dreary for the stars: the same permutations and combinations of questions and answers all the time, back-to-back interviews with journalists passing like cans of peas on an assembly line. Heston at least worked hard at it:

> Mr Heston mints the words freshly each time, even if he has said them a trillion times before. He acts his interviews. Here he is on Ego versus Vanity 'Everyone has an ego. Actors need a very strong ego. But the condition of celebrity is dangerously seductive and corrosive...'
>
> The words, considered, pondered, drawn, were first spoken on *The Gay Byrne Show* just three hours previously, but not a comma seems to be rehearsed.

In general, none of us ever got close to interesting material in that situation; the only hope you had of writing anything decent was if your personal impressions were apt.

There were occasional and unexpected exceptions. In the case of John Denver, I happened to be sitting beside him at an organised lunch in Manchester, during which he gave a dutiful but lacklustre talk about his songwriting and his forthcoming concert tour that was to include Ireland. At the coffee stage, even as the PR person was hinting broadly that it was time we wrapped up, in desperation I lobbed in a couple of off-message questions about skiing. Denver fired up dramatically, and we caught a glimpse of a different man as he rhapsodised about snow, skies and the feelings of sensual freedom engendered by going off-piste. The PR person cut in to tell us, this time firmly, that our time was up. The others were already rising from their seats when I asked him about the space programme: he had been awarded NASA's Public Service Medal and it was rumoured that he had booked a seat on the next space shuttle. Now, despite the PRO's urging him to leave, Denver seized my wrist and poured his heart out about space and the future of space travel, then, speaking faster and faster, segued into his ardent convictions about peace and the state of East–West relations.

I realised that music was no longer this man's primary passion and was confirmed in my view that communal publicity lunches were as much of a penance for the stars as they were unproductive for us. Denver was still talking over his shoulder as he was finally borne away to his next appointment.

Generalisations are dangerous, but I did discover during the course of that work that while most women, however open they seemed and however intimate their confidences, were very much in charge of their secrets, whereas my most forthcoming subjects were middle-aged men.

There were exceptions to this and they were almost invariably artists, usually those who no longer suffered from doubts about their roles in the world. Underneath the 'actressy' posture, I found Siobhán McKenna to be an extraordinary woman who could have achieved a lot in any arena of business or academia. I felt the same about Joan Baez, very beautiful and still as pure-skinned as a teenager, who, in continuing with her lifelong espousal of liberal causes, had, in her own mind, chosen the better part. And Edna O'Brien's focus, determination and dedication to putting her whole soul into not only her art but her image as a writer, to me indicated a steely, even phenomenal strength of character, not least because she persists in writing in longhand on high-grade paper using special pens and inks.

It's not difficult to see why the older men liked being interviewed: their wives and friends had no doubt heard every one of their most cherished anecdotes all too often, were over-familiar with their views on all subjects, and had long ago ceased to probe them about their innermost feelings. But now here was someone, albeit armed with a tape recorder, who was genuinely interested in them as individuals, who hadn't heard their stories before and who, for as long as it took, was prepared to listen to, even discuss, what they had to say. I was always cognisant of my responsibility here in not betraying secrets of a personal nature inadvertently revealed, although where either the media-savvy or politicians were concerned, I felt that they knew the game and didn't need too much minding.

Writers were fascinating to me. I didn't realise it at the time but I was probably attending a sort of serial creative-writing course by talking to them, although some of the lessons I learned were far from esoteric. For instance, I met Hammond Innes when he had just published a novel he had set in Greece. I was very impressed (a) with the notion that here I was, one on one in the tearoom of the Shelbourne Hotel with such a seriously famous and prolific author, but (b) with the 'feel' of Greece he managed to convey in his book. I had fancied that from those paperback pages, I had been able to smell goats and wild garlic; I could hear the sound of quiet Aegean surf on the beaches.

How had he managed this sensory feat? How long had he actually lived in Greece? What were the insider's writing tricks he used?

Innes, smallish, rotund, sitting with one of his little legs bent under him, reacted with astonishment to the question. He had not lived there, ever. He had only once been to the location he used for his novel. He bent his head conspiratorially towards mine, so closely I could see the red lacing in the whites of his eyes. 'What you do,' he said, 'is you take a cheap package holiday to wherever it is you want to write about. You hire a car as cheaply as you can. You buy a good map and a notebook and, for two weeks, you drive around. You stop every so often, at a beach or a bar or somewhere, and you write into your notebook what you see. Bushes and drinks, and so on.'

My memory may not be regurgitating that quote with absolute accuracy but I never forgot the essence and, when my own time came to do location research for novels, I put it gleefully into practice.

In many instances, I did not discover what I had been learning about fiction-writing until I took it up. For instance, the Pulitzer Prize-winning author William Kennedy (*Ironweed*) taught me the necessity for absolute solitude: 'You never know the value of not being interrupted until you're not interrupted.' And, on being asked to describe the so-called joy of writing, the playwright Tom Murphy didn't answer straight away but took time to consider. Then he related, simply, that the true joy arrives when you have sat down at the desk to write for maybe an hour but, when next you look at the clock, you find that six hours have gone by and you have no idea how that happened – that, in a sense, you have gone into another dimension.

I can attest to it: it does happen and leaves you feeling sated.

I believe that one of the reasons writers offer such a wealth of material to interviewers is not necessarily the complex imaginative life they lead – although that is a great plus if they allow you to access it – it is because, like actors, they are accustomed to mining their own lives, motives and experiences for material. In a sense, they are constantly gazing inwards as well as outwards, and when they are relaxed and willing to lift their personal security screens, virtually interview themselves with the aid of empathetic prompts.

Actors were not as easy. Because they were usually being interviewed in the context of publicity for a forthcoming show, they were very brightly 'on', while remaining simultaneously cautious about revealing too much of themselves in case what they said could give them a negative image in the minds of film producers moseying in Ireland and on the lookout for specific 'types'. Having been in the profession myself, however, I could recognise all those complexities, and worked hard to get underneath the public veneer.

This, of course, wasn't necessary in the case of those who no longer needed affirmative personal publicity. I met Dame Judi Dench in her dressing room at the National Theatre in London while she was getting ready for her performance that night as Cleopatra (with Anthony Hopkins as Antony) during a run of the Shakespeare play. With her Egyptian wig on a stand in front of her, she didn't give a hoot that the ugly under-wig binding covering her own hair made her look bald. She was comfortable and chatty, with an open, friendly expression in her cat's eyes. No 'side' to her at all.

In a similar dressing-room situation, I also interviewed Martin Sheen, latterly President Bartlet in *The West Wing*, who was appearing in *The Normal Heart*, one of the first stage plays to explore the dilemmas facing the gay community. He was passionate about his numerous liberal causes, eager to air them, particularly his anti-war work, and absolutely unconcerned about his own reputation, except in the context of how he could use it to gain publicity for his views and his play. I have to say, I adored him.

By contrast, Daniel Day Lewis, who was in rehearsal for his first outing as Hamlet, was beautifully mannered and charming but very wary, as tense as a cornered panther and quite obviously nervous about playing such an iconic role. I was very sad for him, but not all that surprised when he subsequently resigned from the production.

And what can I say about the late Richard Harris?

What can anyone say? The man was irresistible. He was nightly giving a stunning performance on stage in Pirandello's *Henry IV*, but I was in London to meet him in connection with a publicity drive for Noel Pearson's *The Field* in which he played Bull McCabe, a part that could have been written for him and for which it was thought, at least in Ireland, he was a dead cert for an Oscar.

At the appointed time, I turned up at the Savoy Hotel, where he had a permanent suite. He kept me waiting for more than an hour – his privilege – before sending word to the hotel's front desk that he wasn't going to come down but that I should go up. Wearing a badly fitting terrycloth bathrobe, he wrenched open the door, as if he was revealing himself as the Third Secret of Fatima, and ushered me in. My immediate impression of him was that he was too big for the room; that he would be too big for any room. He threw himself backwards onto a chaise longue while introducing me to another man sitting quietly nearby. He referred to this person as 'Doctor' – he could have been there only as minder, foil or witness to nasty newspaper questions.

I didn't get to ask many questions, nasty or otherwise. With an occasional lapse into seriousness – about his childhood, his health or his dead-and-buried life as a hell-raiser – Harris ran the show. While taking on copious draughts of water, he roared, interrupted, giggled, complained, traduced, told raucous stories, frequently sought confirmation of what he was saying from 'Doctor', canonised his ex-wives, challenged me to bet him a tenner on an issue I dared to question, and was disgusted with my lack of appreciation of rugby lore. At a certain stage, he announced that he was hungry, and all three of us went downstairs to the Savoy's dining room where, over lunch, the performance continued, muted a little as a sop to the sensibilities of other patrons. As designated audience, I had a great time and I doubt that my ensuing prose adequately captured the occasion because a lot of what was said, although never malicious, was hilariously defamatory.

Richard Harris promised to write from his beloved Bahamas, and did. In the letter, he acknowledged that he now owed me the tenner.

He got the Oscar nomination but I can barely imagine the degree of his disappointment when he didn't get the statuette.

The tenner got lost in the post.

30

Vincent

I don't mean to trumpet this parade of big names as a tribute to my own achievement. I was merely the conduit.

And I did fail, sometimes spectacularly so.

Twice, having unexpectedly and intensely disliked my interviewees, I was shocked into an inability to write a word about them. Each had agreed to meet me on the basis of my previous work, which, although revelatory, was, I hope, nevertheless empathetic in overall terms. So I felt I could not on principle turn around now and savage them.

On another occasion, although I contributed to the problem, the failure was mainly technological. I went to interview the writer and film-maker Neil Jordan on the set of his movie *High Spirits*. Before I met him, as you might expect, I checked my batteries and tapes, all new.

My custom during interviews was intermittently to rewind the tape a little to check that the sound levels were adequate and that everything was going well. I was, by that stage, quite experienced in meeting famous and powerful people but, for some reason, felt slightly and unusually intimidated in his presence. I was uneasy about stopping the interview even for the few seconds it would have taken to do the checks and so, trusting to fate, I didn't.

Wouldn't you know? On leaving him I checked the tape, and there was absolutely nothing on it except a loud hiss.

And then there was Plácido.

Plácido Domingo is a hero to me. He is the complete package: singer, musician, conductor and actor, not to mention his good looks, intelligence and thoughtful articulacy. Anything I had read or heard about him served only to increase my desire to interview him. Plácido was my Holy Grail.

I worked on it for six months. I had heard he was coming to Wembley in London for a concert and based my requests around this. I wrote, phoned, did everything I could through contacts, agents, publicists and virtually anyone I knew who had any influence in the area.

I didn't get very far. Why on earth, wondered everyone in his retinue, should their star waste valuable time on an Irish newspaper with no circulation in England and therefore no prospect of additional bums on seats for his concerts?

Still I persisted and – hallelujah! – eventually secured a promise that I could have an interview after one of the concerts. A ticket was arranged for me so I could see the show before I met the great man.

Off I went to London, full of excitement and anticipation, with brand-new mini tape recorder and mini tapes, in tiptop condition, obsessively checked and rechecked almost on the hour.

I won't bore you with how, once I got there and tried to pin down an exact time and location for the interview, everyone involved seemed mysteriously unavailable. However, at the last minute, I did get hold of my original contact, who assured me that everything was set. 'Just come round backstage after the concert.'

'Does Mr Domingo know about this?'

'Sure he does. It's all arranged. Ask for me.'

I did. After the concert, I was shown by my contact into a small green room where Domingo himself was setting up a trestle table. His offstage presence was every bit as substantial as the one he projects in performance. He is a large man, strong in body as well as talent; I was particularly struck by the ease with which he hefted the heavy table.

There were others in the room, so I hung back, not wanting to intrude until I was called.

It turned out that his table, behind which he then sat, was for the convenience of the jewel-encrusted punters – and their husbands – who came in to have their CDs and programmes signed. I was nervous, but happy to be there, this period helping me to settle down and gain an entrée into his personality, which seemed charming and accessible. He had a word for everyone and was in no hurry.

When the last of the crowd had left, he pushed back his chair to stand up, and at last I had an opportunity to approach him. 'Mr Domingo? I'm Deirdre Purcell. I'm from *The Sunday Tribune* in Ireland? We're going to do the interview now?'

Domingo frowned. He looked around for help. It was clear he didn't know anything about any interview.

Panicking, I mentioned the name of the man who had set this up.

The tenor asked me to come with him into another room where his wife and some of their personal guests were having a post-concert drink. I followed him but he was immediately absorbed into a group and didn't look again in my direction.

I spotted my contact in the middle of another group, went over to him and asked if I could have a word.

There would be no interview he said. Mr Domingo was now tired.

I argued. Keeping my voice low, because I didn't want to cause a scene in front of the tenor and his entourage, I rehearsed the promises, how long this had been going on, the time and financial resources it had cost *The Sunday Tribune* – but I got nowhere.

Then, quite unabashed, my contact finished our conversation by saying, quite kindly, that he hoped I had got my autograph.

I was dreading the crawl back to Vincent Browne to report all of this.

Vincent laughed. 'These things are good for you.'

Then there was the interview I wasn't allowed to do. I met Charles J. Haughey only once in person while I was at the *Tribune*. I was at a function at the Irish Embassy in Washington and was chatting to someone in a corner of the reception area when the composition of the air in the room seemed to change and a hush descended. Turning around to see what had caused it, I saw him, standing just in front of the doorway, looking this way and that, obviously deciding whom to grace with his presence. He caught my eye and, probably recognising me from my television days, walked straight towards me. Without introducing himself, he picked up a large gold locket I was wearing, looked me straight in the face, and said, 'When is my picture going to be in this?'

It got the laugh.

I immediately asked him for an interview and he agreed.

Back at the ranch, however, Vincent insisted that there would be no interview unless Haughey agreed to talk about the Arms Crisis in 1970. Haughey, of course, told us to take a running jump.

Sometimes, my tendency towards eagerness landed me in situations so surreal that I still can't quite believe they happened.

While interviewing Eartha Kitt at the home of her friend in

London, I had to sit, literally, at the diva's feet, which were soaking prior to her pedicure. And while her manicurist worked diligently on the nails of one hand, Eartha continually squished a hard rubber ball with the other. This, she explained, was to keep her upper arms lithe. She waxed on a great deal about marriage. In her view, the only way to keep a marriage going is to have two adjacent houses, one for each spouse with a communications tunnel running between them.

Then she turned to the subject of her forthcoming Irish concert appearance. 'I love Ireland. I love the real people of Ireland. I want to have lunch in the real people's houses.'

Yep.

Out it came, 'Would you like to have lunch in my house?'

Panic stations when I got home. Paint the hall. Change the carpet on the stairs. Clean the windows.

We had no dining room, so I decided she'd just have to eat in the kitchen like us really real people do.

I borrowed chairs from a neighbour and, to cover all possible conversational lacunae, invited some of the most loquacious people I knew – David Norris, Mary Banotti, Pat Kenny, people like that. And, taking seriously the spirit of what the guest of honour had said about wanting a 'real' and 'ordinary' Irish experience, I cooked a massive container of Irish stew.

She arrived with her driver and squeezed in beside Pat Kenny. She asked for a bowl of garlic bulbs. She peeled and ate them, while picking at the stew on Pat Kenny's plate. She admired my shed, visible in our pocket backyard through the window of our cramped kitchen.

'I love sheds,' she said. 'Everyone should have a shed.'

The greatest kick for me was undoubtedly when I landed the first interview – a world exclusive – with Senator Gary Hart, the ex-candidate for the Democratic US presidential nomination, after he went, in the parlance of those trying to find him, 'into hiding', following the implosion of his campaign. With the primaries in view, he had been a front-runner with an impressive lead over his nearest rival – until he dirtied his bib with the media by challenging them to find and print evidence of marital infidelity.

The version he gave me of how this challenge occurred was that he had lost his temper with a snooping and prurient media. There had been rumours circulating around the various political camps about him and a woman. During a plane journey between campaign stops, he had been trying to discuss policy issues with the press pack on board. They, however, would not engage with him on what he regarded as serious matters, but had persisted in questioning him about the rumours. Frustrated, he had lost his temper and had challenged them to put a tail on him.

No matter how interesting, practical or innovative your policy ideas, if you are a politician seeking office in the United States, you do *not* challenge the American media to dig up dirt on you. So when a so-called friend of a woman called Donna Rice rang the *Miami Herald* and offered to sell them a snapshot of Rice sitting on the senator's lap while on board a yacht called, incredibly, *Monkey Business*, reporters from that paper did follow him and watched his Washington townhouse and, although neither they nor anyone else ever produced evidence of serious wrongdoing, the *Herald* had enough circumstantial stuff from their stakeout to run a front-page story.

From that moment on, Gary Hart's campaign was dead. He resigned from it and vanished from public view, thus goading almost every newspaper and media organisation, including CNN, CBS, ABC and NBC News, into a rivalrous hunt for 'the fugitive' all over the world.

In our humble little Baggot Street office, John Carlos received a call from his mother. His aunt, who lived in Connemara, had heard that, guess what? Oliver North had been spotted in the locality.

It did not take a genius to figure out that this was a case of mistaken identity. Vincent immediately dispatched John and me to the west of Ireland.

John's aunt did not have precise information as to where 'Oliver' might be staying, but we figured that, once we were in situ, it would not be all that hard to locate him. This was a lone American, probably not doing the usual touristy sights, and most likely rebuffing the usual friendly overtures and questions as to where he was from when in shops, pubs and restaurants. This was also a man whose face had been all over the Irish national media, so it was only a matter of time before we came across someone who had spotted him.

It took a couple of days of amateur but careful sleuthing (we didn't want the local hacks to spot us) before we found that the senator was staying in a rented house near the village of Oughterard. And he was driving a rented Opel Corsa. Blue.

Covertly, I checked out the house – no Opel Corsa. He wasn't there.

That didn't matter because I hadn't planned on knocking on the door; I knew that my chances of getting him to agree to talk to me were not great. What benefit would accrue to him? So, rather than confront him on his doorstep, thus giving him too great an opportunity to dismiss me summarily, I had decided to write him a note.

I took my time over it. I toyed with the idea of flattery, offering him a platform to air his views on world affairs, but very quickly discarded the notion: this man was too bright and too experienced not to see through such a blatant overture. So I kept it simple. I introduced myself and *The Sunday Tribune*, giving the paper a gold star for being thoughtful and serious. I asked him for an interview and (with the agreement of Vincent) gave him a solemn guarantee that, if he agreed to speak to me, I would make sure nothing was printed until after he had left Ireland. This was to protect him from the media scrum that would undoubtedly follow publication if he was still there.

Then I went to the house, walked up the driveway and stuck the note to his door with Sellotape. I went back to my guesthouse and waited.

In response, he wrote me a nicely worded, courteous letter declining my invitation.

I allowed an hour or so to go by and then, stomach gurgling with nerves, went up to his house again. This time, I knocked on the door.

> There was another long, long wait, almost as long, it
> seemed, as the preceding four days of 'stakeout', until
> I heard the sound of footsteps approaching the door.

'Good afternoon, Mr Hart. My name is Deirdre Purcell. I wrote you a note.'

> Gary Hart is tall. He wore a striped cotton T-shirt.
> His hair was tousled and his chin grizzled. After a
> further pause, a tiny standoff, he extended his hand.
> 'Come in,' he said.

During that few seconds of stand-off, knowing it could go either way, I kept my mouth shut, my expression expectant yet friendly, and gave no sign that I knew I was being surveyed. I could almost hear the ticking of his brain as it ran through his choices, and the clang as it came down on the lesser of two evils. Any journalist could add to the wreck surrounding him by revealing his whereabouts. I shook his hand and followed him inside. I was elated. While I had passed only a preliminary test and he probably hoped to win me over by explaining why he couldn't talk to me, in my gut I knew he would.

In the end, he even agreed to pose for John's photographs. And in the interview itself, he laid down only one rule: there should be no writing about 'that business in May', the Donna Rice affair.

We met for dinner later in Sweeney's Hotel in the village of Oughterard and we continued talking back in the rented house; I had seen him described as 'an airhead' in a reputable American newspaper. I spent eight hours in his fascinating company. Do not believe everything you read in the newspapers.

On the Saturday morning at home, I had started typing the transcription from my sets of tapes, when Kevin came in to the room to tell me he had heard on the radio news that there had been calls from powerful elements in the US Democratic Party for Gary Hart to get back into the race for the presidential nomination and that, apparently, the senator had not ruled this out.

It wasn't long before Vincent rang me. The deal about non-publication was now off. How far was I into writing my piece? They would need it by three o'clock at the latest.

But Hart was still in Ireland and, to me, a solemn promise is a solemn promise. I contacted Hart and he let it be known that the deal stood.

There followed an exhausting series of hour-long phone calls between the newspaper and me, with Vincent insisting that since Hart had obviously broken cover, the underlying reason for making the deal no longer existed. I insisted it did, because Hart had said it did. I was using words like 'honourable' and 'a matter of principle'; he was using words like 'schoolgirlish' and 'primary duty'.

The fight came down to my contractual obligations to the newspaper. I knew this was reasonable on his part and, eventually, wearied, I succumbed on that basis. It was after midday now and I told him that if he wanted a piece, any piece, by three o'clock, he would have to leave me alone so I could start writing. I would send in the piece by taxi but my letter of resignation would accompany it. This incited another flurry, but I reiterated that if he wanted a piece from me, he would have to get off the line.

I don't know what upset me most: the row itself, resigning from a job I loved or that my final work for the paper would now be a hastily cobbled-together mishmash. I wouldn't even have time to listen to all of the tapes, much less transcribe them. Distressed as I was, the work and the deadline were priorities so I tried to put all other considerations out of my mind and set to.

About forty minutes later, the doorbell rang. It had been rung by Vincent Browne. He had a taxi ticking over outside our house. He had come to talk to me in person.

I dug my heels in at this point and, although the argument raged across my desk, nothing he said or tried would budge me. I continued to remind him that I'd be sorry to resign but if he wanted something for the paper, the clock was ticking…

After three-quarters of an hour or so of this, he shrugged. 'The problem with you is you've no sense of humour.'

'*What?*'

'OK.'

'What do you mean, "OK"?'

'I mean, OK.' He shrugged again.

'You mean you'll hold over the piece until Hart's gone?'

'OK.'

He dashed off back to the office, leaving me like a drowned wasp (I was wearing a cotton jellabiyya, striped in black and mustard yellow that I had brought home from my trip to Bangladesh).

I no longer know who had held the moral high ground in that row. A reporter's duty is to the readers, not to act as a PR for anyone, especially someone like Senator Hart who could never be classed as naïve about media.

However, there is also the not-so-small matter of integrity. Vincent had authorised the promise not to publish. Hart had given the interview on foot of that promise and, on being asked to release me from it because of changed circumstances, had refused, insisting it be honoured since he was undecided what to do next.

Gary Hart left Ireland soon afterwards and the interview was published the following Sunday.

This had been the first of only two serious rows I had with Vincent during my seven-and-a-half-year tenure at *The Sunday Tribune*. The second was when Gay Byrne, through his publisher, Gill and Macmillan, asked me to ghostwrite his autobiography. I was anxious to have a go at it, largely to find out if I was tenacious enough to stick to and finish a long project, but Vincent felt it would be too much of a distraction. This, by the way, from the man who earned a Master's degree in Trinity College and a barristers' Law Degree in the King's Inns while editing his publications and keeping them going despite crisis after financial crisis. He made his displeasure felt for quite a long period, but I kept my head down, did my work and the book and, eventually, we made up.

During my time at the *Tribune*, there were many high-profile departures from the paper but, in general, I found Vincent Browne to be so professionally inspirational that the difficulties some of my colleagues had with his style of management posed few problems for me. And he could be kind: during a time when my personal life was a disaster – simultaneously, Nellie was in one hospital, Mamma in another and my grandmother in a third – he gave me a great deal of leeway.

He is irascible and obsessive, but so are other fanatical and cranky individuals of influence. I hear from those who personally knew her that, in single-minded pursuit of her cause, Mother Teresa could be a termagant.

Vincent is profoundly sceptical but not cynical, a distinction that can be overlooked sometimes by his critics, who would probably dispute this. While he has no tolerance for abuse of power, for pretension or for vanity, and while his permanent crusade for a redistribution of wealth is repetitive to the point of becoming redundant, even while he is ranting about the 'unfairness' of 'society', he recognises that, under the glitz and glamour, the wealthy individual shares a common humanity with the raddled destitute.

I certainly admire his nerve. In the lead-up to the fight in London for the world featherweight title between the Panamanian champion Eusebio Pedroza and the Irish challenger Barry McGuigan, boxing fever was at boiling point all over Ireland and amongst the Irish community in Britain. I know this because, alongside the sports reporters, Vincent was sending me to London to cover the fight that night. (He later sent me to Germany to cover the fans' reaction to Ireland's 1988 European Cup matches: I actually *saw* Ray Houghton's goal against England!)

He wanted to print a colour supplement to wrap around the newspaper, with a huge headline proclaiming 'Champion Of The World!' over a photograph of McGuigan. The problem was that the fight was on a Saturday night and any colour printing for that Sunday had to be done on the Thursday – at a cost of £16,000. The newspaper was not exactly flush with cash and could definitely not afford to lose such a sum in the event the wraparound had to be pulped.

But knowing that if McGuigan actually won the championship, the revenue from the additional circulation engendered by the wraparound would more than equal its cost, our editor went ahead. He printed the supplement and, the story goes, on the advice of Paul Tansey and with a bookie giving him evens, he bet £16,000 on Pedroza.

31

Fairies and Imps

The first six months of interviews with Gay Byrne for *The Time of My Life*, the autobiography I ghosted for him, had not been productive, I thought. Every time he bustled into our room, I felt it was with an attitude of *let's get this thing on the road so we can get it over with as quickly as we can.* I couldn't break him out of it, and I felt I was no nearer to getting to know this Interviewer of Interviewers than I had been after the first hour.

To do him justice, I didn't want merely to string together a fresh collection of already well-worn stories about his childhood on the South Circular Road or of famous people on his shows. In an effort to widen things out, I tried putting to him what other people had written about his life and times, but that didn't achieve much either. He was always polite, warm and friendly, and there were no hiatuses in the way he answered my questions, but in a way this had become part of the problem. The answers were too ready, the anecdotes too practised. Except for a few new titbits about recent interviewees and events, the material I was getting wasn't much different from what he himself had written many years earlier in his own book, *To Whom It May Concern*.

So, although I continued dutifully to turn up to our appointments in an airless, windowless cupboard of a room in RTÉ, having stood out against the considerable antipathy of Vincent Browne to do so, I was beginning to feel I had made a terrible mistake.

To be fair, the atmosphere in that sterile, ugly, glaring little room was not conducive to relaxation or creativity, especially as my subject was fitting in our sessions between production meetings and other important business. But it's a bad workman who quarrels with his tools and I couldn't really blame the environment or even Gay Byrne. The fault had to be mine: I wasn't asking the right questions.

Even as I sat opposite him, I re-examined my interviewing technique. What was I doing wrong? This man should be gold dust for any journalist; through both his radio programme and *The Late Late Show* he had had an enormous influence, directly or indirectly, on everyone in Ireland.

In RTÉ, the newsroom, radio and television divisions are physically separate and, except for saying hello to him as we had passed each other in the grounds of Montrose, I hadn't known him in advance of taking on the commission: could it be that, like most Irish people, I was in awe of his standing and power?

I decided that awe wasn't really the problem; I had interviewed Taoisigh and EU commissioners, the Archbishop of Canterbury – even J.R. Ewing! None of them had caused me a moment's hesitation or soul-searching.

Around this time, I met the snooker player Steve Davis for 'The People Page'. We had a drink together after I switched off the tape recorder and, in the course of chit-chat, he asked me what I was up to these days. I told him about the ghosting.

In response, he put his hand sympathetically on my arm, 'That has to be the most thankless task for any writer. I got my autobiography ghosted and the chap is a really good journalist and he produced a perfectly good, nice book. But my agent and I took it [hands making snatching movements] and we said, "Thanks very much," and then we broke it apart and took out anything we didn't like and put it together again the way we wanted.'

In principle, I knew this was the fate of all ghostwriters and was fully prepared for it but when I heard it put so baldly, it put steel into my soul. I had accepted a commission to write Gay's book about Gay's life, and he could choose what he wanted the public to know about him. But if we were going to continue with this project, my part of it was at least to give him something new and interesting to discard.

Soon after a few inconsequential meanderings at the beginning of our next session, I took a deep breath. 'This isn't working.'

'Is it not, dote?' He was absolutely taken aback.

'No. It's probably not your fault, but you're treating me like a nuisance.'

Now he was appalled. 'Am I?'

'I'm afraid you are ... I certainly feel you are. And that you're impatient with the process. This is your book, Gay. It shouldn't be just a rehash of the last one.'

I don't know what he would say about this episode but, from that moment on, Gay Byrne and I got on famously. His entire demeanour changed and he could not have been more co-operative, allowing me to dig, to draw him out. He worked hard to uncover new anecdotes about his childhood and particularly his mother, who had held very strong sway over his development. To that end, he set up meetings for me with his family – I remember a really lovely family dinner and a lunch with his brother, Al. He arranged for pals to meet me too, and suggested people I could contact to fill in gaps in his own recollections.

I knew he was relaxing with me when he began referring to his wife as 'Kay'. Up to a certain point in our work, he had always called her 'Kathleen Watkins', as he usually did in public: this, I knew, was out of respect for her as a musician and broadcaster in her own right. She was far more famous than he when they had married and he was always sensitive to her status relative to his own. He even arranged for me to travel north with her to see their cottage so that I could understand what he meant when he called Donegal 'beloved'.

I found that while Gay was, and is, prone to groaning about being over-committed, he is intensely orderly and organised and certain to fulfil every last task to his own exacting standards. He does not suffer fools but will happily stretch the boundaries of tolerance to accommodate great talent. Personally, he is generous, and he is great, gossipy company, an excoriating mimic with a wonderful sense of humour.

Although he is modest, he does know his own worth and not only as a broadcaster: while on the surface he pooh-poohs the extent of his influence on Irish society, he is cognisant of it, but credits the programmes themselves and their timely arrival on the scene. Ireland was ready to be influenced, is his way of looking at it, and he pays tribute to the people he was 'lucky enough' to have had on his teams over the years. Loyalty to friends is his overarching virtue.

We worked together for nearly two years on *The Time of My Life*. Burrowing in to inhabit someone else's persona is, in its own way, a creative process; at a certain stage, I felt I knew him so well that had anyone asked me what Gay Byrne's thoughts were about any situation, personal, societal, political, national or international, I could have answered unhesitatingly. I could phrase sentences the way he did, even speak with his intonations.

In the end, of course, he and his family did take editorial control of the book and, having expected it, it was by no means an issue for me. I had learned a lot and I flattered myself that I did manage to write that manuscript, perhaps not totally in the way he would have written it, but certainly with his vocabulary and in what publishers call his 'voice'.

I had also made a friend.

There is a minor coda to this story, minor because it had little effect on the book's sales figures, which were huge.

Naturally, the *Sunday Tribune* wanted the right to run extracts – and because I worked there, I assumed this was a given. But the *Sunday Independent*, far more flush than our paper, made a counter-offer to the publisher; I made strenuous representations to the publisher and to Gay himself that they leave the extracts with us. They agreed.

The *Indo* then ran 'spoilers' in advance of the book's publication and our extracts. A journalist went back to all the primary sources with a brief to write three huge feature pieces to run in successive issues, enough to 'spoil' the *Tribune*'s coup. The brief was not difficult. Information about Gay Byrne was hardly a mystery: a lot of his life had been lived in public and there were myriads of feature articles and opinion pieces about him. He had also given hundreds, if not thousands, of easily accessible interviews.

This was merely the normal cut and thrust of competition in a cut-throat Sunday newspaper market, and there was nothing either unsavoury or unethical about it. What hurt me, though, was that a former colleague of my own was the journalist involved.

I suppose that's showbiz. And that's the killer instinct.

What I got out of that project was not only Gay's friendship but also the satisfaction of knowing that I did have the stamina to complete a project of that length. So, when Treasa Coady, who ran the small Irish publishing company TownHouse & CountryHouse, approached me to write a novel, it was not the prospect of so much work that daunted me, but the serious possibility of failure and public ridicule. I had worked for her before, writing text about the Lough Derg pilgrimage site for a collaborative book with photographer Liam Blake. I knew that her offer was serious. Her company had, up to that time, specialised in non-fiction, so what she proposed was an adventure for both of us: I had never written fiction, she had never published any. She was specific: we were to produce a bestseller.

Her timing was extraordinary because, although I hadn't confided this to anyone, I was having some difficulties with 'The People Page'. I was getting tired.

I still loved interviewing people but my own standards and work methods were burning me out; I felt very strongly that the 301st person I wrote about deserved the same care, attention and hard work as I had lavished on the first, but, more and more, I was finding it difficult to resist the lure of shortcuts. Perhaps I didn't *really* have to transcribe *every* single word? This was still my practice but it was beginning to seem onerous and, although I forced myself to plough on, the temptation to skip this opinion or that quote on the tape was growing. *After all*, whispered the imp on my shoulder, *you'll probably not be using that bit of the stuff anyhow. Why not save yourself the hassle of typing it?*

I worked hard to ignore the imp. I knew from experience that, occasionally, what seemed to be the most pedestrian material on the tape gave the most unexpected and greatest insight when taken in context of the whole piece, and I didn't want to let my interviewees down by perhaps overlooking something crucial just because I was getting tired and a bit lazy.

With all of this going on in my head, a change of direction would have been welcome – although I hadn't yet figured out what kind of change that should be. It should, of course, be within *The Sunday Tribune* or journalism in general.

What Treasa Coady was offering was far too radical and the reason I turned it down was not just the fear of failure. I was intimidated by the notion of working for myself with no salary cheques. Dear God…

She was not put off and, over the next six months or so, persisted, telephoning me every so often. Meanwhile, that imp on my shoulder had changed his focus and was nibbling now at my ear: here was an opportunity being offered to me on a plate. Would it not be myopic, he suggested, not to speak of arrogant, to turn down something that most journalists would consider beyond their dreams? Especially in a city stuffed with journalists telling each other they were going to write a bestseller and retire on the proceeds.

It was a vision of myself at the age of sixty, crying into my gin and tonic about lost opportunities, which finally brought me to my senses. And so, with Frank Dermody's long-ago exhortation – 'If you're going to fail, fail gloriously' – ringing in my ears, I accepted Treasa's offer. So what if I bombed and was publicly ridiculed? Big deal. Today's newspapers, tomorrow's fish-and-chip wrappers or compost filler.

At first, Vincent Browne didn't know what to think, but he was generous. He allowed me to cut down on my commitments to the *Tribune* while I was having a go at the difficult transition from fact to fiction.

And it was difficult. It's all very well thinking, Oh yeah, I'll write a novel – but what do you write about? And how can you fill a whole book?

I had promised Treasa I would come up with a plot outline. Easier said than done. It wasn't a lack of ideas that bothered me – it was that I had too many; once I started prospecting, my head swarmed with them. How to choose?

Then I read a small paragraph in the news pages of *The Irish Times*. The pilot of a small plane had got into trouble just off the Aran Islands and the islanders, hearing him circling overhead in the darkness, had set fires on a flat field to indicate a landing place.

Here was the idea. Forget landing flares. But suppose a plane ditched in the Atlantic a few hundred yards off those islands. Suppose everyone on board was lost – except for a baby who, Moses-like, was carried ashore in a bassinet?

This was the genesis of *A Place of Stones* and it offered endless possibilities. Who found her? Who was she? Did she ever find out? What happened to her when she grew up? Who was her real family and where had she come from? What's it like to think you're one person and find out you're another?

What if…? What if…? As soon as I started with the 'what ifs', I couldn't stop. My plot grew legs and galloped between Chicago, the Aran Islands, Dublin and London. Treasa's outline was labyrinthine: it ran to twenty-two closely typed pages.

Next problem in writing the actual book was length.

Other journalists (Cathy Kelly, Joseph O'Connor, Colm Tóibín come to mind) have made the transition from journalism to novels seem easy. At the start, however, I did struggle to find the rhythm. For instance, when I delivered the second novel, *That Childhood Country*, it was at more than 600 pages and a massive 160,000 words; needless to remark it didn't stay that length!

My interview pieces had been long enough to give me a taste for narrative – there was usually a beginning, middle and end – but, in general, journalism meant compression, succinctness, pithiness: the story in the first paragraph, a character and a life in one page. I now had to allow my sentences to breathe, my story to be like an eiderdown into which readers could snuggle. At the same time, it had to keep their interest. They couldn't get too comfortable, so I had to figure out a way to keep them alert. My instinct was to reveal everything as quickly as possible, but I had to develop patience with my story; I had to spin out the plot and divert readers from their expectations without adding twists that were too outrageous to sustain belief.

My luck fairy was in delightful good humour at that time, however, because Treasa arranged a meeting for us with the London agent, Charles Pick.

Before he had turned to agenting, Charles had been a publisher in the days when publishing novels was a gentleman's game. Canny, charming and clubbable, he was now elderly but still influential in the trade. Treasa had met him in Dublin when he had interviewed her in connection with a report he was compiling for the Irish Arts Council. It had asked him to study the possibilities for expansion by the indigenous publishing industry here. At that time, almost all of the 'big' Irish authors were being published from London.

He agreed to add me to his list, which was satisfactorily short: other than me, he had only one other client – Wilbur Smith, who propped up a good percentage of the profits at Macmillan.

When I did deliver the manuscript for my first novel, unknown to me, Charles sent it on to Michael Legat, a friend of his who had also been influential in publishing and who was known as a straight talker and a perceptive judge of writers' potential.

I have never forgotten two pieces of his constructive criticism.

I had fallen into two of the classic first-timers' traps. First, I had given a life story to every minor character in my highly populated story. Even the single-paragraph postman who delivered a letter to my protagonist had been given an identity and a personal problem. I had thought I was adding depth, interest and local colour. But, in the course of his letter to Charles, Michael Legat warned that to give a life story to every passer-by becomes confusing and obscures the narrative. What's more, each time a writer gives anyone a name, that name remains in the reader's subconscious, hanging around, in Michael Legat's words, 'like a little cloud'. That cloud hovers over the reader's subconscious as he or she assumes that the named character will, at some stage, have something to do with the plot or character development, and when this does not prove to be the case, there is a letdown.

The other crucial observation Michael Legat made in his letter was: 'When this writer makes a scene out of an event or an encounter, the book comes alive.'

I had thought I had understood the old writer's adage of 'show, don't tell'. I hadn't. Now I did. From now on, rather than telling the reader what had happened and what a character feels, I had to let the characters show it: rather than 'she felt angry', it's 'she smashed the glass against the wall'. I can't say that I've mastered the concept, but at least I'm now aware of it and I do keep trying.

What was heartening about the letter overall, however, was that he began it by saying: 'This writer can write.'

Macmillan, through Charles, took me on and my so-far untitled novel was put in the capable and very experienced hands of Jane Wood, a senior editor. Jane, another straight talker, willowy, blonde, tall and intimidatingly beautiful, rang me to introduce herself. 'I understand you're willing to do quite a lot of work on this novel?'

I told her that her understanding was correct.

The real work began.

It culminated in autumn 1991 with Treasa dashing to the border with Northern Ireland to extract two finished copies of *A Place of Stones* from the container truck carrying the books into the Republic so she and I could be the first there to handle them.

In the hand, they felt more valuable than gold.

32

God Chortling

Unfortunately, despite newspaper articles entitled 'How to Get Published', or 'How to Write a Bestseller', there are no sure-fire tips or formulae on which to rely for success. Michael Legat's shrewd reading of my first manuscript was a great boost – and his tips have informed all my subsequent novels – but I learned quickly that, in publishing, there are three types of success for authors: critical, material and personal. Sometimes all three combine, although that is rare.

Critical success admits literary writers to a small select circle where they can bask in respectful admiration but, although some of these authors do enjoy widespread international sales, this is not guaranteed.

The 'mass-market' authors are generally the most materially successful. Yet a new writer here also needs good timing because so-called genres go in and out of fashion. For a few years, it might be Aga sagas or whodunnits, for the next it might be the flippant, lazy and rude categorisation of chicklit; it could be 'women's fiction' for a few seasons but then it might spin on to fantasy or mediaeval thrillers.

The third type of success is personal. No matter what critics say about them or how few books they sell, there are some writers to whom the sight of bound, finished work on bookshelves is all the affirmation or validation they need to make them happy. These authors are few in number and are usually of private means or working in other jobs and so don't need to make a living from writing. Because of the crowded markets in all areas, self-publishing offers the best opportunities here.

On the other hand, all publishers do take chances on new authors and bet on 'the next big thing' (Bridget Jones, Harry Potter), but they are businesses, with balance sheets and profit margins to sustain. So it is vital to have an editor who believes passionately in the value of your work, and also that the latest novel (and if not this one, maybe the next) could be the 'breakthrough', leading to international stardom.

An editor is not only a personal critic and guide: he or she is also a book's advocate within a publishing house. Editors push for attention for the work and authors in their care and try to move them up the pecking order when budgets are being allocated and publishing plans agreed. Therefore it is always traumatic when, just as you are getting used to the language and personality of an editor, he or she moves to a new job and there is abruptly a new person with whom you have to start all over again. It happens all the time; the publishing world rides a carousel, within individual houses and across them.

Contrary to popular belief, editors do not rewrite manuscripts – although I have heard anecdotally about exceptions to this rule. They don't dictate either. A good editor enjoys a priceless skill: criticism is never offered along the lines of 'This doesn't work, fix it'; it comes with suggestions as to how 'it' could be fixed. It is then up to the author to own the work and accept or refuse suggestions about cuts, changes, different emphases and balances.

When I first receive an editorial letter, I scan it quickly to get a feel for the general thrust. My baby has been vivisected and handed back to me for reconstructive surgery. That's how it feels anyhow. Neither experience nor longevity helps with this initial reaction. This is my child we're talking about here.

But if I lie low and don't instantly react like a ninny, within a few days, I'll see sense. My editor is on the same side as me and we have a common goal: to make the book as good as it can be in the time available. So I start at page one, line one and, using the editorial letter as guide and springboard, rewrite the book, usually far exceeding the scale and particulars of the suggestions. And, during this exercise, I'll see that the criticisms were often dead right.

Once each book finally leaves my desk and is in print, I never read it again and, except for enthusiastic co-operation with marketing and publicity departments, I leave the book's fate up to others. Hindsight is too demoralising. I could not bear to find that, despite all the intensity and hard work, there are still aspects of the piece that I could have done better, constructions that could be improved, pruning that should have been done when I had the opportunity. That opportunity has passed and redemption is at least a year away. This is so different from journalism where, in the very next edition of your daily or weekly publication you have a chance to show you've learned from your mistakes. My little assembly of novels and other published work sits on the bookshelf above my desk like a reproachful row of permanently discharged but not wholly cured hospital patients.

At least they act as a spur to improvement!

The daily lives of most writers are not interesting in the normal meaning of the word. I am aware that even some of my friends see my novelist's existence as a whirligig of jet-setting and exotic parties, not to speak of high-level, arcane discussions with fellow artists.

Nothing could be further from my experience. Like most other authors I know, I stay at home mostly, conducting my life at and through my keyboard. When the time comes to attend book parties, give readings or participate in seminars, it is part of the job – far from a social whirligig, it is blinking emergence from hibernation. As for chat with fellow writers, it is rarely arcane and when it touches on our profession at all, the context is usually what's going on with agents and publishers. That holds even when colleagues are friends too, although then, the confidences exchanged are the same as they are within any close relationship: family, friends, health, dreams and plans.

Actually, it's a wonder to me, and a source of immense gratitude, that friends stick with me at all, since I so often turn down social invitations, bleating that I have to work. It's not a handy excuse: for me, once I get into writing a novel, it's like being on a train that never stops.

And yet, when I finally finish and can pull the communication cord, relief is tempered by a feeling of blandness. This book, which for me has been albatross, pal and sumo opponent on board that train for months and months, gets off too and leaves me to my own devices. I miss it.

This might sound as though I am very disciplined, and that is one of the most frequent queries asked of me, and all writers, at public events.

In my case, the answer is that I am. A bit. When the cheeping of beetle-browed deadlines is getting louder. Unfortunately, however,

I am not one of those writers who can, seven days a week, sit down at the desk at exactly the same time every morning to work for a set number of hours. My routines are messy. When there is no other call on me and those deadlines are within sight, I will work virtually around the clock, taking breaks only to eat and sleep.

The rest of the time, although writing takes priority and is the main call on my time most days, I've always had domestic and other outside commitments; it's a juggling act.

'How do you come up with titles?' is something else we are all asked. The quick answer in my case is 'with great difficulty', although I have learned over the years that titles can sometimes have very little to do with what is between the covers.

They are very important for marketing purposes. I envy Patricia Scanlan, who is brilliant in this regard; as she thinks about what her next book is going to be about, an appropriate title pops into her mind and so, before she sits down to write the first line, she has put one vital task to bed. And what's really miraculous is that what she has chosen always encapsulates exactly what the book is about. Ergo: the first line of *Double Wedding* is, 'Let's have a double wedding!', and the plot spreads from there.

By contrast, my titles are always 'working' right up to the last minute. I seem to have no talent in this regard and, with a book close to production, I am usually still to-ing and fro-ing with my editor and, by extension, my publisher.

The first novel went right down to the wire. Treasa Coady came to my home on the evening before it had to go to the printer and we sat in my living room trawling through dictionaries, books of quotations and poetry, a thesaurus and even a Bible until, at about fifteen minutes to midnight, we hammered out *A Place of Stones*.

I took *Falling for a Dancer* from a newspaper headline over a review of a ballet; *That Childhood Country* is a quotation from a poem by Patrick Kavanagh and was supplied in a nanosecond by Professor Brendan Kennelly when I met him at a lunch and confessed that I hadn't a clue what to call my second novel, finished and with the publisher.

'Tell me a little about it.'

'Well, it's about these young twins in rural Monaghan in the 1950s—'

'That childhood country!'

Even during the production process, some of my titles proved to be very much a first draft.

'It might be placed with dance books on the shelves' (*Falling for a Dancer*, changed by an American publisher to *Ashes of Roses*). The same publisher morphed *Francey* ('People might think it has something to do with geography') to *Roses after Rain*.

Then there was *Arcadia*, which was changed after much head-scratching, and help from the playwright Bernard Farrell, to *Last Summer in Arcadia* because in the opinion of those who had to sell the book, '*Arcadia* sounds like a Russian thriller.'

In desperation, I maintain a growing file on my computer with a list of phrases that, in my opinion, could be used as titles for future novels. I have never yet been able to use one, no matter how many ways I have tried to adapt them to suit what I've written.

Speaking of advance planning, one of Gaybo's favourite sayings is, 'When man makes plans, God smiles.' Your writing friends are definitely those to whom you instantly turn when plans in your writing life go askew.

Patricia Scanlan and Sheila O'Flanagan were the two who received panicky calls from me during a period of work in Kilcatherine when I had thought things were going really well on *Tell Me Your Secret*.

Then, abruptly, half of what I had written to that date vanished into the ether and could not be retrieved. Both were exceptionally consoling and did try their utmost to be helpful, as did the guy in Cork's Apple dealership, who, when I brought my machine into him the next day, worked on it for more than seven hours. 'We went on the internet asking for help, we even rang Apple head-quarters in California,' he told me, when I went to retrieve it, but no one could solve the problem. The only clue about what had happened was a small, pie-shaped area of damage on the machine's motherboard.

I leave it to your imagination to figure out how I felt as, with an expensive new laptop beside me on the passenger seat, I drove the long, *long* 100 miles back to Kilcatherine. (Before you ask, I had been backing up, but the backups were gone as well. Too long and boring to explain why.) To add to my misery, as I pulled into the driveway I could see little white horses tricking about on the surface of Coulagh Bay. Dancing over the grave of my poor novel. Not a care in the world. Laughing in the face of my misery. *Serves you right, never coming out here to play in the fresh air, always hunched over your machine in there…* I felt like shooting them.

That night, stunned and despairing, I sat for a long time in the armchair in front of our feeble old television set with its three snowy channels and barely took in what I was seeing. The Pope was dying and the crowds keeping vigil in Rome were growing by the hour.

Each writer has a different method of working. Some start at the beginning of a book and write all the way through until they get to the end. Some write quick first drafts, then spend a lot of time rewriting and polishing. Some prepare very carefully in advance, writing outlines, plot summaries and detailed character biographies before starting on the book proper.

My methods are instinctive and I don't plan in detail. I start usually with one image, something I read, see or hear in passing; this image embeds itself and won't go away until I investigate it. *That Childhood Country* opened up to me when I heard of an enraged man chiselling the name of his brother from a tombstone: such passionate hatred was remarkable and I wanted to build a story around it. *Entertaining Ambrose* started up in my head because I saw an elderly woman, erect as a statue and elegantly dressed in black, using a shopping trolley to run at cars in the middle of a dual carriageway at rush hour. Who was she? What did she think she was doing – and why? Where did she live? Who was her family?

Although there is always a semi-linear track through the finished narrative, I do not write it linear-fashion. Initially, to me the plot development is like a tightly closed rosebud. The initial image is wrapped around it like an outer petal and what is contained inside is initially a mystery. However, I do trust that everything I need is there.

Sometimes, when I get to it, I find that the very centre of the bloom is not the centre of the story at all, and I have to set about re-arranging the petals, pulling them apart, re-layering them, even adding more. My system is like playing circular leapfrog: start with that single image or idea, write Chapter One, go on to Chapter Two: rewrite Chapter One, revise Chapter Two and go on to Chapter Three, rewrite Chapter Two, go back to revise Chapter One – and so on. By the time I've got to Chapter Thirty, I'll have made extensive changes to every preceding one from between ten and fifty times. A week's loss of work carved by this method is a very serious matter; six weeks' loss – ten chapters and six weeks' changes – is a catastrophe.

I decided that this setback had occurred for a reason. It was an omen or a lesson: someone or something was signalling that I should give up writing and seek another challenge.

Or not. I was almost sixty: I had been working solidly since the age of seventeen. That's forty-three years of work. People, normal people with normal jobs, retired after forty.

I have no pension – writers rarely do and, being self-employed, there is no one to fund disability, sick or compassionate leave. When something unexpected happens – a serious illness to yourself, a member of the family or a close friend – you just have to keep going, splitting your concentration between work and the crisis. You shorten your sleep and try to increase your work rate within the hours available to you.

It was time to be practical. The work rate this would demand to fulfil my contractual deadline was not humanly possible. I turned off the Pope's vigil, threw briquettes on the fire in the stove, lit every candle in the house, and poured myself a very large gin and tonic, no lemon, no ice, because neither was available. Then I sat down again in the warm, flickering quietness to review my options.

I had had a good innings.

Yet...

For half an hour, I swung this way and that before accepting that there was no way I could let a stupid technology glitch defeat me. Bathed in the calm light from fire and candles, I sipped my luke-warm drink and tried to settle into a frame of mind where I could go back to the beginning of *Tell Me Your Secret* and rewrite the whole damned thing. And I would just have to confess to the publishers what had happened and ask them to extend the contractual deadline for delivery. That would be personally difficult because I had always prided myself on my professionalism and ability to deliver what I had promised.

So was this to be the lesson? Would I just have to learn to accept that I couldn't please everyone all the time?

Thinking about this, I remembered being sent oodles of similar lessons but I hadn't been paying attention.

'Are you not Patricia Scanlan? Aww. That's disappointing. Where's Patricia Scanlan? Is she not coming?'

'Look at you and you're so demure: how do you write those sex scenes? Where do you get your information?'

'Oh, yeah! You're the one that wrote that thing about friends. I didn't like it.'

'I did read one of your books once. It was in the parish sale, and it didn't sell. So my friend and I took it and we each read it and then we put it back in the box for the next sale.'

'I liked you better on the telly.'

And, by the way, unlikely though it sounds, the only possible explanation for what happened to my computer that afternoon is that either while plugging it in or unplugging it, by a trillion to one accident of coincidental timing, it had been struck by lightning. Much of our part of Béara is rich in copper and our house actually rests on a seam. Copper attracts lightning. It doesn't have to be stormy outside: we've lost a fax machine on a sunny day.

As it happens, and to bolster this theory, I was once told a lovely local story concerning an elderly widow who lived alone halfway up a mountain on Béara. After much persuasion, she finally agreed to the urgings of her relatives that a telephone be installed. With difficulty and the use of a lot of manpower and heavy machinery, over a period of a few weeks a long line of poles was erected at great expense across rough terrain. It reached her house. Her telephone was installed, tested and found to be working perfectly. She was still mistrustful, however, and wouldn't use it.

With good cause. One evening, while she was sitting at her fire, there was a sort of fizz-bang sound and the phone flew past her head and crashed to the ground beside the window.

Whenever God thinks about it all, He not only smiles, He chortles.

33

Colin

So, while there are many wretched days when technology lets you down, when your head hurts, your spine hurts, your eyes hurt, when you can feel a tingling in the dowager's hump you've developed from slumping over the keyboard, this writing life does offer amazing highs too.

Again, I am standing by the French doors in the living room of our house in Kilcatherine, looking out over the bay and the headland fields. One of Raymond and Kathleen McCarthy's lemony calves cavorts, stops, seems to think for a second, then buckleps a half-turn and rushes to butt at its dozy mother. *Wake up, Mammy, wake up, it's great to be alive.*

Yes, it is. The coffee is strong and good. It's July 1996 and it is the opening morning of filming for the cast and crew of *Falling for a Dancer*. My *Falling for a Dancer*. My work on the script is done and is in capable hands – no going back now. The sun, already warm on my face, has started to burn off the sea-mist shrouding the film's principal location at Cleanagh, by Cod's Head, jutting over the Atlantic and safely reached only by four-wheel-drive vehicles. The air over there will be diamond-clear in time for the first calls of 'Speed!' then 'Action!'

That morning was one of the most exhilarating of my professional life. Half an hour after leaving our house, I crested a hill on the mountain road between Eyeries and Allihies and almost crashed the car. Before me, at the base of the swooping, empty landscape normally populated only by roving gangs of hill sheep, I saw that one of the few flat fields had sprouted cars, jeeps, generator vehicles, even a catering bus. I had been expecting something like this, but the extent of it took my breath away.

It was still only a few minutes past six but there were already a few people, some wearing high-visibility jackets, talking quietly in small groups while cradling cups of coffee, uncoiling wires, examining pieces of equipment, The director, Richard Standeven, stood alone beside his car, head bent as though thinking deeply.

I stopped my car to take it all in and to sort out what I felt. I didn't want to make an idiot of myself by oozing down there like an emotional jelly.

But I was emotional. It had taken years of my life to get us all here. The script I had adapted from my novel – with a great deal of help from the script editor, Roxy Spencer – had foundered and faltered many times, through many changes of brass at the BBC and RTÉ, through the search for funding, through wild hope, rumours, shreds of disappointment. What had kept me at it, revising, rewriting, re-creating, accommodating the Eureka-moments of new bosses, was a stubborn vision: I had kept my imagination fixed on the image of a catering bus parked in the village of Eyeries, the nearest big smoke to Kilcatherine.

And now there it was. Not yet in Eyeries, but to be moved to the village when those sequences were to be shot in a couple of months' time.

The hotels, B&Bs and rental properties in the area were full; many of the locals on Béara were to be employed as extras, security personnel, runners, animal handlers, seamstresses and in administration – even the nurse, Teresa Murphy, was from the locality. For the duration of the shoot, £4 million would be injected into the local economy; Eyeries would benefit permanently because, since the film was set in the 1930s, the utility companies had been persuaded to take down their ugly poles and bury an unsightly tangle of overhead wires that had marred the beauty of the place.

And this had all happened because of an idea I had had for a story.

Writers are not normally encouraged to come on set during a shoot – and definitely not in the first days when actors and crew are getting to know each other and settling into temporary family mode. An exception had been made for me because I had worked on the thing for so long with the producers, Jonathan Curling and Peter Norris, and in the last month very closely with Richard, so they knew me and trusted that I would behave appropriately. I had been an actress. I knew the score: as of that morning, the script was no longer mine but theirs.

The changeover had started with the casting, which had had nothing to do with me. I had been invited to the first cast reading and although very few of the players were physically as I had imagined them or described them in the novel, by the end of that session, I couldn't see any of my people being clothed in any but these actors' bodies. The alchemy was under way.

That first, beautiful morning was to be one of the very few during which the sun shone while the series was being filmed. After he became a star, Colin Farrell (never writes, never phones!) who made his screen debut in the piece, was to grumble in a press interview that throughout filming he had been stuck in the back end of nowhere, up to his knees in f—ing mud. I would quarrel with 'the back end of nowhere', but he was factually correct about the f—ing mud; the weather was atrocious for most of the time. But for me that summer, Béara, stormy or not, was Shangri-La and every single day seemed sunny.

There were sunny days too during much of the exhilarating travel I did in connection with writing: book tours to Australia, New Zealand and South Africa, research trips to France, Britain, Canada and, of course, America.

For *Francey*, the novel after *Dancer*, I drove through the lush, posh Cotswolds – Jilly Cooper territory – with my friend Carol Cronin. For *Last Summer in Arcadia* I used the heavenly village of Collioure, next village down the Corniche from Argelès-sur-Mer in the Languedoc where we have our mobile home.

For *That Childhood Country*, the late broadcaster, Treasa Davison, who became a very close friend, came with me to the fire-red earth of Prince Edward Island off the coast of Canada, where we found ourselves tripping over coachloads of happy-snappy Japanese immersing themselves in the home and lore created by *Anne of Green Gables* – and where we found that alcohol was sold only during limited opening times in state-run shops. She came with me too for the first week of my month-long trip to research my fifth novel, *Sky*, in the vast, glorious emptiness and beauty of Montana. Although I loved her company and we travelled well together, the three weeks I spent alone traversing its plains and the Rockies has cemented that huge state permanently into my dream time. For what remains of my life, I will bounce back there at every opportunity.

For *Children of Eve*, with another RTÉ friend, broadcaster Catherine Hogan, I took my cast of new characters through the canyons of Arizona, Grand and many others; we drove almost 3,000 miles through high desert, lush forest, snow bowls, brick-red rocklands and dunes of blinding white gypsum on the White Sands Missile Range. We climbed through forests of saguaro, those amazing cactus oddities that take 200 years to become the three- or four-armed icons of so many Westerns. We visited pistachio farms. Did you know that the reason they cost so much is they take eleven years to mature and each nut has to be harvested by hand?

The choice of those specific locations in America was not arbitrary. I have always been fascinated by local and very specific Irish emigration patterns – for instance, many Connemara and Aran Island people clustered in Chicago. The connection between Béara and Montana is copper mining: the miners from the peninsula travelled to the mines of Butte.

I extended my interest cross-border into Canada (well, into the ocean off its coast) because the antecedents of many residents of Prince Edward Island are in County Monaghan. Just before the Great Famine, a priest from that impoverished Irish county learned that in an effort to populate their empty territories, the Canadian authorities were giving away fertile plots of land. He went to P.E.I. to investigate and wrote back, extolling the virtues of the island and assuring his parishioners that the offer of free land was genuine. A goodly number of his flock took him at his word and went to settle there.

It is not until they appear in my stories that I realise how many scenes I have stockpiled in my memory banks. What I saw while acting as laundry mistress to the cast of *Long Day's Journey into Night* in 1967 surfaced thirty years later when, although it wasn't in the original novel, I found myself including a Magdalen-laundry sequence in the screenplay of *Falling for a Dancer*. Some of it was based on research and was enhanced by my imagination, but one scene in the sequence is an image-perfect reproduction of what I saw once during my days as temporary laundry-mistress to the Abbey Theatre when a horse pulling a laundry-delivery van emerged from behind a set of enormous, high gates. For that script, I also used my memories of those green bus journeys to Durrow when I was just four or five.

The layout of the house on Castle Street has fed into a couple of my novels and it was only having finished *Children of Eve* that I realised my grand-aunt Julia, the woman who was sent into domestic service in Glasnevin, might have subconsciously provided the model – fictionally embroidered to a high degree – for one phase of Eve's life where, starting work as a fourteen-year-old, the character spends a couple of years as a skivvy.

Writing offers small joys too, such as when characters you have created bite back unexpectedly and insist on taking their own course. There is the pleasure of waking up to the realisation that, while you slept, a knotty plot problem unravelled and the solution is now at hand; and there are the Tom Murphy moments, when you look at the clock after writing, you think, for an hour or so, and find that six hours have passed.

And it is gorgeously affirmative when someone approaches me to say, shyly, that they have read all my books and wonder if I might have another one coming out soon?

A sublime high was to find I was nominated for the Orange Prize for *Love Like Hate Adore*. For me, though, far more thrilling even than the nomination itself was the company I kept on that shortlist of six. Would you believe Anita Shreve? Carol Shields?

Carol Shields won it. I had read *Larry's Party* and I knew she would – it would have been a travesty if she hadn't. And so, from the moment I saw her name on that list, I relaxed and went along with the ride and, with no expectations, lived every enjoyable moment of the fuss in London, the gin and tonics, the fêting by my publishers. I particularly enjoyed the public readings in a theatre. Afterwards, crème de la crème, Carol Shields' husband, who was enormously protective of her because she was battling cancer at the time, approached me and accused me jovially of naming one of the characters in my book after him. Which meant he had read it. Which probably meant *she* had read it. Although I didn't dare be so crude as to ask.

And I've saved my very favourite public encounter as a writer until now. It was in a shop early on in my writing life. I was signing copies of *That Childhood Country*, which offers several explicit sex scenes:

> Woman: 'My aunt is in her eighties and she really loves your books.'

> Me (making small-talk while signing): 'That's terrific. That's great to hear that she likes it. In her eighties, eh? How does she handle the sex?'

> Woman (hesitantly): 'Well, she has crutches…'

34

Double Baggers

Real life for me is not only family and work. In some respects, I think I have inherited, from both my parents, a desire to 'give back', either obliquely or in a practical way. So I have been very glad to accept various invitations to serve: for instance, from Lady Goulding and Cardinal Ó Fiaich to join an ad hoc committee to raise funding for Ethiopia. This was a low-key endeavour in the mid-1980s, conducted through meetings held in the cardinal's sitting room in Armagh and culminating in a successful raffle.

Over time, I have also accepted a seat on the board of the Abbey Theatre and membership of the Council for the Financial Institutions' Ombudsman, the Millennium Committee and, at present, I sit on the boards of both the Financial Regulator and the Central Bank.

Declan, too, has inherited this inclination to repay: he is very active in his community and his parish, giving a lot of his limited free time to his choir, his very active amateur musical society, but mainly to his church folk group, for which he composes music.

In addition we are both, I think, double baggers. This is a concept I took away from a 'time management' course I was sent on by Vincent Browne: at a supermarket checkout, the double bagger is the person who, rather than flinging your groceries any old how into a succession of bags, puts one bag inside the other to ensure that the weight of your groceries will be supported. This example was formulated, of course, before the plastic-bag tax. But the idea is clear: enthusiasm for work at hand, no matter how menial and a desire to do it at the best of your ability is what counts.

I adore being involved in projects. My year-long venture for the Millennium Committee tested all of my logistical and project-managing skills to the limit. My idea, which I pitched to the second meeting, was the Millennium Book and I'm glad to say that it did come to glorious fruition. The concept was simple, but the execution was anything but: it involved negotiations with and co-operation from the three main teachers' unions, the Department of Education and Science, the National Library, RTÉ, the Millennium Committee, the Library Service, the managements of every primary and secondary school in the country – and the eventual help of a large number of volunteers.

On 12 May 1999, students of every Fifth Class and Transition Year, having been prepared in advance by teachers, hand wrote on a piece of special, long-life manuscript paper, their own, unedited and unmediated versions of their life stories, their impressions of the world, their vision of life in Ireland and what they would like to leave behind as their footprints on this millennium. The reverse of the page could be used to send us anything they liked: poems, songs, tokens of contemporary life as they saw it. The class teacher then collected the pieces, placed them in a pre-addressed envelope and posted them to us.

On a specific day, the envelopes were opened by volunteers I had press-ganged into service and one page from each was selected *at random*. As I saw it, the incentive for the children was that every participant had an equal chance of being selected for inclusion in this new treasure for the National Library of Ireland. The odds were good: class size to one.

RTÉ agreed to publicise the project via *The Den* (I had to spar on its behalf with Dustin and Socky!) and to supply a co-ordinator, someone who would, with me, source and cost the manuscript paper, the specialist bookbinders, run a helpdesk for teachers, and so on. This turned out to be the excellent John P. Kelly. President McAleese agreed to be our patron.

We received more than 100,000 pieces in total and the pages we selected represent, I think, a fascinating resource. As well as text, we got drawings of the entrants' houses, cats, dogs, trains, landscapes, spaceships, The Spice Girls, Westlife, their mammies, daddies, baby sisters and brothers, an endangered planet and the Manchester United logo. Photographs too – of themselves, their First Communions, their local GAA teams. We got original songs, an Irish dancing medal and collages of product wrappers (as indicators of consumer choice amongst Irish children) – Cadbury's Buttons seem to be right up there. I now believe that the early decision I made – that the entries should be unmediated and unedited – contributed in no small way to the freshness and honesty of the finished book.

While, in some cases, they are laced with sadness and private grief, in general, the pages are permeated with idealism, a sense of place, of parish and of nation, and are an antidote to the poison of cynicism that sometimes pervades our country. Children from special schools sent communal drawings, sets of handprints, a page in Braille. But what was most striking was the optimism and love. With only a few exceptions – and it was clear there was an element of bravado here – those young people saw great futures for themselves. They loved their homes, junior teams, friends, pets, brothers, sisters, aunts, uncles and mentors. They thought their teachers and schools were on their side. They wanted the best for the world and, on that particular day, saw that the best was possible.

On 15 December 1999, during a ceremony in the lobby of the National Library, and in the presence of all who had been involved – including twenty-six students, one selected from each county in the Republic to represent all the schools in it – I presented the Millennium Book to our patron, President McAleese, who, in the name of the nation, in turn entrusted the twenty-three volumes, gorgeously bound in teal and cream calfskin, to the library.

It was one of the proudest moments of my life.

Meanwhile, somewhere in Sierra Leone, on the wall of a domestic-science school, there is a plaque with my name on it.

I had 'sat in' one summer as a substitute presenter for Marian Finucane's radio show and one of my interviewees was a Christian Brother by the name of Noel Bradshaw. Having been declared 'missing' during the appalling genocide in Sierra Leone, after seven months out of contact, he had surfaced with an extraordinary story to tell. When his village was overrun, he had not left the people to their own fate but decided to stay; even if he could not save them from their enemies, he decided his place was to bear witness. To do this, he had to be seen as a neutral, thereby becoming a spectator to unspeakable atrocities.

He subsequently asked me for help – £21,000 to build a piggery, reconstitute the wells and repair the domestic-science school.

I thought of my own comfortable situation, that of my children, and all my friends and associates. Middle-class women of my age, I reckoned, had accumulated lots of jewellery in their lifetime, much of which they did not even wear.

I wrote 100 letters to 100 women, asking them baldly if they would give me one piece of jewellery to auction. I then contacted Sheppard's Auction Rooms in Durrow. Without hesitation, they agreed to do the auction, even print the brochure, without cost or commission.

Believe it or not, this project took almost a year but, with the help of Sheppard's and Joe Murphy, the hotelier in Durrow, whose family now owns our house on Castle Street and who quietly made up the shortfall in what the jewellery fetched at the auction, we hit our target. And the following morning, Minister of State at the Department of Foreign Affairs, Liz O'Donnell, rang me. She had heard about the auction on Maxi's programme and had formed the impression that Brother Bradshaw's project would fulfil the criteria for a grant under one of the headings in the Irish aid budget.

In the end, there was enough money to finish all of the small-scale projects in Brother Bradshaw's village.

The fulfilment of both of these projects means more to me than winning the Lotto or any literary prize ever could.

As for the Abbey, I felt honoured to be asked to sit on its board and regarded it as a privilege to serve.

During my entire period there, the core of the theatre's well-publicised woes was its chronic underfunding. I was deeply frustrated by the sniping from the sidelines – sometimes from people who rarely, if ever, stepped across the threshold to see what we were doing – and, in most cases, were entirely ignorant of what went on behind the scenes.

Some of the criticism was fair and I agreed with it. I have never thought that the artistic director should have a dual mandate as chief executive as well, and I made my views known. But the arguments for and against this are too complex to go into here and have been well rehearsed. As for the overall governing structures, as tortuous and outdated as those of a mediaeval court, during my three successive terms, our boards struggled to reform them. Noel Pearson, as chairman, was beginning the struggle when I arrived. By the time I was re-appointed for a third term, we were making small, incremental progress under the leadership of James Hickey, and the goal was finally achieved under the chairmanship of Eithne Healy after I left and before her board relinquished office. Those who rant about the length of time the process took show scant understanding of the realities of Irish public life.

Politically, Ireland has to decide whether or not it wants a national theatre – and, if the answer is yes, we have to accept that it will be expensive.

But I am well out of the loop now and there is no point in rehashing all of the Abbey's woes. It is not betraying any secrets to reveal that the sad thing for me was to find that, instead of discussing our core business – the making and presenting of plays on the stages – virtually all the time at board meetings was taken up with urgent financial matters, governance and the declining condition of the building in Abbey Street. With a financial rescue plan, a new building in the offing (finally) and fully restructured governance, the future of the place, I hope, is bright. My fervent wish for it is that the state and, even more importantly, the punters, will value and support it to the extent it deserves.

My involvement in the financial world came as some shock. It started with a phone call from Jim Bardon of the Irish Bankers' Federation. He was wondering if I would join the Council of the Financial Institutions Ombudsman, a new body, as one of four independent members under an independent chairman, Ronnie Delaney. The banks and building societies would be represented by four members, so the independents would outweigh the industry on the council.

'Why me?' I asked, dumbfounded.

The answer was incomprehensible to me: 'We asked for suggestions from our members and your name was on nearly all of the lists.'

I couldn't fathom how this had happened. Other than running my own overdrafts, I'd never had anything to do with official financial matters. However, Jim Bardon explained the concept. The ombudsman was being appointed to adjudicate on complaints from customers. With independents in the majority, his council was there to watch out for consumers. The independent members were not expected to be technical experts in banking.

So, with something new to learn again, I happily agreed to take part and set off on thirteen very enjoyable and instructive years as a member of a civilised group under Ronnie's impeccably tactful leadership. The collateral was that, from our meetings and discussions, official and unofficial, I did begin to discern how the financial world worked.

And at the lunches that followed the meetings, I also heard a lot about golf.

I'm not sure whether or not my membership of the council was one of the factors that resulted in an even more surprising telephone call in 2002. 'Is this Deirdre Purcell?'

'It is, yes.'

'Would you hold, please, for the Minister for Finance?'

'Eh?'

But the woman had put me on hold.

I had never met Charlie McCreevy. What on earth did he want?

He came on, his cheery self. And after a few seconds (a very few) of inconsequential small-talk, he asked if I would serve on the interim board of a new body, the Irish Financial Services Regulatory Authority.

'Eh—?'

He explained. And when he had finished, still flummoxed, I asked, if he didn't mind, 'Why me?'

He chuckled. 'I hear you're a fierce independent woman,' he said.

Still stunned, I nevertheless agreed to give it a go and, although nervous, embarked on the steepest learning curve of my life. After that interim year, when the organisation was formally instituted. I was appointed to the authority – and also to the new Board of the CBFSAI (the Central Bank and Financial Services Authority of Ireland – the new name for the Central Bank).

Through this work, which is intense and quite demanding in terms of time, I have had the privilege of meeting, working with and learning from some of the best and most experienced brains in Ireland. And what a privilege it is.

35

And the Turtle a Nest

Two hours after completing the Simplex crossword with me as he lay in bed in the Bons Secours Hospital, Dadda got out of his bed to fill his water glass from the carafe on the bedside locker. His legs folded under him and he collapsed on the floor of his room, fracturing his shoulder and leg.

I raced to the hospital to visit him. He was alert and comfortable: the hospital had ensured he would suffer no pain. But I knew the game was up.

You know that phrase 'my heart broke'? Well, I rediscovered that night that it is actually a physical sensation: a slicing dart of pain deep in the solar plexus. It happened when he said, reflectively, not looking at me, 'I hope everything will be OK for Sitges in May.'

It was not, of course.

Slowly, in the aftermath of his death, the reality of how thoroughly she had depended on him, and that she would not now be going to Sitges this year, maybe never again, dawned on Mamma. I tried to distract her by organising the purchase of an electric scooter so she could regain some independence, at least be able to travel across to the shops beside the Autobahn on Ballymun Avenue.

She couldn't master the kerbs.

Around this time, the Fianna Fáil TD for the area, Pat Carey, whose courtesy and consideration in regard to my mother was exemplary, had the misfortune to put a leaflet through her door. You know the kind: 'If there's anything I can do to help, please don't hesitate to contact...'

Foolhardy man. In Willowpark Grove, the air between the receiver and my mother's right ear burned.

Pat Carey arrives at the house that evening. He finds Mamma at her most dazzling and fluttery. 'The problem is, you see, Mr Carey, I'm a prisoner in my own house. I could get out, I have this yoke here' – indicating the electric scooter – 'but there just isn't enough dishing on the footpaths.'

Enter, within two or three days, staff from the Corpo who assist her into their vehicle and drive her round the neighbourhood so she can show them her intended routes and precisely where the dishing is necessary.

Believe it or not, within days flagged rectangular enclosures appear at the crossing points she had indicated and those dishes are completed within a couple of weeks.

Don't know how many. Never looked. Never had the nerve to count them. Console myself with the fact that a lot of people in that neighbourhood are – or were at the time – aged and those dishes should have been there in the first place.

All for naught as it turned out, because only a few days after they were installed, while standing beside the yoke to chat with a neighbour at the corner of her road, it moved, knocked her off balance and she fell. Nothing major but another hospitalisation and a setting-aside of the scooter. Permanently, as it turned out – she never again used it.

That May, when she and Dadda would have been due to go to Sitges, a loyal friend of hers, Nancy Daly, volunteered to go as a substitute. Kevin and I escorted the two of them to the Romantic. We installed them and then, assured by Nancy and the management that Mamma would be looked after, we left them to it and travelled north to our mobile in Argelès, just over two hours' drive away should we be needed.

We got back to Sitges on the night before they were due to go home and checked ourselves in to the Romantic with the intention of taking them to dinner. Nancy told us that Mamma had been too feeble to leave her room for much of the time but also that everything had worked out. The Romantic had ceased serving lunches and dinners so, after breakfast, Nancy had shopped for them in the local delicatessens so they could have lunch on my mother's sunny balcony; in the evenings, the hotel had organised lifts and escorts to take them to local restaurants when they chose to dine out.

For their last night, Kevin and I had booked a table in Oliver's, a nearby restaurant that Mamma and Dadda had always patronised on special occasions such as anniversaries or the birthdays of their circle of Sitges friends and companions. Dressed impeccably as always and eschewing my arm or those of Kevin or Nancy, my mother made her careful way along the 150 yards between the Romantic and the restaurant, keeping to the middle of the narrow street, her cane wobbling a little. Cars slowed to a snail's pace to accommodate her; pairs of gay men rushed forward to help her negotiate the kerbs, then detained her for a chat. In total, she stopped at least half-a-dozen times to acknowledge the fond greetings of acquaintances. She seemed to know a lot of people very well; more importantly, they sure knew her, and that short journey underlined graphically why she adored that place; there she was granted her rightful place in the firmament.

But that night we were witnessing a lap of honour: still endeavouring to walk like a queen, she was on her last visit to Sitges.

Typically, she didn't accept that, of course, and, although virtually immobilised the next year, continued to plead with me, 'If I could get to Sitges just one more time … If you could just get me there … You wouldn't even have to stay with me. Everyone there would look after me…'

I knew it was absolutely impossible. But I felt her yearning and couldn't bear that she felt she had to beg me. I even booked the tickets.

But we had to let those tickets go. She was taken to hospital a week before the departure date. She had suffered a series of relatively minor strokes to add to her other infirmities and, during 2001, she was in hospital more often than not.

She was in hospital when I went in to tell her that Kevin and I, having lived together for more than twenty years, were getting married. Her gift to me was a pair of old photographs that, with the help of Sheila's daughter, my cousin, Barbara, she had had scanned and mounted side by side in a frame. In this frame, my grandmother and grandfather, as stiff and elegant as yew trees, are reunited and again stand side by side.

With Kevin's agreement, I decided to hold our blessing and reception at her house, notwithstanding its old-fashioned décor and ancient electrical sockets, some still designated for two-pin plugs; she was far too frail and ill to have handled a big occasion in a noisy function room. But I was determined that she would not miss seeing her daughter marry the man she was mad about, and I wanted to make every effort for her. Anyhow, of the generation before Kevin and me, she was the only one left alive.

The judgement had been fortuitous because, ten days before the wedding, I had been sitting with her in her conservatory when she had her final, crippling stroke. Now, she wouldn't be able even for the register office.

We briefly considered postponing the wedding but, although she could no longer speak, she indicated forcefully that we shouldn't do so because of her, so the revised plan now was that, with the co-operation of the Mater Hospital and her doctors, she would come straight to her house by ambulance or wheelchair-accessible taxi to be with us for the blessing in the marquee.

That day, Friday, 14 September 2001, was one of the happiest of my life – paradoxically so, because of Mamma's perilous condition and also because it was Ireland's national day of mourning for the World Trade Center atrocities in New York.

The day before was giddy and it was not to do with last-minute preparations, but because of the announcement that all public offices – including register offices – would be closed for the entire day on the Friday.

I heard the news when I was halfway up a ladder tying balloons into purple swags of fabric that Barbara and I were fixing to the sides of the marquee shoehorned into my mother's back garden in Ballymun. It was far too late to call the whole thing off. The honeymoon was paid for, the caterer was booked, the Portaloos had been erected in the front garden (no room in the back, even if access had been possible), the marquee and every room in Mamma's house smelled like a Caribbean garden because of all the flowers, a wedding present to us from Patricia and her husband, Frank.

Patricia gave me more than flowers: she gave me time. She took a day off work to come with me to the Smithfield flower market where we spent a wonderful couple of hours choosing cartloads of white and purple blooms, so many that we had difficulty fitting them all into the car. For the rest of that morning we had sorted, snipped and placed them in vases, buckets, tubs, anything that would hold water. It had been a marvellous entrée into a great celebration. Patricia is one of those people who enters fully into others' excitements so, when I heard the bad news about the register offices, I ignored it. I wasn't going to waste all that effort and love. Something would turn up, I thought, and on the Auntie Nora principle, I carried on as though I hadn't heard a thing.

And wasn't I right? At the last minute on the Thursday, we heard that Bertie himself, romantic old soul that he is, had reprieved the register offices, but had left it up to the individual registrars to decide whether or not they wanted to work; our esteemed lady in Dublin had decided to give up her bonus day off so as not to disappoint the eight couples booked in with her.

On the early morning of the big day, I got back to Ballymun very early. I still had to tie the last ribbons, blow up the last balloons and recount the booklets I'd made to be sure I'd printed enough. As I pinned and tucked at the top of my ladder, then pulled the hired chairs into rows, my excitement about the coming day was tempered by the knowledge that this visit to her house would be the last Mamma would ever make. She had adored living in Ballymun.

Mamma's lifelong lust was for social interaction and, although many times she had complained to me that she felt imprisoned in her cluttered house, it had been her fortress all the same. She had particularly loved her garden.

Kevin was already in town, breakfasting with his best man and best friend, Eddie Cahill, and I couldn't telephone him to cry all over his rashers, so I tried to keep the sad aspect of the event out of my mind and, instead, focused on keeping the clouds out of the sky. If I concentrated really hard, I thought, I could do it.

Blessings are now quite common in Ireland. Although my own marriage had been annulled as well as dissolved by divorce, Kevin's dissolution had been purely civil and, of course, the Catholic Church would not hear of letting us cross the threshold of any of its premises. I had invited both of my lovely priest-friends, the Finucane brothers, and had asked Aengus, as the senior, if he would do the needful.

At last, everything was as good as I could make it in the marquee and the house and it was time to morph into The Bride.

I wasn't going to be the most groomed or stylish bride ever; because of all the physical work leading up to the day, my nails were as splintered as driftwood and I hadn't had time to get my hair done. I had merely washed it as normal in the shower very early that morning. Bent on enjoying the day, I had chosen my outfit – a flowing, violet creation from McElhinney's of Athboy – for comfort rather than for glamour or a specific 'look'. But when I teamed it with open-toed sandals and a headdress I had made by weaving together ribbons and yarn around a base I'd twisted from a gossamer-fine white wool scarf that Adrian had brought me many years previously from a school tour to Russia, the overall effect did seem somewhat medieval. I wove two similar headdresses for my brides-maids – my sister-in-law Mary and Laly, who was then Simon's girlfriend. They were both game enough to wear them!

I didn't care what anyone else thought anyhow. It was my day, mine and Kevin's. My attitude to parties has always been that I should strain every nerve to prepare for the event and to cover every possibility but then it was up to others to enjoy themselves or not, criticise or not.

When it was time to leave Ballymun for the noon ceremony at the register office, Frank, Patricia's husband, drove me and my two bridesmaids. Frank had decorated his old Ford Escort with white ribbons and, because the streets were eerily empty, we took the long way round to avoid arriving too early and thereby crashing the previous wedding. That journey was magical. We travelled through the deserted streets in a haze of goodwill: on seeing us, the pedestrians who were out did a double-take and reacted with thumbs up or applause. I felt like Cinderella on her way to the ball.

The ceremony, held in stylish, unstuffy surroundings and crowned by our charming, participative registrar, was heralded by the Gerry and the Pacemakers hit – and anthem of Liverpool football club – 'You'll Never Walk Alone'.

Then, after we were pronounced man and wife, I sprang the surprise I had prepared for Kevin. I had asked Declan to arrange an a cappella barbershop version of Elvis Presley's 'The Wonder of You' to be sung by himself, Adrian, Simon and his son Paul. As soon as the registrar had spoken the fateful words, up they popped to sing it.

While they did, I looked across at my shocked new husband and enjoyed his discomfort. This was the man who, in the words of his pal Gerry Barry, could, at the drop of a hat, 'interview anyone at anytime about anything'; who, clutching his microphone while on board the jumbo bringing Pope John Paul II to Ireland, had kneed his way past the notorious Archbishop Marcinkus to get a live quote from the pontiff. Who, having led a public life through journalism, as Director of RTÉ Radio and then as Director of Public Affairs, was now going to the King's Inns to study for a second career in law. But I had managed to throw him.

Like most human beings, Kevin Healy is contradictory. He loves being at the centre of the action and tramping the streets of strange cities, but is never happier than when he is taking our collie, Jack, on the wild commonage above our cottage in Kilcatherine to watch the sun set in the direction of the Skelligs. He tramps our briar patch, loosely termed 'the garden', to measure the growth of the rhododendrons he planted amongst the brambles and the montbretia planted for us by our neighbours, John and Mo Kingerlee. He checks his weather station and the water levels in our old well, reports sightings of hares, badgers, rabbits, and the house martins that, each year, return to build their home on top of the light fixture above our front door. And each August and September, this man, who is subject to seasickness, revels in handling his little open boat as he putt-putts towards the open Atlantic from the harbour at Castletownbere to throw his feathers towards the mackerel harvest.

He has always said that life with me is never boring. I could say the same about him and as 'The Wonder of You' finished, to the laughter and applause of the registrar and as many of our friends and family as we could fit into the tiered seating, we smiled at each other. It was a moment of pure happiness.

Purity, however, can never last and I knew that, for me, that day would always hold an undertone of melancholy.

We were already well into the champagne when Mamma arrived in Ballymun, accompanied by my dear friend, herself now deceased, Suzannah Allen. Suzannah was a nurse and, although I had arranged for an agency nurse to be present throughout the wedding so that Suzannah could enjoy herself, she had volunteered to go the Mater, help get Mamma ready and accompany her in the taxi.

The staff in the Mater Hospital could not have been more won-derfully co-operative. Mamma's favourite colour was red and when she turned up, she was dressed in a red outfit. Her nails had been painted to match, her hair was styled and, to cap it all, she had been placed in a scarlet wheelchair.

I had wanted her to be fully part of the ceremony, so her speech therapist in the hospital had worked daily with her, coaching her to say the line I had chosen for her to speak during the readings: 'The sparrow hath found herself a house, and the turtle a nest.'

When the time came, everyone in the tent, who had been following the readings in their booklets and who knew how ill she was, held their breath.

Although indistinct, she did manage the first part, if very haltingly:

'The sparrow hath…

'Found herself a…

'House….

She stopped.

She made a small gesture of frustration and I could see tears welling in her eyes. Instinctively, I sprang towards her and hunkered in front of the wheelchair. I took her hand. Then, while she made inarticulate sounds along with me, we finished it together: '… and the turtle a nest.'

When the time came for her to go back to the hospital, I could see she was reluctant but I had no option but to see her into the taxi waiting outside. I managed to restrain my tears until I had pulled shut the sliding door of the vehicle. But they were in flood as the taxi slowly pulled away and I saw the oval of her face straining towards the house for as long as possible. We both knew she would never see it again.

I did see her again, but I had to rush home from France to get there in time. Declan and Mary believe she waited for me.

Dear Goncal,
Thank you so very much for your lovely letter received
this morning.

Goncal, as you can imagine, I am heartbroken at losing my mother – she was a maddening person in many ways – she drove me mad anyway! – but now I realise I loved her to bits and I recognise that in many ways, I built the framework of my life around her and her needs – or wants or desires. She was quite special, as you know, a person who should have been born into royalty!

You, Sitges and the Romantic Hotel were a huge part of her life. In fact, I don't believe she was happy anywhere except there. There was always a sort of 'longing' quality about her – it was in her eyes. But Sitges seemed to fulfil that longing in many ways. (Probably because only there was she treated like royalty!)

I miss her terribly, but at least I have no regrets or guilt. I did everything I could to make her last years as good as possible. I tried to 'fix' everything for her – unfortunately, the only thing I could not 'fix' was her health.

I had the last four days with her and was alone with her when she died. She went very peacefully in the end. I put on the radio for her and the Khachaturian piece – 'Spartacus' – was playing. She reacted a little to it and I know she was listening. I whispered into her ear that I loved her and told her to rest now. That I was letting her go. As soon as the piece of music finished, she let out a sigh and didn't breathe again.

She loved you, as I am sure you know. (I think I told you once about moving your photograph aside on the wall of her bedroom in order to put up a clock.

The next time I called, the clock was gone and your picture was back on her wall!)

Thank you for all you did for her and for Bill. I know it wasn't always easy.

Just before her final hospitalisation, I accompanied her to an appointment with one of her specialists at the outpatients' clinic. He was asking her gently about how she was managing at home, how difficult it was for her to cope. She told him that she managed 'as well as could be expected' and described to him the conservatory-extension I built for her as her last bedroom so she could have light and warmth and, in a sense, could live within the garden that she loved so much.

Well, you know how flirtatious she was – even at her age and in her state of health. She looked at this eminent doctor sideways, and, batting her eyes upwards at him, concluded, 'Ah, but, Doctor, I am only a bird in a gilded cage!'

The bird is flying free now, Goncal.

Love
Deirdre

What I did not put into that letter was that when I told her I loved her, her fingers twitched briefly in my hand. I had never before said those words to her, but I know she had heard and understood.

And here is another addendum I did not include because, although I had planned to, at the time I was writing to Goncal about her I was too emotional to continue. At that same specialist's appointment five weeks or so before her death, the man gently asked her if she had any questions. She thought for a moment, then, her effort at conveying strength and brightness all too visible, she summoned every remnant of strength left to her to ask him if there was 'any chance' she might be able to take 'one last flight'.

An echo of Dadda's last hope too.

The family connection with Sitges remains. Barbara has an apartment there now and it is open to us – and, of course, we do go to the Romantic.

I love it, but being there is bittersweet for me. I see both of them everywhere: when I look up from the breakfast garden of the Romantic, I can see the balcony where she was so happy; I can see them sitting at 'their' table in the garden or at their other table in their favourite bar, he happily pontificating about the state of the world to whichever cronies they have with them, she slightly aloof, watching the door to see who else might come in. I can see her smiling upwards at the proprietor in that fey way she had, asking that he give her a 'small', a 'very small' portion of *patatas fritas*. 'And if possible,' head slightly inclined like a little girl's, 'a fried egg?'

I see her standing with her nose figuratively pressed to the plate-glass windows of the stylish shops. I see him lying on the lounger he hired always from the same lady on the beach, Walkman on his belly, earphones plugged into his music.

With the Romantic as one of its hubs, Sitges has, in recent years, been advertised by travel companies specialising in holidays for gays and lesbians and, whenever I want to smile about my parents, I return to a picture coruscating in my memory. It dates from about 1996 and is in complete contrast to that image of the two of them sitting alone and silently in the auditorium of the Abbey when I couldn't bear to approach them.

I turned up unexpectedly at the Romantic or elsewhere in Sitges now and then to surprise them – usually for their wedding anniversary. One of these occasions was at breakfast time and, from a vantage point on the steps leading down into the hotel's garden restaurant, I spotted them immediately at their regular table. With sunglasses covering their eyes, they were both tanned and obviously relaxed: he in shorts, a short-sleeved T-shirt, runners and a battered white baseball cap; she, her white hair glistening in the dappled sunlight filtering through the foliage above their heads, wore a canary-yellow sundress and espadrilles.

With head bent over his plate and bony elbows splayed like chicken's wings, he was, as usual, laying into his food. She, a morsel of bread in one hand paused in mid-air, was dreamily fluttering the fingers of the other at a tight-shorted, muscle-armed male couple who, smiling and waving back, were crunching through the gravel towards the breakfast buffet under its blue and white striped awning.

Every other table was occupied by pairs of men. My elderly mother and ostensibly strait-laced, conservative father were perfectly at ease.

In later years, he even took to carrying a man bag.

36

This Shoulda Been Different

I find that something unexpected has happened to this memoir, the idea for which arose during an initial conversation with Hodder Headline Ireland over a lunch to talk about publishing plans for *Children of Eve*. That done, with all of us in high good humour, I was expounding in anticipatory detail about all the terrific jaunts and exciting adventures I had planned for my year of turning sixty. I was going to celebrate and celebrate hard for a full twelve months.

As publishers will, they became interested in 'The Year' as a possibility for a book, particularly when my plans did not seem to include bungee-jumping in New Zealand or having a makeover.

Travel featured hugely in the plans, to many of which I was already committed – a trip to Boston for the christening of Declan's first grandchild, an Amtrak train trip from that city to Chicago to visit the Spataforas and C.Sue, a visit to Anfield to attend a match involving Liverpool FC. The basic idea for the book was that I would write a jolly account of my travels, building them around anecdotes and stories about journalism, theatre and all my other lives, plus selected memories of childhood. And of course Things I Have Learned over the course of sixty years of living. Sure, the book would practically write itself! Its core was to be a really special six-week trip to fulfil three personal ambitions: a voyage to America aboard the *Queen Mary II*, a seat at a live concert given by the Mormon Tabernacle Choir and, crème de la crème, a road trip in a motor home through the wide spaces of the northwestern US.

Hugs all round. We were all set.

Then there was the actual birthday. As I did for our wedding, I took on the organisation of this too, in our own house again, with a marquee and another gift of a ton of flowers from Patricia and Frank.

To say I enjoyed myself at that party has to be the understatement of the past sixty years. I wafted around in a haze of delight that so many people had taken the trouble to celebrate with me, particularly as we now live outside Dublin. There they all were, my new neighbours in Mornington, friends from every profession I've had. The apogee for me was when John O'Conor played 'Happy Birthday' on the piano I'd hired. Now there's a lifetime's honour. And looking at all those smiling faces as they sang, I acknowledged to myself how fortunate I've been in my friendships. From every age and stage of my life, I've garnered at least one close friend, sometimes more and, despite my wonky schedule and reclusive habits while I'm writing (which must drive them mad), they have stuck with me.

I did take every trip mentioned above, but there should have been a lot more … That computer crash wrecked more than my writing schedule.

But six weeks after that party, on *his* birthday, Kevin and I set sail on the *Queen Mary II* from Southampton bound for New York. This was a quadruple celebration: my sixtieth, his fifty-eighth, his retirement from RTÉ and his graduation from the King's Inns as a qualified barrister.

His lifelong dream had been to enter Manhattan from the sea. And, boy, did it ever live up to his expectations – and mine!

The captain had urged us to get up early for the experience and so, at 4.30 in the morning, there was quite a sizeable group gathered as, flickering like fireflies through the heavy mist, the distant lights of the New Jersey shoreline slipped silently past us. Kevin had been up long before that to watch the pilot being taken on board, something he has always wanted to see at close quarters. He had spent his childhood summers on the clifftops in Crosshaven above Cork Harbour, logging the movements of the great liners – and their pilots – to and from Cobh.

Clustered on the observation deck at the bow, we all strained to catch our first sight of Liberty's torch through the windows. 'There she is,' someone who had been there before and knew where to look, pointed at a speckle of orange light, diffused by the mist. And there, indeed, she was.

The ship had slowed to a crawl when at 5.00 a.m., as dawn light was seeping through from the east behind us, the statue itself emerged, ghost-like, from the mist. It was one of those eerie, hair-lifting moments. All the watchers, who had been chatting quietly, fell silent. Some held each other while, dwarfing her, we glided past and gazed down at her face and torch.

Half an hour later, the captain speeded up a little to get under the Verrazano Bridge, linking Brooklyn with Staten Island, and entered the Narrows. Manhattan, like a Lego concoction, lay ahead; in the vapour, the same colour as the river, it seemed to have no anchor to the earth. By this time, we had been joined by escorts, a police helicopter above and two coastguard boats alongside.

Gradually, the mist lifted as we proceeded slowly up the Hudson river with the helicopter circling closely overhead and the coastguard boats keeping pace. The skyscrapers, whose tops seemed close enough to hit with a golf ball, were now etched angularly against a hazy sky of deepening pink and lemon. A swarm of cars, insects in orderly formation along the quayside highway, was increasing by the minute.

Then, so suddenly it gave me a fright, a full red ball of sun fired at us through a gap between two of the buildings. All the nearby glass reddened and, from then on, windows flashed and glowed at us in random sequence as we moved past warehousing and piers until, in high, hot sun, we eventually reached Pier 90. Then we looked down at a dinky aircraft carrier and, on a pontoon attached to a museum, a Concorde aircraft that, from our perspective, seemed small enough to fit into one of our onboard restaurants or theatres. The drawn-out process of inching our behemoth into position alongside its mooring took a good two hours.

The live concert by the Mormon Tabernacle Choir, 300 voices with a forty-piece orchestra, also fulfilled my expectations. The Tabernacle in Salt Lake City was being refurbished, so we flew to Boise, Idaho, where they were appearing in the Taco Bell Arena ('Next Event: Basketball Hoop Camp').

We sat in the front row of the balcony, just above the orchestra, from where I could see every feature of every face of the musicians and choir, even the smallest of their movements.

They started with an a cappella version of 'The Star Spangled Banner' – tippy-toeing through it at half volume but sending tingles up and down the spine nevertheless. And then, at full blast, they launched into their first hymn and blew the hair off the back of my neck.

From then on, I levitated through the classics and spirituals and an amazing Nigerian carol in which the eight timpanists took off their jackets and sat in a row in front of the ululating choir to play traditional African instruments. Behind them, the singers rattled their hands and bracelets and swayed rhythmically in exact unison, blue and black waves on an inland sea.

Naturally, we were all waiting for the finale, and it didn't disappoint. For 'The Battle Hymn of the Republic', the choir started as softly as a quiet wind, then, bit by bit, the sound grew until, finally, they were manipulating hand bells and clappers to augment their voices, with the thundering of brass, drums and every other instrument played at full volume.

And then…

The orchestra members put down their instruments and stood up, joining the choir. Instead of watching the conductor, they turned to us, the ovals of 340 faces like eyes in an open fan. Each face targeted segments of us in that 2,000-seater arena while in unison, smiling tenderly, issuing a song that wished us well and bade us farewell until we all met again at the feet of God.

In black and white like this, it sounds hokey and mawkish and, of course, it was rehearsed, but what emanated from that choir during that piece was a waft of human goodness, kindness, understanding, forgiveness and sincerity. During the final elongated note that hung in the air like a silver thread until it dissolved, I saw, rising between me and the smiling singers, the distinct faces of my mother and father, of Nellie – and of my friend, Suzannah, who was dying of cancer. I started to cry and couldn't stop.

I took with a vengeance to RV-ing (driving long distances in a recreational vehicle) and got hooked for life. That's all I can say about it here because, as we drove through the spectacular whitewater canyons, mountains and national parks of Idaho, Utah, Wyoming, Montana, Oregon and Washington State, that ribbon of road in front of the squat diesel hood of our van became forever my drug of choice. To start describing it all now, despite what I promised Hodder Headline Ireland a year ago, would lead to a separate tome.

As I've said, this memoir sure turned out a lot differently than I thought it would. I should have paid more attention to the experience of Nuala O'Faolain, who set out in similar jaunty fashion to compile a collection of her journalistic pieces. When she sat down to write a foreword to the collection, she found this growing exponentially until, journalism ditched, the entire book became *Are You Somebody?* the outpouring of grief and pain that struck such a chord with people around the world.

For me, the memoir experience has been similar to hers in one practical respect: I had not planned to write at such length about my childhood and early experiences as a young woman and find that these have taken up half the book and spilled across the other half.

What is utterly dissimilar, however, is that where Nuala found grief, I found tenderness. Just as those sunflowers burst through what I had thought were my permanently grey and black memories of the 1950s, I discovered them blooming all over the memories of Mamma and Dadda too. In writing about them, about Nanna and Nellie, even about our teacher and Frank Dermody, I discovered the real people under the edifices I had constructed around them from my own reactions.

What a marvellous discovery.

But what life lessons have I learned during these first sixty years? Never to plan – that's for sure. I'm not referring merely to the computer crash that scuppered so much of my merry scheme for the year of becoming sixty. But if, when I left Gortnor Abbey in 1962, I had developed a five-year, ten-year or even life plan – and had stuck rigidly to it – I wouldn't have taken any account of all those unexpected jammy offers flying in from the sides to turn me in other directions. Look at all I would have missed!

What else?

That I dearly love my family, past and present. That I love and value my friends. That I'm contrary and frequently odd. That what keeps me going is the prospect of new challenges; and what makes me happy is to feel that those I love are thriving and happy too.

And what's next?

Who knows? Learning new things. More novels for sure. Certainly more projects. I'll maybe take my clarinet out of its case and finally learn to play it.

Or maybe what's next is something I have not yet even imagined.

Acknowledgements

I hope that for those named in it, the body of this memoir can be taken as a public acknowledgement of the help, support and love with which they have blessed me over a lifetime. There are very many names, too many to list here, but I trust that all relatives, friends and colleagues, past and present, will know how truly grateful I am. If I have not actually mentioned you, be assured you are in my heart.

In the context of the book itself, however, I'd like particularly to thank Tiddle Walsh from Durrow, whose memory of times past is prodigious; my cousin Laura Butler, whose work on our family tree was of great help; Pat Laffan, whose memory of the Abbey Theatre days is better than mine; John Carlos, who has been generous with his photographs; Martin Moloney, who helped with some tricky wording; and my brother, Declan, who was able to supply details that had eluded me.

In addition, I should like sincerely to express my gratitude to Claire Rourke, my patient and kind editor who had a lot to put up with! And as ever, Pat Brennan came up trumps when help was needed. Thanks are also due to Hodder Headline Ireland – Breda, Ciara, Ciara, Ruth and Peter – and, of course, to my agent, Clare Alexander.

As for my dear Kevin, Adrian and Simon, there would be no point in any of it without you.

Deirdre Purcell
October 2006